Paul Ramsey's Political Ethics

Paul Ramsey's Political Ethics

David Attwood

Rowman & Littlefield Publishers, Inc.

ROWMAN & LITTLEFIELD PUBLISHERS, INC.

Published in the United States of America
by Rowman & Littlefield Publishers, Inc.
4720 Boston Way, Lanham, MD 20706

British Cataloging in Publication Information Available

Library of Congress Cataloging-in-Publication Data
Attwood, David (David T. E.)
Paul Ramsey's political ethics / David Attwood.
p. cm.
Includes bibliographical references and index.
1. Ramsey, Paul.
2. Christian ethics—History—20th century.
3. Christianity and politics—History of doctrines—
20th century. I. Title.
BJ1231.A87 1991
241'.62' 092—dc20 91-18626 CIP

ISBN 0-8476-7685-4 (cloth : alk. paper)
ISBN 0-8476-7686-2 (pbk. : alk paper)

Printed in the United States of America

To Gillian

Contents

Part Four: Nuclear Weapons and Nuclear Deterrence

Preface

As I write at the end of 1990, much of the world hovers anxiously on the brink of a major war. Churches in many countries debate heatedly whether they can approve open warfare by UN forces to free Kuwait (or what is left of it) from Iraq. As I follow these debates, I am struck again by my sense of the magnitude of Paul Ramsey's achievement. In his writings on the just war, he rescued these old and disused principles of Christian thought and gave them a new and lively existence. It is a tribute to him in very large measure that these principles are presently given so much attention, in Protestant as well as Roman Catholic churches.

Meanwhile, the nuclear stand-off has faded in public consciousness with the continental shifts that have taken place in Europe in such a short time. Nevertheless, nuclear weapons remain a serious and dangerous concern. Ramsey's rehabilitation of just war thought addressed this concern in particular, and his work deserves our careful attention just as much now as it did a generation ago. The theological and political basis that he fashioned to handle this question is a powerful one.

Sadly, firsthand knowledge of Ramsey's writings remains the prerogative of comparatively few specialists. There is very little secondary work that offers a way into Ramsey's writing, which demands sustained and careful attention from the reader. This book aims to offer such a way in. It is offered in the hope that it will lead a fresh generation of students to Ramsey himself. Those who do return to his works will, I believe, find ample grounds for answering the charge that his work is now out of date. Some would say that Ramsey held hopes too high for politics today. They allege that the political world no longer looks to the theologian for analysis, and cannot sustain the high level of reasoned argument that Ramsey employed. I do not think this is the whole truth, for Ramsey's analysis of political power and armed force sets out how politicians do behave as well as how they should behave. The new setting of international politics in the 1990s does not invalidate his analysis either. Of course principles may have to be transposed, but an understanding of Ramsey's moral Christian realism offers resources for this task in any age.

I have accumulated too many debts in writing this to acknowledge them here, or as they deserve. Directly, I owe the most to my supervisor, Oliver O'Donovan, for his wise and patient oversight. In other ways I owe much to colleagues and friends in parish life in Swindon, and in college life at Trinity College, Bristol. From them, from students, and from my family, I have received the resources for this task. It is a task I have richly enjoyed, and I hope my readers will gain some of the enjoyment and enlightenment it has given me.

David Attwood
December 1990

Introduction

It might seem rash to say that Paul Ramsey offers the most coherent and theological approach to the tasks faced by Christian ethics in our day, for his work displays neither of these qualities very obviously. At its most profound and most helpful (e.g., in *The Just War* and *Ethics at the Edges of Life*), it seems to be caught up most of the time in an intricate technical argument accessible only to specialists. Ramsey's only book on theological ethics, outlining a general approach or introduction to the subject, was the early *Basic Christian Ethics,* which is far from representing his most mature and valuable thought.

Yet the way he draws together central themes of the Christian faith, and allows them to bear on knotty and pressing twentieth-century problems in a deeply penetrating way, substantiates the claim that he is to be considered among the foremost Christian thinkers of our time.

The fragmented character of Paul Ramsey's writings hides a thoroughly thought out theological ethic. His thought has a profundity and a unity that result from the fusion of three major streams of thought— a theology within the Reformed tradition, a moral casuistry with a strongly Roman Catholic feel, and a political theory owing much to Reinhold Niebuhr's Augustinian political realism.

This book attempts to display the coherence and lucidity of Ramsey's casuistry of Christian love, first in its roots, then as applied to the just war theory, and, consequently, to the ethics of nuclear deterrence.

Love is one of the central themes of the whole Judeo-Christian tradition, from the Pentateuch onward, and Augustine did much to ensure that the idea of love has been at the heart of Western Christian ethics ever since. So it was for all the great theologians. To list but a few, one could name Thomas Aquinas, Martin Luther, John Calvin,

Jonathan Edwards, Karl Barth, and Paul Tillich. This impressive list also makes clear that to say that love lies at the center of Christian ethics may not yet say enough. How is "love" to be understood, and in what framework is it to be interpreted? Ramsey's answer to this question will go a long way to show us how he combines the various aspects of his thought in a coherent whole.

Ramsey is determined that love should be not only central, but basic and essential to all else. Whatever other sources of moral understanding there may be, none can take priority. All must be understood in the light of love, and on that base alone. To be able to bear this weight, however, it is important that the idea of love be fully and accurately filled out. This must be done theologically; that is, we must learn the nature of Christian love from our understanding of the nature of God, Father, Son, and Holy Spirit.

Ramsey wrote little that is directly concerned with theology, but we can glean a great deal from the important indications he gave of his theological allegiances. In fact, he was always ready to learn, but there can be no doubting the importance for him of the American theologian Jonathan Edwards.[1] Though he was continually in dialogue with many, from Roman Catholic theologians to political theorists, he was always a Protestant Christian at heart, a Methodist by upbringing and continued membership, and had a genuine appreciation for the Reformed tradition. He had a great admiration for the work of Karl Barth.[2]

God's love for us is best encapsulated in a single word as *faithful*. It seems that one of the reasons Ramsey liked the words "faithful," and "faithfulness" is that they enable us to talk with the same word of God's love for his people, theirs for him, and for one another.[3] More importantly, the idea of faithfulness allowed Ramsey to pick up and enlarge and apply certain biblical themes which he felt particularly apposite to trends in contemporary thought. Before expanding this, it is important to be clear that in selecting this aspect for particular attention, Ramsey does not mean us to overlook other dimensions of the meaning of love as we learn them from the love of Christ. Moreover, the word "faithfulness" is given a rich and strong content.

Faithful Christian love is first and foremost oriented to the needs of the neighbor. It is prepared if necessary to sacrifice its own interests. It is incarnational—it has regard to the flesh and blood realities of human life. As we shall see, the themes of human frailty and mortality are especially significant for Ramsey.[4] Love is also virtuous; it is wise, prudent, just, courageous, self-controlled, etc. All this is in service of the neighbor—the person standing before us, toward whom our actions are directed. Human love for our neighbor is to be patterned on God's love for us; it is to be forgiving, patient, enduring, always caring and respectful of the other.

For instance, to be faithful in marriage is, for Ramsey, a rich and positive way of expressing our patient love, which sticks by the marriage partner in all his or her frailty, weakness, and need.[5] For a doctor to be faithful to the patient means that he is always to care for and respect the patient, putting the needs and concerns of this patient before all other good objectives, if necessary.[6] Faithfulness in times of war means respecting the immunity of the enemy innocent, never directly attacking those not engaged in fighting, whatever military advantage it may appear to bring.[7] These three are examples of the way that faithful Christian love is embodied in principles. In each of these three areas these principles offer penetrating challenges to opposing moral viewpoints.

In Part One, which sets out the general background, we will survey the development of Ramsey's understanding of Christian love as the key to a grasp of his thought as a whole. Most of our attention will be on the years 1951–68, from the publication of *Basic Christian Ethics* to *The Just War*. In searching for the roots of Ramsey's casuistry and his just war theory of politics in the theology of Christian love, we will find that the essay he wrote on Reinhold Niebuhr in 1956 is of particular importance.[8] Reinhold Niebuhr was of enormous significance for Ramsey, but the question we are driven to ask is whether the correction Ramsey makes to Niebuhr's thought leaves us able to describe him as still a follower of Niebuhr. This discussion leads to a schematic presentation of Ramsey's understanding of politics as a rational and moral task.

No ethics, least of all an ethics of Christian love, can do without an understanding and analysis of rules and principles, and how they are to be applied to human acts. In other words ethics needs casuistry. At the heart of Ramsey's casuistry is the claim that there are some virtually exceptionless moral rules.[9] He also defended a version of the principle of twofold intentionality ("the rule of double effect"), that allows that we do not always intend all the consequences of our actions, which may sometimes be allowed as merely permitted. We will approach our exposition of Ramsey's casuistry in Part Two by seeing how his treatment of this principle advanced during the course of his work. In the course of this exposition we will have to enter some of the intricacies of Ramsey's arguments, especially the debate with Richard McCormick over consequentialism and double effect. It is, of course, the way in which any theory can defend itself when strenuously attacked that provides a major test of its validity.

Christian love also expresses itself in an ethic of resistance. When claims are conflicting, love will not stand by if it has the power to come to the aid of one who is unjustly oppressed. If it needs to, love will itself use force to defend another. In this use of force, love will be careful that it never unjustly oppresses others, but will always direct its own use of force at the unjust oppressor. This concern provides the basis for the principle of discrimination. The defense of others is the key concern of the proper use of power, the proper concern of politics.[10] It is the use of power that makes politics what it is.[11] Political theory thus requires, as a central element, an analysis of the morality of the use of force, a vital, but not the only, component of power. Politics also require an understanding of the goals for which power ought to be used. These include the qualities of justice and order, qualities that do not always simply walk hand in hand, but that can often conflict or work in different directions.[12] Judging the hard choices that arise from these tensions is part of the work of political prudence, guided by the principle of proportion.

Ramsey's analysis of the principles of politics exemplifies his understanding of moral casuistry. Love seeks, for instance, justice. Where this requires the use of force, it is guided by the principles of discrimination and proportion. Ramsey's handling of these principles is most clearly grasped in the light of his careful exposition of love-inspired rules. In Part Three I will attempt an exposition of the way Ramsey handled these twin principles, giving some examples in specific topics, and offer defenses of his position against some of his critics. Part Three functions as the linchpin of the whole book. It prepares the way for the discussion of the ethics of nuclear deterrence in Part Four.

Ramsey's debates on deterrence were involved and difficult, and my aim in this section will be to clarify and examine the expression of his thought. The difficulty is of course no accident, for here Ramsey reaches to the heart of the moral conceptual difficulties which any serious treatment of deterrence must encounter. My claim is not therefore to give anything like an adequate account of this vast debate as it has developed over nearly thirty years, but it is my belief that the way Ramsey was drawn into it, and the propositions he advanced, still have a very great deal to offer to the contemporary discussion.[13]

The debate about the morality of nuclear deterrence has inevitably continued to revolve about a few central issues: Can nuclear weapons ever be justly used? How does nuclear deterrence work? Does it actually work? What kinds of threats does deterrence entail? Are they really meant or not? What is the morality of such threats? What moral differences are there between first use and retaliation? If the strategy of the West for the past thirty years or so has been unjustifiable (as very many moralists conclude), is there any way of mounting an effective justifiable deterrent?

No moral discussion of nuclear deterrence can avoid these questions (though they are rather broadly expressed here). Ramsey's answers to them, and the debates in which he participated, attempt to show that there could be a just nuclear deterrent. We do not have to conclude from the immorality of present strategy that the only moral alternative is immediate nuclear disarmament. The importance of this discussion justifies our attention to it in Part Four, as does the obscurity of some of Ramsey's expression and style.

Ramsey's Prose Style

The foregoing outline is heavily simplified and schematic. It cannot, of course, do justice to the range and subtlety of Ramsey's writings in trying to condense its basic shape in a few pages. Nevertheless, there is good reason for offering a schematic outline, for Ramsey's presentation of his thought must be described as fragmented. This is evident in at least two senses.

From a literary point of view, the political ethics appears particularly fragmented. The major book, *The Just War,* is a collection of articles written over a period of about eight years. It is often repetitive, it contains shifts of position,[14] and it makes little reference to the theology, or to the moral theory, which underlie it, and comparatively little even to his political inheritance.

The moral theory is even more awkwardly presented. Even the book *Deeds and Rules in Christian Ethics* is a collection of diverse essays, and this important book is superseded in various ways in later articles (especially "The Case of the Curious Exception").

In addition to this it must be admitted that there are grounds for complaint in both the literary style and the structure of many of Ramsey's significant writings.[15] The style is often convoluted in its concern for precision, and the reader has sometimes to work very hard to see the overall plan of an essay.[16]

One cause of all of these complaints is Ramsey's very evident enjoyment of argument. In the arguments he conducts (or wages), his thought is most tested and most profound, but the argumentative setting and style contribute much to the difficulty of the writing. This is particularly true of debates we will examine—on nuclear deterrence, on exceptionless moral rules, or on consequentialism (to give just three examples).[17]

Any secondary exposition of another thinker's work must always try to place him in context. This is particularly important for an expositor of Ramsey because of the development of his thought, the way he addressed particular issues and arguments, and the way he aimed to contribute to public discussions, both using and adapting the language of contemporary public life.

It is a pity that Ramsey so rarely offered systematic accounts of his thought, but we should not complain too loudly. He had good reasons for not doing so. Mainly, of course, it was his enthusiasm to be involved in pressing and vital issues. No one can do everything, and Ramsey's choice was to "write on" into the real issues of political, medical, and moral importance.[18] He took for granted the foundations he considered firmly laid in order to be able to build a superstructure capable of addressing real issues in a penetrating and relevant way. In doing this, though, he was no ivory tower theorist, for he was always ready to return and rephrase formulations made earlier. If I were pressed to single out one quality of Ramsey which has most impressed me, it would be this. His ability to criticize the work of others was directed also against himself. If his criticisms of others sometimes seemed harsh or excessive, it was clear that he always remained ready to criticize himself.[19] In fact the same concern for truth and accuracy also sometimes led him to interpret others by attributing to them the points he himself is making. Sometimes this appears as a kind of generosity, at other times a kind of barely veiled criticism.[20] Both sprang from what the *London Times* obituary called "his sense of the dignity of argument."[21] This quality of rigor, so often commented upon,[22] meant that he had to change his views comparatively rarely.

It is this humility that marks Ramsey. His pugnacity in argument should not be opposed to his willingness to learn, to give credit, and to change his mind. Both are indeed the two sides of the same coin, namely, his concern for truth, and the service of the truth in love for his fellows. When convinced of the truth, or of error, he was single-minded in pursuit of either. Truth was also important for him because it was vital in the service of others, for their well-being, and always ought to be embodied and lived out. Reason must, therefore, be in constant dialogue with experience, and moral reasoning especially needs a wise flexibility as well as a love-inspired firmness. This helps to make Ramsey's thinking both profound and relevant. I do not think that we can in fairness ask him also to have presented his work as a neat, systematically contained package.

It appears that Ramsey learned these qualities from his father, if we can fairly judge from the son's obituary tribute. Therefore, it is thoroughly appropriate that we should begin a sketch of the relevant aspects of Ramsey's intellectual life at that point. Thus, we begin with one or two comments on the early years, before taking up the account more thoroughly with the publication of *Basic Christian Ethics* in 1951.

Part One: The Development of Paul Ramsey's Ethics

1

1913–1951

Little need be said about Ramsey's life before he began to teach in 1944. He was born the son of a Methodist minister, in 1913, in Mississippi. Ramsey wrote an obituary tribute to his father, the Rev. John Ramsey, in 1949, and it seems clear enough from this article that there are very significant traits in common between the two. There is the same rugged independence of mind and spirit, especially as regards "modern" thought. Other qualities passed on were a deep spiritual and theological conviction as well as a rigorous and inquiring habit of mind. In his tribute Paul Ramsey hints at a striking combination of pugnacity with a willingness to listen and give credit:

> Still he was not content to let what he believed stand simply as a matter of faith or passionate reiteration. He displayed exemplary willingness to "reason together," exercising reason in its own right, logically explicating and defending the great truths of the faith.[1]

This combination is one of Paul Ramsey's own strengths. The enjoyment of argument almost for its own sake shines through in everything he wrote. But we should not be misled. Argument is never for its own sake, but is there to serve a deeper and better understanding of truth, that we may be instructed by one another and change our minds. The ability to change one's mind is a great virtue (though somewhat frustrating at times for critics and expositors).[2]

It is interesting to note that Ramsey changed his mind over pacifism. He was in fact a pacifist as a student. In 1935 an address given by Ramsey was published in the *Christian Advocate* (Nashville). He was at the time president of the student body at Millsaps College (Jackson, Miss.). The address is a plea for Christian pacifism, and it ends:

11

to love peace enough to be willing to die for its preservation against the forces which tend to create war is Jesus' method of projecting his ideal into reality. Have we the courage to follow Jesus completely? Upon the answer we give to this hangs the destiny of our civilization.[3]

This maverick piece was Ramsey's only pacifist publication although he never stopped wrestling with a pacifist conscience.[4] This early evidence shows that the wrestle with pacifism is first conducted by Ramsey with himself, before it is expressed in argument with others. In his last book, *Speak Up for Just War or Pacifism*, there is a remarkable ability to understand and criticize pacifist positions seemingly from within. His estimate of pacifism is not easy to express accurately. He repeatedly admitted that pacifism is a choice made in all sincerity and intellectual honesty by some Christians. He thought it a hard choice to make consistently, but still a tenable one.[5] However, he also maintained that pacifism is wrong, both morally and intellectually. It is a misunderstanding of the Christian way, which requires us to protect the oppressed, by force if necessary.[6]

In 1942 Ramsey began to teach Christian ethics. Out of this teaching came a number of published articles, and then in 1951, he published *Basic Christian Ethics*. Some of the approaches and openings in this book were later ignored or superseded,[7] but there are a number of emphases in direct continuity with later writings. In particular, two strong themes should be noted: the theme of covenant love as providing the basis for ethics and the link from theology to morality, and the idea that love has to prefer one neighbor to another, even to the point of resistance and bloodshed. These two connected ideas are fundamental, and Ramsey's understanding of them scarcely changed at all.

Basic Christian Ethics: Christian Love

The main concern of *Basic Christian Ethics* is Christian love. Ramsey undertook to show that obedient love, love for the neighbor, is the foundation for ethics. Although the roots of Ramsey's distinctive approach are here, the picture is not complete. A brief sketch of the main elements of the book will be a helpful way to introduce his mature understanding and how it developed. In *Basic Christian Ethics* Ramsey tackled a variety of views and problems, and we can only pick out some of the leading themes, with a view to later progress. We choose six themes that seem most important.

(1) Gods Love as the Pattern for *Agape*[8]

In the first and last chapters of *Basic Christian Ethics* Ramsey laid a heavy stress on the theme of covenant. He wrote:

For a proper study of the origin and nature of Christian ethics, a distinction may be made between (1) God's righteousness and love and (2) the reign of this righteousness in the Kingdom of God. These are the two sources of "Christian love." Never imagine you have rightly grasped a biblical ethical idea until you have succeeded in reducing it to a simple corollary of one or other of these notions, or of the idea of covenant between God and man from which they both stem.

So, for instance, we learn "how to be perfect from God's care for the just and unjust, the good and evil alike; the meaning of Christian love by decisive reference to the controlling love of Christ."[9]

In a straightforward, traditional way, then, Ramsey found the motivation and the content of Christian ethics in central biblical themes. There is no need to elaborate at this point, but we should note that there is a significant inference that is not drawn in *Basic Christian Ethics*. It was not until later that the quality of "faithfulness," of steadfast concern for individuals, became a central theme in the exposition of *agape*.[10] This feature of the nature of covenant love was not noticed in *Basic Christian Ethics*.

(2) Neighbor-Love as Disinterested Love for the Other

We condense at least two large questions in a few comments here. Ramsey's discussion partly sidestepped the old question about the relation between the love of God and the love of the neighbor. The upshot of the discussion is that neighbor-love forms the basis for Christian ethics. For instance, he corrected Augustine's picture of the virtues as forms of the love of God by suggesting that they are forms of the love of the neighbor.[11]

Another cluster of questions surrounds the right view of self-love, self-sacrifice, etc. Here the ground was prepared for the later critique of altruism as necessarily the highest form of Christian love.[12] The example of Jesus means that we should always be ready to put the other first, but it does not rule out care for oneself enabling one to look to the needs of others later.[13]

Again, we note briefly that progress remained to be made in exploring precisely what Christian love for the neighbor means. In *Basic Christian Ethics* Ramsey insisted that it is the "true need of the neighbor" which motivates love in action.[14] In later works Ramsey takes it that the paramount needs of every human being arise from our mortality and frailty, and our need of protection from those who would harm or abandon us. It is these needs that constitute the driving force of his major fields of concern, namely, war, medical ethics, and marriage.

(3) The Sovereignty and Flexibility of *Agape* in Ethics

The more general any principle is and the more it has to cover, the more flexible it must be. Ramsey, we have seen, claimed for *agape* that it includes and controls everything in ethics. It has therefore to be flexible enough to apply to everything. We can illustrate this theme in *Basic Christian Ethics* by giving two short excerpts from Ramsey's long and approving quotation of Paul Tillich:

Love, *agape*, offers a principle of ethics which maintains an eternal, unchangeable element but makes its realization dependent on continuous acts of a creative intuition.

Love alone can transform itself according to the concrete demands of every individual and social situation without losing its eternity and dignity and unconditional validity.

Ramsey himself put it more simply, though no less rhetorically:

Only one thing is necessary: for love's sake it must be done. All things are now lawful, all things are now permitted, yet everything is required which Christian love requires, everything without a single exception.[15]

How flexible is *agape*? In *Basic Christian Ethics* the impression was given for the most part that love can do without rules. The dominant note was an attack on legalism.[16] Only later were the themes of faithfulness and the human need for protection brought together in opposition to the teaching of situationism. To this, we will, of course, return.

(4) *Agape* as the Source, Measure, and Unity of the Virtues

This theme provides an apt illustration of the way in which *agape* is viewed. Making clear that love includes the virtues gives Ramsey's exposition of love a rich, diverse, but also flexible quality.

James Gustafson and Paul Ramsey were both students of Richard Niebuhr. When Gustafson accused Ramsey of "love monism,"[17] Ramsey claimed their teacher's authority in the following way: "There is little or no significant difference between listing obedience, gratitude, hope, faith, humility, etc., *alongside* love and an understanding of love rich in diverse aspects or elements bearing those same-named virtues."[18]

This means that Ramsey's understanding of Christian love is open to a richness of biblical and theological content. Ramsey gives a variety of instances and examples of general (pure) rules, including love in 1 Corinthians 13, the fruits of the Spirit, the virtues in Thomist ethics, Christ's teaching on justice, marriage, and truth-telling, and general prohibitions of vice in Scripture.[19]

The relation of love to justice is a matter of particular interest—this is a question allied to love's relation to natural law. It is clear that the way in which Ramsey was to develop his view of the relation of love to "rules" of various kinds is closely analogous to his view of the relation between love and the virtues.

(5) Love as Prudent, not "Unenlightened"

Ramsey argued strongly for a hardheaded view of love, especially when there is conflict and the actor must choose between neighbors. He quoted Augustine to the effect that it is not enough merely to be kindhearted.[20] Nor is love characteristically spontaneous in action, for its actions may more commonly be guided by forethought. Love is not simply an emotional response, though, of course, it may be in appropriate circumstances. Allied to this is the concern that the avoidance of bloodshed per se is not a priority—it is moral evil that is most unlovely, not physical evil.[21]

(6) Love as the Root of an Ethic of Resistance

Apart from the early piece we have already referred to, dating from the 1930s, his student days, and the height of Western pacifism before

World War II, Ramsey's opposition to pacifism was clear and unwavering, though always in a way sympathetic. His exposition of just war theory can clearly be seen to begin in Chapter Five of *Basic Christian Ethics*. The main point here is to establish that an ethic of resistance is not merely compatible with *agape*, it actually should be derived from it. Love requires us to choose between neighbors when they are in conflict, not to turn aside and abdicate from tough and bloody choices. Ramsey turns to Ambrose and Augustine and examines the logic of their thought in refusing the right of *self*-defense, while still expecting the Christian to take part in warfare when called on to do so in a just cause. We will return to Ramsey's exposition and argument in due course.[22]

Our survey of some of the major themes discussed in *Basic Christian Ethics* has trailed advances in basic ethical theory which did not appear in Ramsey's writings until the 1960s. Before tracing the lines of development, we may pause to look at one or two further general characteristics of Ramsey's work.

A Biblical Thinker

It is easier to make a general claim that Ramsey's ethics is biblical than to substantiate it in detail.[23] He is biblical usually only in a general theological way, and rarely appeals to particular biblical laws or commands. In "The Biblical Norm of Righteousness," for instance, there are only five or six biblical references—on the treatment of strangers, God's love for Israel, Christ's love for us, and a general reference to Paul on marriage in Ephesians 5. This is typical. Ramsey himself summarizes:

> The message of both the Old and the New Testament is that God means to mold human life into the action of God; human righteousness into God's righteousness; man's frequent faithlessness, or maybe his fragile faithfulness, into the faithfulness of God himself.
> Now let us simply summarize these models, this pattern, this final norm of Christian life, by using the words Christian love or Christian charity.

And to cite Ramsey's biblical "poetry" once more:

> just as we know the heart and needs of a stranger from God's care for us while we were yet strangers, we also know the heart and need of a dying

one from God's care for us who live always in the midst of death. This means that the perfection of love is a working knowledge of another as a creature of flesh and blood whose fate it is to live always in the valley of the shadow of death.[24]

Although we have jumped nearly twenty years, and we find now the characteristic concerns with faithfulness and human frailty, the continuity with the thought of *Basic Christian Ethics* is readily apparent.[25]

Ramsey would no doubt agree with Gustafson when he says, "The biblical writers were not ethical theorists."[26] Ramsey clearly embraces all the pluralism that there is in the Bible, even if his narrow aims sometimes seem to obscure this. Ramsey's creative use of the Bible can also be illustrated in his writing on abortion, or in his sparing use of Bible stories in political ethics, or in his hypothetical retellings of the parable of the Good Samaritan, but the general quality shares with the biblical writers a robustly objective view of morality, as for example, Fletcher, McCormick, and Gustafson do not.[27]

Ramsey and the Christian Tradition

To establish the centrality of *agape*, Christian love, Ramsey draws not only on the Bible, but also on the greatest theologians, including Augustine, Aquinas, and Luther. This is pursued with interpretations (and corrections) of others including Barth, Tillich, Brunner, Maritain, and the Niebuhr brothers.[28]

In other respects, he uses the Christian tradition quite freely. It is worth noting that he likes to return to the great thinkers direct[29]— Augustine, Aquinas, and Luther in particular—remaining untroubled by the weight of scholarship and conflicting interpretations that have (rightly) grown up around these figures. His expository uses of Augustine on noncombatant immunity, and of Aquinas on the killing of an unjust aggressor have not been accepted in the relevant fields.[30]

Just as in his handling of modern thinkers in *Nine Modern Moralists*, Ramsey's interpretations tended to be constructive rather than historically strict. He tried to reach the central dynamic of thought which inspired each writer, and in the process developed his own views. It is, for instance, probably better to regard his understanding of the basis of just war theory in Christian love, and his view of the relation between love and justice, as inspired by Augustine rather than simply as historical interpretation.[31]

One of Ramsey's inspirations is scarcely ever explicit. This is the debt he owed to Jonathan Edwards (whose *Freedom of the Will* and *Ethical Writings*[32] he edited and introduced) although he scarcely ever cited him—a couple of times in *Basic Christian Ethics*, in "A Letter to James Gustafson," where he calls Edwards "America's greatest theologian,"[33] and on the frontispiece of *Nine Modern Moralists*:

. . . The tendency of general benevolence to produce justice, also the tendency of justice to produce effects agreeable to general benevolence, both render justice pleasing to the virtuous mind. (*A Dissertation on the Nature of True Virtue*)[34]

2

1951–1961

Richard Niebuhr characterized the position of *Basic Christian Ethics* as "love transforming natural law."[1] This was a label Ramsey accepted and used. It raises immediately a number of related questions—perhaps especially the question of the relation of Christian love to law. In the 1950s, working in a number of different areas, and reading fairly widely, the center of his attention was claimed by this question. In various ways we can see how the attention he gave to it led him from various points of view to a new perspective, differing from that of *Basic Christian Ethics*.

Although "natural law" is the subject that prompted a new perspective in Ramsey's thinking about law, he found other ways of expressing it. The rather loose dialectic implied by talk of "transformation" was open to misunderstanding, and the phrase "natural law" is itself understood in a variety of senses. We now prepare the way for examining the charge of inconsistency by outlining the terminology Ramsey used in this connection.

Apart from the phrase "love transforming natural law," other formulations are favored by Ramsey to express the foundational place of *agape* in Christian ethics. These include the use of the idea of the complementarity of creation and covenant. Ramsey took the "creation-covenant" expression from his reading of Karl Barth in the late 1950s (i.e., when successive volumes of the *Church Dogmatics* were published in English), though his application of the idea was not in the direction Barth intended.

Another phrase, which Ramsey came to use much more than "love transforming natural law," was "in-principled Christian love." As we shall see, the latter expresses the substance of what Ramsey wants to say much more helpfully and directly than the idea of transformation.

Alongside this exploration of the key ideas on which Christian ethics rests, Ramsey highlights the importance of faithfulness as a way of explicating the meaning of love.

In 1961 and 1962 Ramsey published three books: *War and the Christian Conscience, Christian Ethics and the Sit-In,* and *Nine Modern Moralists.*[2] In the 1950s Ramsey also worked a good deal on the theology and ethics of sex and marriage.[3] The diversity of this work makes it clear that the development of his theoretical ideas took place partly under the pressure of thinking through specific ethical issues. In this process he considered and commented on other thinkers and theories. While we separate out the various themes to comment on, we must remember their interconnection and the context in which they were set. This includes not only the questions raised by war, marriage, and politics, but also the emerging vogue for forms of situationism and contextualism which were crystallized by Joseph Fletcher in the 1960s.

"Love Transforming Natural Law"

In the introduction to *Nine Modern Moralists,* Ramsey claimed that his aim was to "lift this motif into fuller view as the real groundwork of Christian ethics in the thought of many of its greatest contemporary exponents." In order to do this, of course, a good deal of attention had to be given to what natural law really means. This inquiry is the guiding thread of the book. By trying to show that a concept of natural law is implicitly foundational to many of the thinkers he examines, Ramsey explored and expounded his own views.

Ramsey's summary in the introduction sets out his view quite modestly: "I affirm that there is some virtue in man's ordinary moral decisions, and, as it were, challenge the reader, who may have an ingrained prejudice against a wrong conception of the natural law, to say whether he means to deny this." Writing approvingly of Tillich's discussion of the relation between love and justice, Ramsey argues that "[Tillich] does not allow fully for a natural capacity on the part of man for deciding justly and rightly *within* the actual encounter when he has before him, concretely in the prism of the case, the claims of persons."[4] It is clear from the phrasing that this is Ramsey's way of putting it. Basic to his view of natural law is that it rests on the rational expression in particular cases of the sense of justice, or the sense of injustice.

Whenever Ramsey made these relatively modest claims for the

natural law, he immediately affirmed the need for love to transform and complete, "to sensitize, enlighten, direct and extend." He examined this in detail in the two chapters on Maritain and Cahn entitled "The Egypt of the Natural Law" and "Man's Exodus from Natural Law." The metaphor seems to imply that we all must start in Egypt, with our created sense of injustice and our ordinary moral sense, but that our goal is the exodus into covenant-righteousness and love. This is bound to raise questions for the permanent validity or usefulness of the "Egypt" we must be redeemed from:

> The question to be raised is whether the morality of Exodus into covenant is not needed as the *explicit* theological premise *actively at work* in the moral life of men in every Egypt of the natural order in order to sustain any proper ethics, to comprehend and interpret it adequately, or even to restore it in this hour of moral and political disorder.[5]

Ramsey effectively abandoned this metaphor from this point on. It is unnecessary to spend time here following the twists and turns of the detailed and searching dialogues and critiques in *Nine Modern Moralists*. The causes of the change can be surmised with reasonable confidence.

The first reason is that the phrase "natural law" fails to convey any precise meaning without a good deal of further elaboration and discussion. Ramsey was careful, for instance, to distance his understanding not only from that of official Roman Catholic doctrine,[6] but also from any extreme or erroneous rationalistic interpretations relying on rational-deductive schemes. This point is almost inseparably connected to a second. Ramsey's reason for rejecting any claim that natural law can itself supply "a certain and a sufficient indication of right and wrong action in any area" is that *agape* "provides the supreme and controlling determination."[7] It is not only, then, that Ramsey has to explain what he means by natural law, but he also has to explain how it is transformed by Christian love. It might have been simpler, in other words, to begin with love and work outward from that in the first place. The two expressions Ramsey used for this movement were "in-principled Christian love," and the complementary relation of "creation-covenant."

Creation and Covenant

When Ramsey read Barth's *Church Dogmatics,* especially Volume III on the doctrine of creation, he felt he had found a much better way to express the relationship between love and natural law or justice.[8] Barth speaks of creation as the basis or precondition of covenant, and covenant as the meaning and goal of creation. Barth's concern is a wide and general one, and Ramsey borrowed his language in order to use it in social and political ethics in a way that Barth never did, and indeed would have resisted.[9] The language of creation and covenant expresses the thought of transformation and the asymmetry of the relation between natural law and love extremely well.

This solution is first found in *Christian Ethics and the Sit-In:*

> The state and its law as an ordinance of creation, natural justice, human and legal rights, and social institutions generally, so far as these have a positive purpose under the creative, governing and preserving purposes of God—all are the external basis making possible the actualization of the promise of covenant; while covenant or fellow humanity is the internal basis and meaning of every right, true justice, or law.[10]

The clear advantage of this formulation is that it holds together the various points that Ramsey wished to make. He wanted to affirm the value and importance of natural justice, natural law, in moral thought and social life. Justice provides the basis in the social order for the promotion of love's aims, but it is at the same time the rules of justice that give social expression to Christian love. He wants to say that these form a foundation for, and expression of, the action of Christian love so love itself is the inner meaning and basis of natural justice, etc. It is because love is this basis that it should also transform and control the content of natural right and justice.

> The order of charity thus interpenetrates the order of justice—affirming and confirming justice and fundamental rights as first and also required of a Christian by the saving love of Christ by whom we and all men have first been loved, and then elevating, transforming, definitely shaping, and fashioning what justice may mean, if possible more in the direction of the requirements of charity.

In this way Ramsey underwrote his formula "Christ transforming natural justice." We should note the emphasis that justice is not sovereign: "In addition to trying to determine what justice requires, even the requirement of a love-transformed justice, [the Christian] may and can and should also ask again what love requires."[11]

It is a bit of a puzzle that Ramsey talked of creation and covenant so rarely after 1961.[12] We may hazard two conjectures about this. It is possible that Ramsey partly felt that the solution to the questions he had been dealing with was so completed by the notion of the relationship between creation and covenant that there was no need for him to continue to pursue these questions (especially as his attention was drawn away to the specific topic of just war theory). This suggestion finds no support in any comment Ramsey himself made, and so we are driven to make another. Ramsey's concern to protect the idea of the sovereignty of love in Christian ethics made him wary of natural law language or formulations. He came to prefer to speak of in-principled love.

Even if creation-covenant language is rarely used by Ramsey subsequently, the substance remains, as we see in a later article: "Faithfulness claims and canons of covenant loyalty may be the profoundest way to understand all our concepts of justice and fairness."[13]

In-Principled Christian Love

The sovereignty of Christian love, which Ramsey at no point wavers from, perhaps made it inevitable that his own substantial contributions to moral thought should be built on a basis rather different from "love transforming natural law." Instead of beginning with ideas of natural law or justice, Ramsey's political ethics takes another course. He begins with love, and seeks to see how love can be embodied in practical action, and in rules and principles to undergird action. The phrase he used to describe this was "in-principled Christian love."

This phrase made its appearance in 1960 in an article entitled "Faith Effective through In-Principled Love."[14] It is used in significant places in *Christian Ethics and the Sit-In*. For instance, at one point he glosses justice as "the justice that provides an in-principled expression of divine charity." Summarizing at the end of the book, he writes: "This entire movement of charity into justice may be termed 'faith effective through in-principled love.' "[15]

Charity does not take shape only in justice, of course. Love is the basis for some of the key terms of Ramsey's thought. One thinks immediately of "discrimination" in just war theory, or his use of the word "care" in medical ethics. In both areas, Ramsey employs a word in fairly general use, but then gives each principle a precise content and definition derived from Christian love.

In this way Ramsey satisfied his concern that moral language should be in touch with the everyday social ethos—to correct and reshape it,

but still to be in basic continuity with it. His procedure here expressed
his confidence that the society to which he spoke was still sufficiently
grounded in its historical Christian foundations to be able to learn
much from a rigorous explication of the meaning of Christian love. In
his intricate wrestlings in politics, in medical ethics, with legal judgments,[16] he entered into the public arena, using the concepts and
language in an everyday sense that at the same time he brought into
correspondence with his own theory.[17] We will also see this concern in
his debates with situation ethics and with consequentialism, for moral
language rests on good moral thought.

Faithfulness

In *Basic Christian Ethics,* Ramsey made much of God's faithful
covenant love as the source of Christian ethics, but it was not until
1958 that he used this as the controlling theme with which to characterize Christian love: "Hence we may summarize biblical religion as
faith in the *faithfulness* of God; and we may summarize biblical ethics
as the molding of human action into the action of God's faithfulness."
He adds in a footnote that this is the way in which we can grasp the
central coherent meaning of the twofold love command: "Faithful,
faithfulness, *hesed,* is the single, univocal biblical concept in terms of
which the meaning of 'love' in Jesus' twofold command has to be
understood."[18]

Allied to the emphasis on faithfulness is the idea of "covenants of
life with life." Faithfulness belongs to relationships, and the covenant
relationships here are those into which we are born, and which we
enter. Ethics is not only interested in "decisions," but in the fabric of
our enduring lives in which all our decisions are set. The examples
Ramsey is fondest of using are the marriage relationship, and that
between doctor and patient.[19] In war, this leads him to focus on his
concern for the noncombatant, to whom we have an obligation. Our
relationship to him of course is only defined negatively, but it requires
of us that we should not be unfaithful to his life by directly attacking
him.[20]

Faithfulness is the concept that lies at the heart of Ramsey's work.
It leads very simply to the concern for rules and principles,[21] and to
his concern for the ethics of marriage, as well as to the direction and
character of his work in medical and political ethics.

Since this is the key to a grasp of Ramsey's thought, we should pause for a moment to consider it. How might we object to this portrayal of Christian love and Christian ethics? It would, I think, be hard to doubt its correctness as a central part of any analysis, and here it is important to remember that faithfulness is always thought of positively, not negatively. (We are not thinking of a "faithful" husband merely as one who does not commit adultery.) To possess the virtue of faithfulness means to be forgiving, caring, steadfast, loyal, concerned for the other, and in principle to embrace all the Christian virtues of human love and relationships. Perhaps it might be objected that, for all its importance, faithfulness cannot be considered the sole or dominant feature of ethics. It must be clear that Ramsey would not want to call it the only consideration in ethics, but for him it is unquestionably the dominant one. Is his emphasis justified?

Much (indeed, almost everything that follows) is in principle at stake here. In response, it is important to note that the emphasis on faithfulness is central to Ramsey's interpretation of the theology of Christian love. It is not a matter of more or less, but an implication of the nature of love. Ramsey conceived the task of Christian ethics to be the determination, as accurately as possible, of the meaning of love. Here we can allude briefly to the general theological and philosophical reasons that led Ramsey to his view of Christian love.

We make two general kinds of remark. First, this is the way Ramsey read the Bible, Christian theology, the central ethical thrust of the gospel. Second, by placing the emphasis here, he undertook to place certain facets of Christian theology in contrast with certain trends of contemporary thought. The two are interconnected, and we simply separate them for convenience.

In theological terms, the doctrines Ramsey wanted to emphasize include the sovereignty of God over human life and destiny, the steadfast self-giving love of God for humanity, the physical mortality of human life, and the frail sinfulness of human beings. We could summarize these as the doctrines of God, covenant, creation, and fall, I suppose. Of these, the significance of covenant will be clear enough already, but the others need a word of explanation.

To refer to the doctrine of God is to say little more than that we are concerned, after all, with *Christian* ethics. But this is not to be taken for granted. It means that we must be concerned with each individual person as one whom God loves. It means, also, that we are concerned with obedience to God in the place where we are now rather than a general concern for the human race or the future. This is not to say that such concerns are ruled out, but rather that they are to be derived from, and rest upon and be subject to, the sovereign providence of God. Christian ethics, therefore, is primarily interested in the quality of actions and relationships, and only secondarily with their consequences.[22]

Each of these elements of Christian theology was drawn out in implicit or explicit contrast with Ramsey's reading of contemporary culture. His view of the sovereignty of God led him, of course, to many attitudes in significant contrast to modern ones, but there are some specific comments to be made also. He drew attention, for instance, to the problem of how an ethic for which human life is the source of value can give any justification for the sacrifice of a single human life.[23] He reminds us that sin is a spiritual, not a physical, phenomenon.[24] One cannot deduce moral evil from the mere causation of physical suffering or evil. Christian ethics cannot rest content with arguments based fundamentally on the survival of the human race.[25]

The doctrine of creation should draw our attention to the nature of human life. Men and women are body-soul unities, living in particular histories and neighborhoods.[26] Human life is mortal and precarious, vulnerable and in need of protection. These themes deserve greater exploration and exposition. All we can say here is that the frailty of human life is one consideration that leads to Ramsey's emphasis on faithfulness.

Ramsey's understanding of the doctrine of creation is tied up with his opposition to "Cartesian dualism" and voluntarism. Christian anthropology perceives that human life is a unity, and that physical realities are inseparable from mental ones; we are "embodied souls" and "ensouled bodies." He opposed individualism and utopian idealism with the truth that we live in a particular time and place, with particular neighbors and responsibilities. He vigorously opposed modern tendencies to think that man should be his own maker.[27]

The doctrine of the fall plays a smaller, but a significant role. Its importance can be illustrated by the use Ramsey made of it in his view of marriage vows. Two of the reasons we make vows are to commit ourselves to be faithful to the other in the event of their failure and sin, and to bind ourselves against the likelihood of our own temptation. A similar pattern could be traced in the basis for other social institutions,[28] but it is important to notice that these also have their roots in the positive doctrines of creation and providence.

The doctrine of sin becomes particularly important in the political sphere when Ramsey is concerned with the question of power and its restraint. It led him to oppose those who believed that it is desirable for the world to be freed from war or its possibility, and those who argued for world government.[29] He argued rather for a realism that sees political power being restrained by opposing power, and that sees dreams of lasting peace as enticing us to immoral and dangerous planning and thinking.

These perceptions about the nature of Christian truth, and its challenges to modern secular thought, are inextricably linked to his choice of the key term "faithfulness" to characterize Christian love, which is the basis for his ethical thought at every point. Whether his outworking of this theme is right at every point is a matter for careful judgment, but two concluding comments (or warnings to would-be objectors) are called for. We will find, irrespective of emphasis, that the truths from which Ramsey started were cogently and powerfully addressed to controversial questions. It may prove insufficient, in order to overthrow the conclusion, to object only to the degree of emphasis placed on the initial assumption. It is usually the truth of the assumption that must be questioned. We will also find that Ramsey connected these broad and central Christian themes with the intricate and perplexing questions of modern life, and that he did this in a way which does justice not only to the intricacies but also to the quality of moral demand that one would expect to follow from the searching character of God's love.

3

Developing a Protestant Casuistry

From the late 1950s through the 1960s Ramsey worked principally in the fields of ethical theory and just war theory. The two tasks are intertwined, and indeed sometimes indistinguishable, for instance, in discussion of the rule of double effect. Nevertheless, for purposes of exposition, they have to be separated. In terms of systematic exposition of a body of thought, it is clear that it is more convenient for ethical theory to precede its outworking in a particular area. This should not be taken to imply that that is how ethical theory can be or should be developed, and this is certainly not how Ramsey himself worked in these years. On the contrary, he believed that the moralist has to continue to work backward and forward, from theory to practice and vice versa.[1]

Ramsey articulated his theological ethic in the 1960s in the debates over situation ethics. Every so often an apparently unorthodox view of Christian belief challenges traditional thinkers to set out their own understanding more clearly and in new ways. Paul Ramsey took up the challenge of situation ethics very vigorously, perhaps partly because his earlier book, *Basic Christian Ethics*, could certainly be read as an expression of a situationist view.

Indeed, his ethical methodology sets out from what look very like the concerns of Joseph Fletcher.[2] Both would agree that Christian love has a fundamental priority in ethics, and would also agree on the importance of an understanding sufficiently flexible to handle properly the complex diversity of real life. From these concerns Ramsey, for his part, developed an approach which is too easily labeled "deontological."[3] It is a confident and firm ethic, and in particular it is at the opposite pole from Fletcher in developing a powerful analysis of rules and actions. Here is a rational casuistry which is much more reminis-

cent of Aquinas, or perhaps Suarez, than Luther; it is sharp, sophisticated, and thoroughly and carefully reasoned out.

The ideas that Fletcher put forward so bluntly and strongly in his
Situation Ethics were by no means brand new. Ramsey had already
taken some of these tendencies to task in a number of articles before
he published the first edition of *Deeds and Rules in Christian Ethics* in
1965.[4] Further chapters were added for the second edition in 1967.

The major theme of Ramsey's continuing opposition to forms of the
"new morality," contextualism, situationism, etc., remained the
same.[5] He insisted that a true assessment of the requirements of love,
and of the implications of our sense of morality, always sees the
propriety and necessity of the place of principles, rules, and careful
casuistry in Christian ethics. In various ways he undertook to show
that the exponents of situationism are confused, or inconsistent, or, at
the least, insufficiently careful to weigh the implications of the different
statements they make (and mean to make).

Some examples of his critiques will illustrate his method and help us
to sketch the development of his thought. Since the foundations for
Ramsey's critique of situationism were laid as he thought through his
views on natural law, we return first to 1956, to a key essay on the
moral thought of Reinhold Niebuhr.

In 1956 Ramsey contributed an article to Reinhold Niebuhr's festschrift entitled "Love and Law."[6] This is a definitive article for any
grasp of Ramsey's thought, especially to see the emphasis change in
the 1950s after *Basic Christian Ethics*. It is perhaps the most significant
of the essays in *Nine Modern Moralists*, in which Ramsey first developed clearly the major themes of his advocacy of a radical revision of
natural law. It also marks out the lines of Ramsey's divergence from
Niebuhr, from whom he learned much of his political theory. In moral
theory Ramsey's debt to Niebuhr is that the latter provided clear and
articulate views from which Ramsey could learn only in the process of
overthrowing them.

In "Love and Law," Ramsey responds first to Niebuhr's article
"Love and Law in Protestantism and Catholicism."[7] The main section
of the latter, "The Transcendence of Love over Law," gives four
points at which the transcendence of love is clearest (or perhaps really
three—Niebuhr concedes "one point may really belong to the rule of
law"). These include "Love as Sacrificial" and "Love as Forgive-
ness." On sacrificial love, Niebuhr had written:

> It is the completion of the law of love because perfect love has no logical
> limit short of the readiness to sacrifice the self for the other. Yet it is a

point which stands beyond all law, because the necessity of sacrificing one's life for another cannot be formulated as an obligation, nor can it be achieved under the whip of the sense of obligation.[8]

With this point about the transcendence of love, Niebuhr combined his understanding of the indeterminacy of human nature. Theories of natural law, he contended, do not allow for this indeterminacy, nor do they allow sufficiently for historical contingency and relativity.

Typically, Ramsey uses Niebuhr's own language and expressions to make his critique. He shows that much of Niebuhr's claim for the transcendence of love relates to the subjective aspect of morality. By "the subjective aspect" he means the way in which love is understood by the actor, and the way in which love should be taught and encouraged. For instance, we see in the excerpt above that sacrifice "is the completion of the law of love," but it cannot be "achieved under the whip of the sense of obligation."

Just as pertinent to Ramsey's critique of situationism is his wrestling with Niebuhr's understanding of indeterminate human nature. Ramsey was concerned to make two points that, he believed, need to be carried through more clearly and straightforwardly, without the issues being clouded by Niebuhr's dialectic style of argument.

Niebuhr had conceded, at one point in his argument, that man "is a creature of nature who is subject to certain natural structures." Ramsey comments: "That one sentence will have made plain that the minimal, negative, and most universal aspects of morality are grounded for Niebuhr in certain immutable aspects of human existence."[9] But for the most part Niebuhr's interest was in the indeterminate aspects of human nature, its freedom and transcendence. Even here, however, as Ramsey points out, Niebuhr admitted that moral obligations can still be encompassed in terms of law, if law is properly expressed: "Yet they do not stand completely outside of law, if law is defined in terms of man's essential nature. For this indeterminate freedom is part of his essential nature."[10] Ramsey brings these two points together, arguing that more can be made of them than Niebuhr typically allowed. "What can be more grounded in nature than the assertion that man is made for life-in-community whose quality is love?"

This then gave Ramsey an approach to his own idea of a radically revised natural law theory. It incorporates a theme which was a continuing part of his critique of situationism, i.e., that principles and rules in ethics (forms of law) are to be based on the patterns and continuities of human and social life. These are given in nature, and are there to be discerned, not invented.

One of Ramsey's severest criticisms of situation ethics was a short
article in 1960 responding to Alexander Miller in *Christianity and
Crisis*. In this article Ramsey pleads for rigor and reason in ethics.
Miller wished to reject principles, and he also dismissed "any systematic morphology of man." Yet, Ramsey claims, Miller had to bring
both back in, either openly or smuggled. Miller, for instance, admitted
that we need "something like a morphology of man," and that "one
marriage is in salient respects much like another." Miller's proposal
was for "a prudential calculation reinforced and corrected by an innate
impulse of justice and compassion,"[11] which Ramsey claims is well on
the way to restoring the natural law principles Miller thought he had
jettisoned. Ramsey's general judgment is a severe one:

> Only in appearance is faithfulness to the Gospel-ethic to be secured by
> lack of rigor and completeness in elaborating the substance of every
> crucial decision.
>   The fact is that recent Christian contextual ethicists have been content
> with Pyrrhic victories, obtained by absent-mindedness, or by failure to
> make a part of their conscious thought the principles that are actually
> present.[12]

A persistent topic in the discussions of the early 1960s was marriage,
and the proper circumstances for the full expression of sexual love.
Two examples from *Deeds and Rules in Christian Ethics* show how
Ramsey's point here is a practical outworking of the theoretical arguments with Niebuhr, Miller, and others. The situationists claimed that
love cannot be "confined" to marriage, but two significant exponents
of situationism (the Quaker document and John Robinson) set out
conditions for sexual intercourse that Ramsey showed amounted to
marriage in all but name.[13] In exploring the conditions in which sexual
intercourse should take place, the Quakers asked, "Could we say also
that at least in spirit each should be committed to the other—should
be open to the other in heart and mind?" But they would not draw
from this the conclusion that marriage is the place for sexual expression. Ramsey comments:

> But these Friends drew back when they saw that to ask what they were
> driven to ask from within the interior of an ethics of responsibility was
> "to ask nothing less than the full commitment of marriage." They chose
> act-responsibility when a rule of action embodying responsibility ap-
> peared on the horizon and was obviously required by their own analysis.[14]

In a similar critique of Robinson, Ramsey made another important point about marriage. He argued that most, if not all, of Robinson's reservations about insisting on marriage are due to a misunderstanding of what at heart constitutes a marriage. Robinson had objected to what Ramsey calls a "bourgeois" conception of marriage, which assumes that marriage is defined by the legalities, rather than by the full commitment of one person to another. In rejecting the bourgeois understanding, Ramsey makes a typical claim for his own approach. "It is in fact what Christianity has always meant by marriage, or the responsible consent to one another that alone makes marriage."[15] Ramsey's crediting Christianity with this view is somewhat optimistic. As we will see, Ramsey's point is typical of his "radical revision" of natural law categories and rules (e.g., in asking about the meaning of rules or about the use to be made of "double effect").[16] The importance of seeing what Ramsey understands by the *meaning* of moral rules can scarcely be overestimated.

Ramsey also attacked another general feature of the ethos of the early 1960s—the proneness to make particular moral judgments on issues of social and political morality, attempting in the process to work out a casuistry of principles, rules, and application. At the same time a similar task in personal ethics was avoided or rejected.[17] Against this, Ramsey insisted that it is usually more difficult to formulate general principles in social ethics, and work through to application, than in personal ethics: "It would seem that if Christian ethics can get down to concrete cases, *prima facie* it can do this in the realm of personal morality better than amid the complexities of economic and social policy.[18]

We can now summarize some key aspects of Ramsey's criticism of situationism. He charged it with overlooking the continuities and similarities of human life and overestimating the difficulty raised by the creativity and indeterminateness of human nature, the variety of human life, etc. It underestimated the moral importance of themes like commitment, faithfulness, truth-telling, promise-keeping, etc., often reading the Christian tradition here too literally.[19] It was characterized by a lack of rigor, a tendency to be content with inconsistencies and easy generalizations, which are not sufficiently explicated and pursued.

All this is mainly negative, and it does not yet get to the real problems which prompted the popularity of situationism. We must now set out the question at the center of the debate with a little more precision in order to introduce the detailed scrutiny which will occupy us in Part Two.

What was the basic challenge of situationism? The question that it posed may be expressed as follows. If Christian love leads to principles and rules, based on human nature, and reasoned out with care and thought, how can those rules survive the undisputed existence of situations where love clearly seems to suggest a different course of action from that specified by the appropriate rule? This was the unresolved question of *Deeds and Rules in Christian Ethics*. The question was most clearly expressed in that volume in Ramsey's use of Frankena. Frankena had offered different types of "agapism," namely, act-agapism, modified act-agapism, summary rule-agapism, and pure rule-agapism.[20] The problem is stated in the way that pure rule-agapism is defined. In this moral method, *agape* leads to rules that must then be applied without further reference to *agape* itself. Thus, according to pure rule-agapism: "we may and sometimes must obey a rule in a particular situation even though the action it calls for is seen not to be what love itself would directly require."[21] Ramsey agreed that there are pure rules through which *agape* expresses itself. He gave a number of biblical examples. At the same time, negatively, he showed that summary rules will be forced either to slide back to act-agapism (since the rule is always potentially in question), or be shown to be pure rules all the time.[22]

But can the pure rules thus devised then lead to acts which are not in themselves love-fulfilling? In *Deeds and Rules in Christian Ethics* Ramsey went a long way to answering this, but he did not do so conclusively. He took the route of examining virtually all the exceptional cases offered by Fletcher.[23] Sometimes it is clear that Fletcher had mistaken his understanding of the rule (e.g., marriage, where Ramsey attacked his bourgeois conception of it). At other times, Ramsey argued, the problem is a wrong description of the act concerned (e.g., describing self-sacrifice to save others as suicide—or even euthanasia!).

These points were made in the essay on Fletcher in the second edition of *Deeds and Rules in Christian Ethics* in 1966. By this time, then, it seems that Ramsey was near to showing how rules can always express Christian love. We need to look more closely at the meaning of a given rule, and, the other side of the same coin, the way in which an act is described and subsumed under the rule.

This way forward was clearly indicated in 1966, but it still remained for Ramsey to show in theoretical terms that there can be pure rules, to which there are no (or virtually no) exceptions, on the basis of Christian love. This task, which means more than the defeat of situationism, for it amounts to the spelling out of a method of casuistry, was undertaken in 1968.

The essay that filled the gap was "The Case of the Curious Exception." In this long and convoluted article Ramsey defended the possibility of exceptionless moral rules.[24] At its center is the discussion of how apparent exceptions to moral rules are to be handled. Ramsey offers two ways of doing this: either to specify the exceptional cases by examining what considerations will override others, and so on, or to inquire more deeply into the meaning of the rule, and the principles that underlie it, and so attempt to gain a fuller understanding not merely of the situation, but also of the rule itself. Ramsey favors the latter, and this understanding of casuistry is at the heart of his thought.

Our summary of Ramsey's critique of situationism sets the scene for a more detailed scrutiny of Ramsey's casuistry. That we will come to in Part Two, along with the principle of double effect, which we have omitted from our outline so far. Ramsey's work on this principle is actually more to be found in his writings on war. It is now time to survey Ramsey's progress in the 1960s in the fields of politics and war.

4

Political Ethics and the Just War Theory

As far as political ethics is concerned, Ramsey's claim to greatness does not rest on the originality of his leading ideas. For the most part he was content to remain with the ideas and concerns of those from whom he learned. Perhaps the only major original idea that he advanced in this area was the analysis of the origins of noncombatant immunity in the underlying patterns of thought of Ambrose and Augustine. The stature of Ramsey's just war theory is rather to be found in the particular combination of ideas he drew together, and the way he held them together as a convincing whole and used them to penetrate complex and difficult practical issues in an illuminating way.

This is the heart of our inquiry, and we can now see how it forms the center of our essay. This section surveys the context for Ramsey's central political assertions. It will proceed by looking at some of the major figures whose writings and thought particularly went to the making of Ramsey's. Ramsey fashioned a coherent political morality from three Christian traditions which are often seen as mutually separate or in tension. These three traditions are a characteristically Protestant ethic of Christian love, a sharp-edged rational casuistry, and an Augustinian political realism. (Tracing the shape of Ramsey's realism is part of our task, but for now it is perhaps sufficient to say that by realism we mean an attitude to politics which emphasizes its limitations. In particular it emphasizes the human propensity to wrongdoing and the need for the restraint of wrong, by force when necessary.)

Our survey of Ramsey's political ethics, with its combination of moral rigor and political realism, prepares the way for Part Three. That will focus on the derivation of just war political ethics within an ethic of Christian love, and then examine his articulation of the twin principles of discrimination and proportion. These have to be grasped as an instantiation of his ethical method. An examination of the outworking of the theory in relation to the Vietnam war will then precede a fuller exposition of his concern with nuclear deterrence, which will occupy Part Four.

It will be impossible in a short survey to do justice to the full range of questions Ramsey addressed as well as give any account of the subtlety and rigor of his thought. Ramsey rarely started from square one. Instead he tended to assume a grasp of the theological and moral basis for political ethics that he had established elsewhere. He also assumed, and here particularly he is liable to be misread by critics, a liberal concern for social justice which looks for the maximum improvement in political life of conditions of freedom, respect for the law, open political debate, equality, etc.[1] That Ramsey seemed to lay little explicit weight on such things is due partly to his dislike of repeating what seems obvious, but perhaps more to his concern that these things be not advocated naively and without regard to the sometimes harsh realities of social and political life.

Ramsey's first concern in politics is with the morality of right, or just, political action. For him the acid test of this is the morality of the use of force, in particular in armed conflict. The question whether Christian love may engage in war was a concern in his first book, *Basic Christian Ethics*, and in his last, *Speak Up for Just War or Pacifism*. Should the Church be pacifist? Throughout his working life, Ramsey insisted that it should not. But with his continuing debate with pacifism came his insistence on very carefully defined limits for the conduct of war. Though the Christian may and should be ready to fight, one who is motivated by Christian love to fight for good political ends will also be controlled by love in the way he fights.

Development

Two of the key figures who influenced Ramsey's understanding of politics were Reinhold Niebuhr and John Courtney Murray.[2] There can be little doubt that Ramsey's immediate debt to Niebuhr was much greater than his debt to Murray. Nevertheless, one way of approaching the essential shape of Ramsey's political ethics would be to ask whether he was closer to Murray's moderate Catholic realism or to Niebuhr's pragmatic Protestant realism. It does not take long to see the answer to this way of putting the question. While Murray never spelled out his views in detail or at length, it would seem that Ramsey's differences from him were only matters of emphasis, as far as their basic position is concerned. On the other hand, Ramsey differed from Niebuhr in important matters of substance. A brief inquiry into Ramsey's relation to these two major figures will help clarify Ramsey's views, and it will also teach us about an abiding division between different approaches to Christian political ethics.

We must first acknowledge briefly the importance for Ramsey of the vital work of John C. Ford. In *Speak Up for Just War or Pacifism*, Ramsey acknowledged the key influence of Ford's article on "The Morality of Obliteration Bombing." It was from Ford that he learned the perennial truth and contemporary urgency of the principle of noncombatant immunity.[3] This principle is not outdated or irrelevant in the modern age. Rather, it is all the more essential in modern warfare where the temptation to overlook it is so strong. Nevertheless, its widespread rejection by contemporary political theory and ethics means that much work has to go into its clarification and presentation.[4] It looks at a first superficial glance to be difficult or impossible to combine with a realistic political emphasis. Maybe for this reason Ramsey gave a lot of time to clarifying the meaning of the principle.

He spells out the principle in full as follows: "definite limits [are] placed upon the conduct of war by surrounding *non-combatants* with moral immunity from *direct* attack," or "[love] requires that non-combatants be never directly assaulted."[5] Ramsey gave close and repeated attention to examining the meaning of the words "deliberate and direct," and "non-combatant."[6] He showed how carefully and subtly these meanings must be inquired into, and he aimed to show that this principle is one that may never justifiably be violated when properly clarified.

Ramsey also learned much from John Courtney Murray (also, of course, a Roman Catholic). Although Murray knew the principle of discrimination, he chose to emphasize the crisis in modern political ethics in another way. He insisted that modern political thought had lost touch with the vital truth that morality and politics are properly thought together, not separately or in continual tension. Murray wrote:

> There are . . . the two extreme positions, a soft sentimental pacifism and a cynical hard realism. . . . Both of them are condemned by the traditional doctrine as false and pernicious. The problem is to refute by argument the false antinomy between war and morality that they assert in common, though in different ways.[7]

In place of the tension between politics and morals, Courtney Murray argued for a "far more vigorous cultivation of politico-moral science." Politics is the place where power and morality meet: "Policy is the hand of practical reason set firmly upon the course of events. . . . Policy is the meeting place of the world of power and the world of morality."[8] This insistence on the unity of morality, reason, and politics is vital to the thought of Ramsey. He made a number of points in common with Murray, including the one we have noted about the similarity between some forms of pacifism and political realism. With Courtney Murray, Ramsey also considered that the contemporary problem is to make war possible by limiting it, not to abolish it. Ramsey agreed that the abandonment of traditional moral doctrines does not make them irrelevant. Rather, as Courtney Murray put it, "there is place for indictment of all of us who failed to make the tradition relevant."[9]

Ramsey also learned from another who was much influenced by Courtney Murray: Thomas Murray, who made a number of similar points. For instance, T. Murray also noted the underlying connection between the extreme opposites of pacifism and realism: "The extreme pacifist and the extreme belligerist positions are equally irrational, for they both make an absolute disjunction between military strategy and ethical value."[10] We may note a number of further points made by Thomas Murray that Ramsey endorsed.[11] In indicating the moral and rational limitations that needed to be placed on modern war, Murray argued for a distinction between force and violence, for counterforce rather than counterpopulation fighting policies, and for weapons programs to be controlled by policy rather than technology.[12]

Ramsey's defense of a just war theory is set within the tradition of Christian realism of which Reinhold Niebuhr was the foremost contemporary exponent. Ramsey was closest to Niebuhr in the latter's Augustinian phase (remembering that Niebuhr changed his mind and his emphasis on major issues throughout his career).[13] We will now sketch the realist understanding of politics that Ramsey learned from Niebuhr, and then consider the significance of Ramsey's differences with Reinhold Niebuhr.

Niebuhr's influence on Ramsey is very clear. Ramsey paid tribute to his political mentor as follows: "All in all, Niebuhr almost single handedly took the irrelevance out of Protestantism and restored Christian categories to widely acknowledged social and political importance."[14]

Niebuhr's political thought is dialectical, quicksilver in its pace and changes of tack and in its movement from practical illustration to high abstraction. We can only venture a few very selective comments. Niebuhr "took the irrelevance out of Protestantism" with his trenchant critique of naive and overoptimistic liberalism. He insisted on the sinfulness of man, which needed always to be restrained, but he also insisted strongly on the human capacity for goodness, for social and democratic progress. Both aspects of human nature spring from man's essential freedom, a concept at the heart of Niebuhr's thought. The complexities and unpredictabilities of human social life mean that politics is always for Niebuhr a matter of practical possibilities, of not aiming too high, nor aiming too low either.

R. H. Stone has offered a brief and helpful summary of an essay of Reinhold Niebuhr:

> The argument of the essay exposes the dangers of overly consistent realism or idealism. Man is both self-seeking and inclined towards a moral life. His moral ideals can be achieved only through policies which account for the self-seeking aspirations of various men and groups. He does not expect the realization of man's political ideals, not even of his own liberal democratic ideals of toleration, liberty, and representative government. However, man cannot succumb to cynicism, and the wisest policy is one which strives to maximize the degree of possible justice. Justice, as a principle for Niebuhr, consists of both equality and liberty. The goal of tolerable justice for a society involves the achievement of the maximum possible degree of liberty and equality within a framework of order. The ideals of political liberalism are utilized by Niebuhr, but he does not confuse what he regards as normative with his description of political reality. Political reality is necessarily separated from the ideal, but it is in need of constant improvement and criticism by reference to the ideal.[15]

In judging what is practical in politics, the politician should not lose sight of the human capacity for good, and the possibility of relating the moral ideal to the difficult realities of human situations. The way in which Niebuhr related moral ideals to practical questions makes his work continually fascinating, but in the end deeply frustrating. It is frustrating partly because Niebuhr's gift of insight into contemporary politics can only be admired (despite the occasional mistakes) but not passed on.[16] There is greater frustration in Niebuhr's moral method, relying as it does solely on calculations of greater and lesser evil. His dialectical method, as I will try to indicate, rested upon a mistaken understanding of the nature of Christian love.

Ramsey took from Niebuhr his critique of liberalism, and to a very large extent, his broad analysis of the nature and goals of political action. This we learn more from Ramsey's own comments on his work than from any very explicit acknowledgments in the body of it. The reason for this is not far to see. A comment of Ramsey will begin to explain it:

> In all that I have ever written upon the justice of war I have been quite consciously drawing upon a wider theory of statecraft and of political justice to propose an extension within the Christian realism of Reinhold Niebuhr.[17]

It is this "extension" that claimed the larger part of Ramsey's interest. His first concern is the problem of what constitutes just conduct in war. This is determined by the twin principles of discrimination and proportion. Here Ramsey's keen interest was always primarily in the former and its relation to the latter. The principle of discrimination is a kind of pure rule, while the principle of proportion is a broad summary rule.[18] Indeed, Ramsey continually insisted that the principle of proportion must be kept as widely flexible and encompassing as it ought, in order to do justice to the variety of political questions that arise. There is, therefore, less that the ethical theorist, *qua* theologian or churchman, can say at this point; his interest is in clarifying the theoretical moral questions that arise, and these always arise first in relation to the principle of discrimination. But, and this is the point, Ramsey saw Niebuhr as dealing only with the principle of proportion:

> The second test of justice in war is the principle of proportionality. All that Reinhold Niebuhr ever said about politics and war falls under this heading, since the principle of proportion says simply that nations, statesmen, and citizens are acting responsibly when they choose and vigorously support policies and decisions which are likely to secure the lesser evil (or the greater good) among their mixed consequences.[19]

The framework for political goals that Ramsey adopted is very similar to that of Reinhold Niebuhr, but the style is different. Niebuhr was forever trying, often with penetrating insight and judgment, to inquire into the relation of these tensions to contemporary political events and circumstances. He related justice to the transcendent ideals of love and equality, seeking to see how the detailed stuff of political life could be related to the ideals of Christian faith. The subtlety and historical strength of Niebuhr's grasp of politics meant that this was rarely done too simplistically.[20]

For Ramsey, however, the impact of Christian love in politics comes primarily in a quite different place. He agreed with Niebuhr that deciding on the best course of action, by weighing what will most likely bring the best outcome, is something that can only be ventured. It cannot be simply deduced from ideals such as equality, or freedom, or the desire for peace, etc. No doubt many things have to be considered, and these related back in one way or another to moral and theological concerns. But Ramsey considered that Niebuhr's great gift of historical and political discernment offers a very misleading model for the work of the Christian moralist or churchman. The first and essential task of the church in politics is to clarify and advance political doctrine. It is not its task, except in exceptional cases, to make specific moral judgments.[21]

The initial impact of Christian love upon politics is on how power, especially the use of force, is to be employed. Ramsey's analysis insists that the use of force must only be employed "discriminately." Ramsey's insistence on the principle of discrimination served to give his political ethic a radically different cast from others in the school of Christian realism.[22] This is such an important divergence that it seems worth inquiring further into Ramsey's critique of Niebuhr's view of the basis for political ethics—his analysis of Christian love, equality, and justice.

We must turn again to Ramsey's seminal essay "Reinhold Niebuhr: Christian Love and Natural Law."[23] We have found there the roots of Ramsey's concern with the weakness of situationist approaches to ethics in his argument for clarifying the connection between Christian love and human nature. This connection led him to espouse a radically revised natural law theory. In later sections of the essay he took up the connection made by Niebuhr between love and justice, and the meaning of Christian love.

Niebuhr's view of Christian love was that in its essence it is to be considered as self-sacrifice. The fundamental example of love is the death of Christ on the cross. Love is an impossible ideal against which we measure and find wanting all our more or less loving actions. This does not deny that love is truly to be found in other forms, especially mutual love. In social and political life love is more and less expressed in a scale of qualities, that Ramsey summarized as freedom, equality, equal justice, justice, and schemes of justice.[24] The best approximation to love is freedom, but given the realities of social life, human competition, etc., the next best is equality, and so on. Love is relevant to all these, both as motive and critic, encouraging and rebuking our politics. Ramsey illustrated this theory with quotations from *An Interpretation of Christian Ethics*, such as:

> As the ideal of love must relate itself to the problems of the world in which its perfect realization is not possible, the most logical modification and application of the ideal in a world in which life is in conflict with life is the principle of equality which strives for an equilibrium in the conflict.[25]

Ramsey agreed with Niebuhr's concern to base social ethics on Christian love, but he was more concerned to correct Niebuhr's characterization of love as essentially sacrificial and suffering. We should not measure love by reference to its results for ourselves, argued Ramsey, but with reference to the others whom we are loving. That a loving action results in advantages for the actor does not thereby make it less loving. Love stands always ready to make the sacrifice, but it is also ready to be prudent in order to be more loving in the future.

> No doubt love is "heedless"; but there is also nothing more heedful, careful and flexibly wise than love. No doubt love "suffers" all things; but also love rejoices with those that rejoice.[26]

This correction means that it is possible to say without qualification, for instance, that it is love itself which is expressed in institutions and principles of justice:

> there are principles of equality and justice by which love takes shape for application to historical situations; and . . . there are relative schemes of civil law and economic and other institutions which fully embrace the particularities in various constellations of human relationships in history.[27]

This amounts to little more than a systematization of Niebuhr's lively dialectic. The correction becomes much more substantial when it comes to the morality of international politics. As is well known, Niebuhr believed it was very rare for social groups to act in a truly loving way, for they never, or hardly ever, have the imagination and the altruism to act in a sacrificial manner.[28] The morality of collective action, therefore, could never be for Niebuhr more than the calculation of more or less good, more or less selfish action, more or less evil. Against this Ramsey insists that proper concern for the national self-interest is among the real concerns of a statesman motivated by love. For a leader to sacrifice the interests that he is responsible for safe-guarding is not loving at all, rather the reverse. The statesman is "bound to sacrifice sacrifice, regardless of what he might be willing to do were his own life alone at stake."

> The point is not that the motive of love can ever be taken alone, any more than self-interest can, but that we ought not to say that only the admixture of collective self-interest prevents love in group action from leading on to overt self-sacrifice.[29]

The significance of Ramsey's correction of Niebuhr on the nature of Christian love can hardly be overemphasized. Here is to be found the root of Ramsey's difference with all those realist approaches to politics (many contemporary exponents of realism were, of course, greatly influenced by Niebuhr), which rely wholly on an ethic of greater and lesser evil, more or less good. Ramsey's connection of the demanding and rigorous morality of *agape* with the everyday stuff of political action in the real historical world means that it is unnecessary to despair over the selfishness of collectivities. Instead, the first moral test of political action, and in particular the use of force, is the manner of that action. Niebuhr's view of love as an impossible ideal made such a view of political morality impossible to hold, for if all our politics is inevitably self-interested and thereby immoral, all that is left is to weigh up the more or less immorality.

We can go further than this. It is surely a Niebuhrian type of analysis of the inevitability of the immorality of politics which leads all too many to conclude, in sad or happy agreement with this analysis, that if this is the nature of politics then the fewer Christians who are involved in it the better. Now not every pacifist views politics as immoral in the way Niebuhr did, but there are many varieties of pacifist opinion that condemn politics as immoral in blanket terms, having a view of Christian love that condemns them to such a view.[30] The reverse side of Ramsey's rigorous understanding of love's moral demands is a concern that moral demands be not applied indiscriminately. His articulation of love's casuistry not only calls for exception-less rules, but also for wide areas where it is right to seek the greater good by all legitimate means, for it is precisely love which is embodied in the politician's prudential concern for justice, for order, and so on.

We have spent a good deal of time on Ramsey's debt to Niebuhr, and his disagreement with him. It is now time to attempt to characterize the main lines of Ramsey's political theory and ethics.

The Just War Theory of Political Ethics

For Ramsey, four things are inseparable in political thought. They come together in a working Christian politico-military doctrine.[31] Politics is about the use of power, which cannot be split apart from military strategy. Reason brings these together in a responsible Christian doctrine, and this means a moral reason. Good political theory is rational, and it is also moral. Morality is not to be extrinsically imposed on political reality as if it belonged to some other realm of thought. Of course, to say that these four aspects are inseparable is not to say that they are the same thing. Politics, the use of power, is connected to military strategy, to moral doctrine, and to clear reason. Each of these three connections is now examined.

(1) Politics Is Inseparable from Military Strategy

Ramsey more often expresses this by saying that politics is defined as the use of power, and that the possible use of force is at the heart of power.[32] In contrast to this view, Ramsey saw two groups separating force from politics. Conservatives do so by threatening the use of force without political purpose, to defend by strength of will, by resolute declaration and posture. Liberals, on the other hand, think political purpose can only be positively advanced by peaceful means. Correct doctrine, against both of these kinds of approach, will see force, and its possible use, as a way of using power to fulfill good political purposes.[33] This means that military, strategic, and weapons policy must be subject to proper political policy and decisions.

(2) Politics Is Inseparable from Moral Doctrine

We consider Ramsey's view of the relationship between moral and political theory under four heads, beginning with the morality of the use of force.

(a) The Use of Force

The use of force for political purpose can be an expression of Christian love. Borrowing a term from Luther, Ramsey once called this an alien work of love[34]—to resist some in order to protect others. Since the aim of love here is the protection of third parties, love will also be rigorously careful to use force only against those who are themselves the bearers of force. The question of the possible use of force is the clearest prism in which to analyze the question of the use of power of any kind. The use of power of any sort should always be aimed at the bearers of power who are to be resisted in the cause of justice. (One particular issue Ramsey had in mind here was the question of general economic sanctions, e.g., against South Africa.[35])

Christian love generates the principle of discrimination, in other words, and this principle is to be held to be exceptionless. (Ramsey much preferred this word to the term "absolute."[36]) This has, of course, enormous implications for the military and strategic doctrines underlying the possession and design of nuclear weapons. Ramsey believed the recovery of the principle of discrimination to be of profound importance. This should be a cardinal point in the clarification of political thought that is the church's primary contribution to general political life.[37]

(b) Justice and Order

Love also generates the political goals for which power is to be used. The just war theory teaches us that there is a presumption in favor of the righting of wrong, the correction of injustice.[38] But justice is not the only goal of politics, for the preservation of peace, law, and order may and often does conflict with the demands of justice. Balancing these up is the work of political decisions, practical wisdom, or prudence. Some good aims may only be achievable at some other cost. There are decisions to be taken where our guide can only be the aim of bringing about the greatest good, the least evil. Such a guide also governs whether or not to employ a discriminate force in a particular instance. The test of proportion, of which we are now speaking, is not essentially different whether as one of the tests of *jus ad bellum* or as one of the tests of *jus in bello*.

Ramsey only sketched briefly and broadly, nonetheless powerfully, how he understands the framework within which the greater good and the lesser evil are to be secured. Although there are indications and

discussions of this throughout his political writings, the clearest statement is to be found in the article "The Uses of Power."[39]

The article sets out from the point we have already sketched: that
politics is defined by the fact that it has to do with the use of power.
Power is inseparable from the possibility of the use of force.

> The use of power, and possibly the use of force, is of the *esse* of politics,
> and it is inseparable from the *bene esse* of politics. This entails no
> derogation of the uniquely human ends, the generic values, the *bene esse*,
> of political community. Quite the contrary. This puts power in its place
> in our understanding of politics by definitely placing it within the pursuit
> of the common good.[40]

That politics is about the use of power must never be forgotten. Any
political action is likely to affect the power position of a nation, as well
as attempting to further its purposes. Both must be considered. This
means that it is not obligatory always to do good, for there is the
obligation also to be able to do good (to maintain power to do good) in
the future. Allied to this is the point that the statesman has to consider
the national common good along with the international common good.
The two do not necessarily coincide.

> Every responsible political decision involves some precarious determina-
> tion of how the circles of the international common good are to be drawn.
> This is the mode in which the ideal humanitarian good (all of which, by
> definition, ought to be) specifies itself for political choice.[41]

Some critics have been concerned that Ramsey stressed order too
much, and at the expense of justice. However, his argument for the
possible justice of war always considered that justice could be worth a
considerable degree of disorder (rather a mild term for war). In *Speak
Up for Just War or Pacifism* Ramsey draws out the significance of that
assumption. He denies that there is a Christian presumption against
violence and war, and in favor of peace. "Instead, *the presumption is
to restrain evil and protect the innocent.*"[42] There is then a prudential
limitation to be placed on the use and scale of force. In an age when
war is soon likely to be disproportionately destructive, that limitation
must receive careful attention. This does not in any way remove the
proper concern for justice, but it does provide a vivid illustration of
the problem of trying to seek for justice and order at the same time.
These two are often in tension with each other:

Order is not a higher value in politics than justice, but neither is humanitarian justice a higher value than order. Both are in some respects conditional to the other.[43]

Ramsey's analysis of the tension between order and justice is typical of a Niebuhrian kind of analysis.[44] This tension Ramsey sees as closely similar to the tensions between the need to preserve power and the concern to use it for good, and between the national common good and international common good. It is within this framework that the political decision maker has to weigh up what will bring about the greatest good.

> This may not tell him what to think, but it is how he will think. He will know that "order" and "justice" both are the effects of his action. He will count the cost of one effect upon the other. He will ask how much disorder is worth a calculable preservation or extension of justice (which in turn will make for a new or better political order), or he will ask how much of the injustice in the world (none of which *ought to be*) it is his responsibility to expunge at the cost of disordering the political order in which alone political justice obtains embodiment.[45]

The generality and flexibility of this is deliberately intended. Ramsey believed that great harm could be done by mistaken moral views of politics in two principal ways. One danger is to aim too high, without reckoning with the historical and social realities of politics, especially the power realities. Another is to restrict the moral boundaries of action too narrowly. They come together, typically, in political advice which is too ready to see ways of avoiding conflict, or conversely of bringing about improvements in justice without reckoning on the costs to the social fabric of ordered and lawful peace.[46]

This discussion of political goals, which represents the heart of Ramsey's political thought, has necessarily been rather general. It is possible to indicate some of the general directions that Ramsey offered about the ways in which he saw his doctrine applying to contemporary American responsibilities in the world.

One of his main concerns was to argue the case for possible military intervention to right injustice.[47] This follows from his basic argument about the paradigm case for the use of force—that it is first and foremost to defend third parties. He objected in several ways to the overly simple notion that "the aggressor is always wrong." If this is taken to rule out intervention, then it is particularly misleading.

The notion that the aggressor is always wrong leads directly to the claim that the defender is always right. In particular, it tends to lead the defender to claim that defense is so much right that anything may be done in its cause. We have seen why Ramsey strenuously objected to this claim. He saw it as one of the confusions of thought that had led the West to its dependence on a doctrine of nuclear deterrence by threat of massive retaliation.[48]

If Ramsey believed very strongly in the just war presumption against injustice, he also held a very strong presumption in favor of order. Ramsey explored the theological basis for "law and order" most fully in *Christian Ethics and the Sit-In*. In this book he questioned whether those engaged in law-breaking protest, even in a just cause, have thought deeply enough about the question of order. Ramsey explores both positive and negative reasons for respect for order and legality. The positive reasons are derived from the created nature of humanity. We are created for covenant, and in order to enter into covenant with one another we need a place to stand, involving human rights, freedom, and property:

> I need some things to call my own in order to be with or for fellow man. Otherwise, I would be without a place to stand with him. He would then be without me, and I without him.

The negative reasons are derived from the fall. Social institutions and the legal order are provisions of God's restraining grace:

> The distance between man and man has to be *increased* in a fallen world, . . . precisely in order to preserve in extant social orders the possibility and promise of covenant.[49]

Ramsey proceeds to argue that those who wish to advance the cause of justice should recognize the point of a legal order, only breaking the law for sufficient reason, such as to challenge and so clarify it.[50]

Although Ramsey usually spoke of justice and order as complementary, potentially in tension, the relation between them is not a symmetrical one. Justice is the higher, but it depends on order:

> Order and justice condition one another, although justice is the superior value in the scale of excellence. No one should ever voice the belief that anarchy (the opposite of order) and tyranny (the opposite of justice) are equidistant alternatives on an abstract continuum—as if when reduced to

it tyranny ("law and order") would not be the first and only choice if ever a society is reduced to choosing one over the other.[51]

Both justice and order come together to lead to a powerful case for conducting counterinsurgency warfare. This case allied to his readiness to advocate intervention made him very ready to hear the case for the Vietnam war. Still, his main concern over Vietnam was not whether it was a just war, for he did not see how the moralist *qua* moralist could be in a position to make such a judgment. Rather, he considered how the principle of discrimination should be applied to the conduct of counterinsurgency war, where it seems difficult or impossible to conduct military operations without attacking civilians.[52]

(c) The Church and Politics

Ramsey frequently opposed what he took to be the liberal church consensus on their political attitudes and pronouncements.[53] We can now see the main point of his opposition. It did not lie in his own political allegiance, nor did it lie in any version of the view that the church should keep out of politics. What concerned him was the manner of the church's involvement. The church's political duty does not lie in making specific recommendations. Instead the church's task is to clarify the basis and nature of political doctrine—to offer to statesmen and voters a proper framework of thought by which they would be better informed for the making of political decisions.

If the church makes specific policy pronouncements, then that has a number of serious dangers. Perhaps the greatest of these is that it may obscure the essential work of clarifying political doctrine. At the same time, specific pronouncements are not, and cannot be, as specific as they seem. The reason is that particular decisions can only be taken at the point of decision, that is, by political authority. The churchman or moralist is not there at that point, and is not informed as fully as the one at the point of decision. Therefore, Ramsey argued, even specific advice from churchmen is still necessarily abstract.[54] Particular pronouncements made by those who do not have to take the decisions and bear the responsibility for them are prone to seeing the gains of a course of action without its costs. Ramsey illustrated his concerns with an analysis of his attendance at the 1966 Geneva Conference on Church and Society. Finally he was concerned to point out that church pronouncements on specific policy matters run the risk of unchurching those who conscientiously come to different conclusions.[55]

It is important that Ramsey's views on the role of the church are not overstated. He admitted that the clear line he advocated between the general and the specific could not always be clearly drawn, but the existence of twilight does not abolish the difference between night and day.[56] Besides, his criticisms of church statements on politics were very often substantial criticisms of their understanding of just war theory or political doctrine. In *Speak Up for Just War or Pacifism* Ramsey does not criticize the Methodist bishops for attempting what they did in *In Defense of Creation*. His very severe criticism is directed at the substance of what they said.

(d) Deferred Repentance

These, then, are the connections between morality and political doctrine. Morality is not imposed on an alien political sphere, but works in political thought to help shape and direct our thinking. The morality of politics is not to be set apart from the morality of any other subject, but neither is the morality of politics identical to private morality. In the same way, we might say that the morality of marriage is not fundamentally unlike the morality of friendship, but the two are not identical either. There is, in addition, one very special feature about the morality of politics as Ramsey sees it—that is what he called "deferred repentance."[57]

Normally, anyone should repent immediately of anything they perceive to be wrong. This also applies in general to political repentance, but there are circumstances in which it may not be true. In his discussion, Ramsey had in mind preparations for nuclear war and the weapons of nuclear deterrence.[58] A statesman who is convinced that his nation is pursuing wrong policies may nevertheless stay in office and support those preparations while working over a period of time toward justifiable policies. A nation may have to take time to await the right political moment to put its repentance into effect, all the while aiming to deter war and working to limit the means and ends of war. None of this is to say, Ramsey insisted, that repentance may be deferred forever.[59]

We have sketched in a broad and schematic way Ramsey's approach to political theory. In Part Three the burden of our concern will be the detailed understanding of Ramsey's account of the principle of discrimination, and the way in which it relates to his overall view of politics. We now return to the third of the inseparable elements that are all aspects of politics. It is so much a part of moral and political thinking that it is artificial to separate it out, but there is, I believe, a particular point to be made about the rationality of nuclear deterrence.

(3) Politics Is Inseparable from Reason

Ramsey's whole corpus of political writing bears this out in a rigorous and thorough way. For him the work of morality is always a work of love-informed reason. Perhaps one of the notable aspects of this in Ramsey's work is his reluctance to concede the existence of moral dilemmas not amenable to rational clarification.[60] In such cases, he worked back to higher levels of generality to see what was at stake and to see how an apparent dilemma might be clarified. This, at least, is what he undertakes to do in considering the great moral dilemma of our age, the dilemma of nuclear deterrence. His fundamental conviction is that this should not be an insoluble moral dilemma.

The apparent moral dilemma can be simply stated. On one hand, there is the duty to be prepared to contain the possibility of unjustified nuclear threats, nuclear blackmail. It is a moral duty to be ready to protect the free world from the possibility of such threats. On the other hand, there is the duty only to use discriminate force to resist such threats. Many believe that such force is bound to be insufficient to contain or counterbalance them. Ramsey's attempt to solve this dilemma took him deep into the logic of nuclear deterrence strategy. In the final analysis, he believed, it must be true that no good could come of doing evil, even to try to bring about good. He also believed that no political purpose could be achieved by behaving or thinking irrationally.[61] Even if an enemy behaved irrationally, no good could come of responding in kind. But is it possible to deter an irrational opponent by rational moral means? The answer to this question must depend on the extent and nature of the enemy's rationality. Ramsey felt that in some respects, anyway, the Communist nations had a more rational view of military strength than the West, and he also believed that a moral, rational, deterrence policy would actually be a sufficient one.

Political Institutions

Ramsey's main focus of interest in politics was the morality of political action. As we have seen, he saw power and the possible use of force as constitutive of politics. This view naturally has implications for his approach to political institutions. His views, though, on the nature of democracy, on political obligation, on nations and international authority, are not very explicitly and fully developed. We can sketch the main lines of his thought from the indications he gave.

In Chapter Six of *War and the Christian Conscience*, Ramsey outlined the development of the Calvinist tradition of justified revolution.[62] This saw lesser magistrates as having a right and a duty to oppose the unjust tyrannies of higher authority. By a natural extension, the common man himself became a lesser magistrate, with the right to oppose injustice under certain conditions. Ramsey noted that the logic of this extension of political rights to every citizen added to the impetus toward democratic control of government. Democracy is seen from this point of view as institutionalizing in a ballot the right of each citizen to resist the government, and collectively to overthrow it and replace it with another. The concern with the control of power is the point that characterizes this view of democracy. From this point of view, Ramsey then went on to argue for the right of selective conscientious objection, long before this became a concern in the United States in the mid-1960s.

It is the question of power from the other angle that exercised Ramsey when it comes to the matter of political obligation in a democracy. Here the concern is not so much the control of the state's power by the citizen as the need for the state to maintain sufficient power for coherent action. The relevant discussion here is the full and careful consideration of selective conscientious objection. Ramsey wanted very much to argue for such a right, as we have just noted.[63] But, in the later discussion, the point that also concerned him was that no government can give up the right to require military service. If the conditions are right, and it is highly desirable that they should be, the state can grant the possibility of conscientious objection. But the state may need to be able to call people up in order to be able to fulfill its purposes. Fortunately, it is able to concede to general conscientious objectors the possibility of objection, partly because of their limited numbers. However, a recent Supreme Court decision had significantly widened the boundaries of who might conscientiously object.[64] This, Ramsey feared, significantly aggravated the difficult question attached to pleas for selective conscientious objection. The difficult question is how to test genuine conscientious objection to particular wars. In particular, is it possible to distinguish political opposition to a war from serious moral conscientious objection? Ramsey felt this to be a very significant difficulty. He proposed that it might be possible to consider allowing selective conscientious objection on the basis of moral objection to the conduct of war, and to indiscriminate military conduct. Ramsey's analysis illuminated clearly the realities of the political issue that actually faced the United States at that time. It illustrates equally clearly how his approach to politics enabled him to enter into the real issues and balances of political life.[65]

An issue to which Ramsey devoted careful thought over a period of years was the desire for a world political authority. His first comments on this were in his reaction to the papal encyclical *Pacem in Terris*.[66] Ten years later, his views appeared to have changed, at least in emphasis.

In 1963 Ramsey appeared to accept the goal of a world political authority, as proposed and argued for by John XXIII. Ramsey was far from accepting the argument put forward by the pope; he especially took issue with the easy optimistic tone of the argument, and the tendency to overlook the problems and realities of power. John XXIII all but withdrew the right to go to war, without, as Courtney Murray pointed out,[67] sufficiently confronting the realities of such a prohibition. The pope's argument seemed to spring too lightly from the hope, even necessity, of a world political authority, to the view that it can and should be provided, and on that basis the nations ought to give up their own ability to promote justice by force. The pope seemed to argue that justice can never be safeguarded or advanced by warfare in the nuclear age. Even if that were true, Ramsey argued, still the right to use force cannot be withdrawn before there is a world government.

> Only the public authority of a world community can provide the legal transcription of the tendency of papal teachings to withdraw, morally, the right of war. These two things are opposite ends of the same seesaw: the moral right to use force cannot go down faster than the public authority and enforcement of a world community is organized.[68]

In the light of what Ramsey said in 1973, we are driven to go back and consider the precise phrasing of this and other earlier discussions of world government. In 1973 Ramsey argued decisively against the goal of establishing a single world political authority. Ramsey's views on world government in the articles collected in *The Just War* could be read in two ways. They could be read as affirming only that certain things are not possible until a world political authority is actually a reality, or they could be read as affirming the duty to bring about such an institution.[69] However, other articles make clear that Ramsey definitely advocated a world government in the early 1960s. For instance, in 1963 he wrote: "We need to give ourselves world public authorities and alienate ourselves of the right and the power to judge the justice of our own cause."[70]

In rejecting this advocacy a decade later, he leaned on the opinion of Helmut Thielicke. Thielicke's objection was that there would be no power to balance a world government, and that the monopoly of power so established would be very dangerous. Ramsey comments on Thielicke's fears of an "unbridled upward expansion" of a world state: "To prevent that vertical turn towards unbridled upward expansion, the law of move and countermove, the limitation of power by further power, was established for the good of mankind always."[71]

We should not overestimate Ramsey's dependence on Thielicke. Thielicke's objection is couched in typically theological language. The state for Thielicke is "an emergency institution between the fall and the judgment." The danger of a world state is not so much the danger of a universal tyranny as it is the danger of a Babel-like rebellion against God. A world state would "be led to play the role of Antichrist." Of course, we must not read Thielicke wholly negatively in this area. He does not want "to discredit the idea of a league of states or a union of nations."[72] Thielicke recognized the positive functions entrusted to states. Ramsey was also ready to recognize in typically Lutheran language that the use of force is an alien work of love.[73] All this said, there is a world of difference between the typically positive way in which Ramsey speaks of the state's concern to preserve justice and order, and the way in which Thielicke speaks negatively of the state as an emergency institution. Apart from Thielicke's marked reluctance to enter anything looking at all like casuistry, it is the place he gives to justice which marks him out from Ramsey. It is not that Thielicke is without a working concept of justice but that he gives it a much less prominent place than Ramsey. Ramsey's concern for justice, on the other hand, is both genuine and unswerving throughout his career, even though he felt so often compelled to lay stress on the necessity of order.

5

Political Ethics in Debate: Nuclear Deterrence

It is not quite accurate to say that Ramsey changed his mind about deterrence. In one sense he did, in that whereas *War and the Christian Conscience* had appeared quite firmly to rule out the moral possibility of nuclear deterrence, *The Just War* unmistakably argued for it. On a closer reading, however, it is clear that the earlier book argued only against types of deterrence that rely on irrational and incredible threats of city-exchanges, leading on to total destruction.[1] In *The Just War* this type of deterrence was just as fully rejected, and the basis for deterrence to be found there is elaborated from the principles in *War and the Christian Conscience*.

Ramsey's earlier critique of nuclear deterrence is to be found principally in Chapter Eleven of *War and the Christian Conscience* and in Chapter Eight of *The Just War*. In these chapters he draws attention to the central conundrum of the conventional wisdom about deterrence. The difficulty, which has, of course, formed the center of debate for some thirty years (at least since the work of Kahn, Schelling, and others[2]), is easily enough stated. Nuclear deterrence (as commonly proposed) rests on the assumption that neither side will start war because both sides have the power to annihilate the other completely. Therefore, both are deterred from fighting. The difficulty is stated by asking the question "Would you really use these weapons?" Neither answer, "Yes" or "No," is quite possible or credible, for the former implies readiness for complete mutual destruction, and the latter implies that deterrence was all along merely a matter of words and threats.[3] Ramsey sets out to show that "*neither* deterrence *nor* warfare with these immoral means is or can be made feasible."[4]

To demonstrate this Ramsey took up the work of Herman Kahn, who believed that for deterrence to be effective, it must rest on credible war-fighting capability, and not merely on declaratory threats and the assumption that war could no longer be fought. After analyzing Kahn's critique of merely declaratory policies, Ramsey turns to his proposals for war-fighting policies. He focuses on some of the grimmer possibilities suggested by Kahn if we are to envisage the feasibility of actually fighting a nuclear war, and then on Kahn's proposal for deterring the enemy in the event of the destruction of more than 80 percent of our forces. In this event, said Kahn, turning away from the direction of his analysis up to this point, "we should devote the remainder of our force to malevolent (i.e., countervalue) objectives—to punish the enemy in that way which was most hurtful to him."[5]

Ramsey sees this passage in Kahn's argument as essential to his whole view of deterrence, perhaps somewhat unfairly. At this point only, Kahn relied on a "Rationality of Irrationality" policy in which we arrange in advance, if possible, for machines that will effect automatic retaliation and take the decision wholly out of the hands of decision makers at the time. On the premise that Kahn's analysis provides no basis for a credible or moral deterrent at the upper levels of war, Ramsey first concluded that none can be found.[6]

At other places Ramsey simply opposed deterrence policies that rest on holding enemy cities and populations hostage. It was Ramsey who devised the "babies-on-bumpers" analogy, which argues that even if tying babies to car bumpers were an effective way of enforcing safe driving and preventing accidents, it would still be an immoral way to achieve the desired end.[7] In place of these policies, in *War and the Christian Conscience*, Chapter Twelve, Ramsey made suggestions as to where he thinks a line might be drawn between weapons with rational counterforce purposes (e.g., lower kiloton bombs) and those with only indiscriminate uses (e.g., megaton bombs).[8] As for deterring an enemy who possesses larger weapons as well as the apparent readiness to use them, "there is in no case any other recourse than to stand firm in the right as God gives us to see the right and to stand firm with arms that are the arms of a national purpose."[9]

By 1963, however, Ramsey thought he could see a moral way to deter even such threats, if necessary. In *The Limits of Nuclear War*, he proposed an alternative way of deterring city destruction than by answering with the same.[10] He proposed three ways in which the deterrent effect of counterforce warfare could be justly augmented. These were (1) the threat of collateral civilian damage; (2) the threat inherent in the mere possession of nuclear weapons, from which the possibility of countercity use could not be removed; and if necessary (3) a readiness to appear to be ready to use weapons to attack cities (the deterrence of bluff).

Ramsey's proposal was vigorously challenged by a group of Roman Catholic thinkers, in discussions of the work of the Second Vatican Council in this area. The debate that took place was published as *Peace, the Churches and the Bomb*, which was followed by Ramsey's reply, *Again, the Justice of Deterrence*.[11] Two of those with whom Ramsey debated stand very close to him in their basic moral assumptions. Walter Stein is a nuclear pacifist, who came very close at some points to holding a fully pacifist position. On the face of it, Justus George Lawler stood even closer to Ramsey in the first of his two articles. He agreed on the basic moral position—the doctrine of noncombatant immunity, together with the view that it is wrong to threaten a wrong action, even conditionally. But he also appeared to agree that some nuclear weapons may not be condemned by these tests, for use and for deterrence.[12] However, Ramsey's exchanges with Lawler are much more heated than those with Stein, sharp as the latter are. The reason for this appears to be that although Ramsey and Lawler argued from similar premises, Lawler came to the personal conclusion of "the immorality of any nuclear war." On the whole Ramsey succeeded in defending his position against Lawler and Stein, except on the subject of "bluff."[13]

This debate illuminates the way in which Ramsey held together a traditional (Roman Catholic) moral casuistry with a Christian political realism. The approach of Stein, Lawler, and others lacks that element of Augustinian realism.[14] For them, ultimately, we must say that morality is imposed on its subject matter from without. The rather rigid interpretation of natural law methods of moral reasoning that they use does not allow them to penetrate sufficiently into the realities of political life. By contrast, Ramsey's analysis of politics, based as it is on the vocation of love in conflict situations, allows him flexibility to try to hold together the political concern to protect the oppressed with the concern to do this without oppressing others. It is this analysis that allows him to claim that he is actually pursuing a natural law interpretation (albeit radically revised), since he has attempted to grasp the nature of politics and the way in which right political action is inspired and controlled by love.[15]

The debate is theoretical, indeed highly theoretical at times, but its heat was partly fueled by its relation to very pressing contemporary politics. (One may suspect that it was partly fueled also by Ramsey's apparent attempt to correct Roman Catholic theologians on their own premises.) How far did Ramsey mean to defend contemporary U.S. policy? He was clearly attracted, for obvious reasons, to the declarations of McNamara in the early 1960s that the "principal military objectives" should be the "destruction of the enemy's military forces, not his civilian population."[16] However, this did not remain a foundation of U.S. policy for long. By the early 1970s Ramsey was one of the first to protest against "MAD" (Mutual Assured Destruction) nuclear deterrence policies, and in 1988 he declared that MIRVed nuclear weaponry was inherently disproportionate.[17] In fact he turned away somewhat from his support of counterforce policy (claiming that the meaning of the word had shifted too far) toward seeing countercombatant targeting as possibly the highest that weapons should proportionately go.[18]

1968–1988

Nineteen sixty-eight saw the publication of *The Just War*, and in the same year Ramsey took up medical ethics declaring that he had stopped writing in the field of politics.[19] With characteristic thoroughness and enthusiasm he undertook to learn sufficient medicine to enable him to write medical ethics.[20] Over the following ten years he tackled a variety of issues—the most prominent were those surrounding abortion and death. They also included the meaning of consent, transplant surgery, genetic engineering, in vitro fertilization, fetal research, and infanticide.[21]

Finally Ramsey did return to political ethics and to the just war. He was provoked to write *Speak Up for Just War or Pacifism* by a statement of the United Methodist Bishops, *In Defense of Creation*. The book takes off from a critique of that statement, but it ranges much more widely. It includes Ramsey's only published response to the pacifist writings of John Howard Yoder, as well as further reflections on the U.S. Catholic Bishops' letter "The Challenge of Peace," and on the proper manner of the church's speech in political life. In this book he also went to some pains to spell out his understanding that "creation" is not a name for the universe or for our planet. Creation is the name given to the theological conviction that God created the world, and that this means also that its end is in his hand, thereby giving the context for human aspiration and purpose.[22]

The doctrine of creation was also an essential foundation for Ramsey's work in medical ethics. The realities to be analyzed are created realities. Human life is not a human project, but a given. It is within created structures that we find the application and meaning of covenant love. The modern tendencies of dualism and voluntarism are interlinked, and both must be resisted. Body-soul dualism thinks of the body and soul as separate entities, with the body merely instrumental to the soul, or mind, which is the seat of human freedom.[23] Voluntarism is a label we can conveniently give to the tendency to see all human purpose as matters of the free choices of human will.[24] In this connection, Ramsey particularly questioned some of the assumptions underlying proposals for genetic engineering, in methods of procreation, and policies for infanticide of the handicapped.[25]

These concerns are to be thought of in alliance with Ramsey's concerns in politics to recognize the reality of force and the meaning of an "arbitrament of arms." Human conflicts cannot always be settled by a mere conflict of wills, or in the abstract, or simply by negotiation.[26] Ramsey's concern for realism and rigor in medicine and in politics raises the question of the place of the doctrine of creation in his thought. We have already glanced by this question in relation to his exploration of moral method in the late 1950s, as he worked with the theme "love transforming natural law," and as he came upon Barth's terminology of covenant and creation.[27] It seems that he was reluctant in the 1960s and after to talk of natural law, and of creation, for fear of misunderstanding, and for fear of displacing Christian love from its sovereign place in Christian ethics.[28] Nevertheless, both the doctrine of Christian love and the doctrine of creation are indispensable for a full grasp of the basis of Christian ethics as Ramsey understood it, and as he worked at the political and medical issues confronting him. Even more clearly, they are vital to an understanding of Ramsey's ethical method, to which we turn in Part Two.

Part Two: The Rational Casuistry of Christian Love

6

Love and Rules

The survey of Ramsey's thought in Part One gave some attention to the debate with various related ethical theories—situationism, consequentialism, etc. We saw how crucial Ramsey's ethical method is to his articulation of a contemporary just war theory. However, we have done no more than indicate the positive position that Ramsey holds. Clearly it is not enough for him only to show the weaknesses of others; he has also to show that the version of traditional theory that he wishes to defend is capable of avoiding the criticisms of his opponents.

In this part we will take up some of those objectors and their attacks. At the same time we examine some of the most difficult and intricate argumentation, where Ramsey argues out with himself and others the best way to account for certain difficulties or dilemmas for moral thought and action. Chiefly these are the rule of double effect, and the problem of apparent exceptions to moral rules.

The argument of these chapters will proceed as follows. They begin with an analysis of the basis for a careful casuistry in an ethic of Christian love. This analysis is centered on a refutation of those who found a serious inconsistency between the love ethic of *Basic Christian Ethics* and the rule ethic of *Deeds and Rules in Christian Ethics*. This leads on to the main exposition of Ramsey's casuistry. This exposition is undertaken first by examining Ramsey's continued discussion of the rule of double effect, and second, by taking up some questions arising from his article "The Case of the Curious Exception." We will then examine of some of the objections to Ramsey's position, most notably that of Richard McCormick in the volume *Doing Evil to Achieve Good*.

At the outset, we can try to express the heart of Ramsey's casuistry in a nutshell by saying that the shape of moral thought is governed by the shape of human action. For the most part, broadly speaking, the description of human action is unproblematic, but there are occasions when we are forced to closer attention by a difficulty in reaching a moral account of what someone does or should do. Ramsey considered two general types of such difficulties: rules and intentionality.

In considering the question of rules and how to handle them, Ramsey gave his own account of how action should be properly described. Understanding an action means knowing about the context of the action, including not only the circumstances in which it is performed, but the thought which lies behind it as well. Only then can it be properly described. The importance of description is that the description is fundamental to the question of whether a particular rule applies or not. This also implies, of course, that the rule must be carefully and accurately framed. For instance, Ramsey suggested that the forbidden lie should be defined as "withholding the truth from someone to whom it is due."[1] He then argued that the practice of using different words for "justified killing" and "murder" suggests the possibility of calling justified instances of telling untruths as something other than "lying." This offense term could be reserved for unjustified actions.

The question of what outcomes are "intended" by action, which foresees what it will bring about, is handled by the rule of twofold intentionality. The difficulty of saying that one does not intend something one causes is a real one. Yet Ramsey argues that it is inevitable if we are properly to describe human action in moral terms. Moral analysis must respect this obscurity of the nature of human action.

In both these areas, moral theory must be articulated to match the realities it deals with. It needs general principles, flexibly and situationally interpreted, but more specific "virtually exceptionless" rules are also warranted.

Love and Rules: Is There an Inconsistency?

The core of Ramsey's thought did not alter in its essentials, but he frequently returned and revised or altered particular applications and opinions. He admitted this much: "True, as a doctoral student paper written for Oliver O'Donovan at Oxford memorably affirmed, 'The quest for consistency before all else has never been one of Ramsey's failings.' "[2]

Do the admitted and apparent shifts of emphasis amount to a serious inconsistency?

First we return to the shift of emphasis that took place during the
1950s to examine the debate over situationism and the development of
the importance of rules in the moral life. We follow through the way
Ramsey developed his casuistry and ethical analysis from his view of
Christian love. At the back of our minds throughout this exposition is
the question whether Ramsey held together a major concern of situation ethics coherently with his rational casuistry. The key concerns of
situation ethics can be summarized in two stages. In Fletcher's words,
first, "We are commanded to love people, not principles, so that the
needs of human beings come before adherence to any rule," and
second that the validity of general rules is questioned "actually to the
point of rejecting any claim of absolute or universal validity for any
rule."[3] The first of these was supported in every respect in *Basic
Christian Ethics*; the second, however, as Ramsey continued to maintain, was not.

Ramsey insisted on the primacy of Christian love throughout *Basic
Christian Ethics*. For instance, discussing the attitude of Jesus to
Jewish law, he commented:

> Jesus completes in such fashion as entirely to annul the law. This also
> means that Jesus Christ "finishes" any ethic of conventional respectabil-
> ity, any customary code of conduct into which at least every man is born,
> any more or less philosophic definition of good and evil in which "*at least
> everyone* claimeth to be an authority."[4]

Again and again Ramsey insisted that Christian love alone is the
foundation, the final arbiter, the sole source of authority in Christian
ethics. For instance:

> Jesus in effect affirms the love commandments to be *incommensurable*
> with all the rest and declines to measure their importance by comparison
> with any other legislation. . . . [5] Everything is quite lawful, *absolutely
> everything* is permitted which love permits, everything without a single
> exception."[6]

Luther was quoted with approval:

> Therefore, in all his works he should be guided by this thought and look
> to this one thing alone, that he may serve and benefit others in all that he
> does, having regard to nothing except the need and advantage of his
> neighbor.[7]

Similar considerations also apply to any thought about natural law or natural morality, a topic that Ramsey left at least partly open: "Whether or not there is actually a natural morality inscribed in every human heart, this much is certain: this law also Christian ethics transcends."[8]

There can be no mistaking that this was the dominant emphasis of the whole book. No other basis can be found for Christian ethics than that of love. At the same time, it is quite clear that this is the source for an ethic of obligation:

> While love frees from the law it binds a man even closer to the needs of others, even as Jesus Christ was bound; and precisely that which alone frees also binds.[9]
>
> In place of rules for conduct, instead of "the law" which Christianity entirely finishes, comes not irregularity but self-regulation, and not merely the self-regulation of free, autonomous individuals but the self-regulation of persons unconditionally bound to their neighbors by obedient "faith working through love."[10]

The repeated opposition to law is not an opposition to all forms of rule and discipline. It is opposition to all forms of legalism, inflexible programs, social conventions, and so on: " 'What love teaches' cannot be identified for all time and all historical or social circumstances with any particular program of action such as prohibition or socialism."[11] Love is likely to need other guidance, though it yields supremacy to no other source of understanding: "Although much needs to be added from many sources to complete the whole edifice of Christian social ethics, no other foundation can be laid than that which has been laid."[12]

In the discussion of social policies in Chapter Nine, Ramsey argued that love may enter into "coalitions" with other schools of thought, but always as the senior partner, and never permanently:

> Christian love must, indeed, enter into such alliances; it must go in search of some social policy. Yet in the relationship between Christian love and the principles of an acceptable social ethic, Christian love remains what it is, dominant and free.[13]

For establishing standards of social justice, biblical justice is supreme. We need to remember in this discussion that Ramsey believed that righteousness, justice, and faithful covenant love in the Old

Testament (*mishpat*, *tsedeq*, and *chesed*) are "not at all clearly distinguishable in their meaning and never separable in fact."[14]

Christian love must seek to find out whatever may be known concerning the just ordering of human life. It cannot be too often said or too strongly emphasized that biblical "justice," when it begins to establish some order, can make use of any of the ideas or norms for determining "worldly justice" which happen to be convincing.[15]

Ramsey here laid the basis for a social ethic that is capable of great flexibility, but also of a high degree of definition and firmness. Although *Basic Christian Ethics* is not the place to find the mature and considered thought of Ramsey, it remains in many ways a foundation that he never moved away from.[16]

It does mean we must raise two connected questions about Ramsey's ethical theory. Is his theory self-contradictory and inconsistent? If we can answer this charge, the second is raised: Is Ramsey's ethical theory a unity, or is there a dualism in his approach? We might wonder if he is in fact developing and using a "two-level morality."

These questions are best illustrated with reference to political ethics. A number of commentators, as we will see, have found it hard to grasp Ramsey's combination of political pragmatism or realism with his unwavering insistence on the principle of discrimination. The difficulty here is more often a difficulty with Ramsey's moral thought than with his political theory. The point is that a clear understanding of Ramsey's casuistry (its combination of flexibility and firmness) is essential to his political thinking.

A number of critics have charged Ramsey with inconsistency in ethical method. They have brought this charge in varying forms, but the typical theme is that the ethic of Christian love is at variance with his insistence on rules, in general and in particular. Curran and Gustafson made this charge in a somewhat indirect way: they see his ethical method as a "love deontology" or as "the knitting of love to a deontological method,"[17] implying that Ramsey has to introduce some extraneous methodological assumptions. Neither, it should be noticed, found Christian love actually inconsistent with Ramsey's ethical method, but neither thought that love needs to be understood in this way. Curran also alleged: "I think Ramsey does not really prove any distinctive contribution of *agape* to the principle of discrimination."[18] In a similar vein Curran accused Ramsey of leaving considerations of Christian love out of his thought on wider concerns of political ethics.[19]

Curran seemed to look for a "Christ transforming culture" theme that Ramsey never claimed for his own work.

We now need to examine this charge, to see how Ramsey could answer it, for he insisted on the basic unity of his work. The task of exposition is made easier for us in that Ramsey himself undertook it in response to various critics. The key point is that Ramsey characterized love as faithful, and derived rules and principles from the nature of faithful covenant love. Love is articulated and applied in an "in-principled" way. We can illustrate by quoting Ramsey's answers to his critics. First, in answer to Curran:

> Can anyone deny that it is a strong sense of *care*, derivative from covenant love, with which I seek to illuminate the justice due in doctor-patient relations; or that this explains for me the origin of the principle of discrimination in war and the imperativeness of that principle today?[20]

And in answer to Gustafson:

> . . . covenant-love drives on to some rigorist deontic principles, not the other way round, i.e., . . . the distinguishing feature is the role Christology plays in moral analysis and in life. . . . Fidelity to covenant impels the most searching and relentless effort in extending love's light upon our human pathways, to discover not only permissions but also requirements; and if we find the latter to include some principles or rules of practice that should be held closed to future possible, morally significant exceptions—so be it![21]

We can see in these two quotations something of the combination of strength and flexibility in the characterization of love as faithful covenant love. We can explore this further by considering the critique offered by Dewey Hoitenga.

Hoitenga compared *Basic Christian Ethics* with *Deeds and Rules in Christian Ethics*, and suggested that Ramsey in 1950 was a proponent of situation ethics—"among its earlier spokesmen." He quoted from *Basic Christian Ethics*:

> While love itself never submits to external rule and does not proportion its benefaction according to some rule, it never becomes unruly, since the needs of other persons are the rule of love and quickly teach such love what to do.[22]

But, argued Hoitenga, in *Deeds and Rules in Christian Ethics*:

It appears, indeed, that he has actually moved away from his earlier position, if we may judge from the main thesis . . . viz, that "the Christian life may still take two forms: it may be productive of *acts only* or of *rules also.*"[23]

Hoitenga had several criticisms of Ramsey's later book, including that "he does not himself appear to have a definite constructive theology of creation."[24] This could perhaps be answered by referring to a strong hint about the correct understanding of the place of creation in theological ethics. When discussing what he calls "mixed agapism," Ramsey refers to the debates in theological ethics over "mandates," "orders of creation," etc. He insists that *abusus non tollit usum*:

There remain legitimate and important differences among these systems of theological ethics, but these differences are confused and not focused by all this effort to avoid using the word "order" or even "order of creation." The question is not the usefulness or the need for these categories in any full elaboration of Christian ethics.[25]

Evidently this is insufficient to satisfy Hoitenga. In the main he felt that Ramsey does not move far enough away from situation ethics. Ramsey wants to maintain the theme of the sovereignty of love, whether working without rules (act-agapism) or with summary rules or pure rules. Hoitenga comments "Ramsey's resistance to a pure rule ethic must be due to a persistent orientation to his original situationist position."[26]

We have already indicated the emphasis on love to be found in *Basic Christian Ethics*, along with the emphasis that love makes its rigorous and exacting demands. We can now give some examples from *Deeds and Rules in Christian Ethics*, which read with a new emphasis, but little substantial disagreement or inconsistency. In his critique of the document *Towards a Quaker View of Sex*, Ramsey writes: "The Friends reached the border where *Christian love embodied in an act* had to become *Christian love embodied in a general rule*, or where act-agapism, fully explored, was about to be replaced by rule-agapism."[27]

In Chapter Five of *Deeds and Rules in Christian Ethics*, Ramsey delineates four types of agapism.[28] These are act-agapism, summary rule-agapism, pure rule-agapism, and combinations of the first three. He then makes his own view clear:

It would seem, in fact, that if a Christian ethicist is going to be a pure agapist he would find this fourth possibility to be the most fruitful one, and most in accord with the freedom of *agape* both to act through the firmest principles and to act, if need be, without them.[29]

Ramsey then asks rhetorically: "The question is simply whether there *are* any general rules or principles or virtues or styles of life that embody love, and if so what these may be."[30] Ramsey answers his question by referring to 1 Corinthians 13, and continues with examples including the fruits of the Spirit, virtues, justice, marriage, promise-keeping, and the prohibited seven deadly sins. There are ways in which love will always behave, and things it will never do.[31]

Now clearly there is a shift of emphasis that Hoitenga, in the main, describes correctly.[32] It is also clear that Hoitenga's criticism of situation ethics is still substantially leveled against *Deeds and Rules in Christian Ethics*, and this bears out Ramsey's claim that there is an essential continuity between the two books.[33] Ramsey's claim is that while *Basic Christian Ethics* is capable of being read to support act-agapism, it also leaves room for rule agapism, or other principles in ethics than agapism only.

It is clear that we are not forced to read *Basic Christian Ethics* and *Deeds and Rules in Christian Ethics* as mutually contradictory. There are different emphases. But this does not mean that Ramsey has in any way weakened one of the keynotes of *Basic Christian Ethics*: "that only *agape* is primary and distinctive." This provides the foundation for the basic consistency, the lack of internal contradiction, in Ramsey's moral method.

Ramsey's admission that there is room for act-agapism and rule-agapism side by side in ethics allows us to raise another, weaker objection: that he has two bases for morality. By rule-agapism Ramsey means rigorous, exceptionless rules, which express the meaning of *agape* in any situation. By act-agapism we mean any moral decision covered simply by *agape* in action for the neighbor's good. Act-agapism also includes summary rules which guide *agape*, but which are not invariable or complete guides.

The importance of answering this objection does not consist merely in its significance for a grasp of Ramsey's ethical methodology. It is only when we understand this that we can make sense of his political ethics. The obvious instance of pure rule-agapism is the principle of discrimination. And when we talk of act-agapism (or summary rule agapism) we are thinking particularly of the areas covered by the principle of proportion. That principle itself is rigorous (*agape* never acts disproportionately or foolishly), but in discerning the best possible political action, *agape* can only be guided by the political wisdom enshrined in the political goals of justice, order, etc. We cannot expect to follow the way in which Ramsey understands the principle of discrimination without an understanding of his method of moral casuistry, of the place of exceptionless rules, and the principle of double effect, nor can we appreciate the principle of proportion as he expounds it, and its relation to discrimination, without grasping his analysis of the morality of action, and his careful critique of consequentialism, which does not deny the importance of consequences in moral analysis. The roots of his insistence on keeping these two principles clearly distinct are also to be found in his underlying theological and moral convictions. So, too, is any answer to the objection that this is a divided theory.

In order to tackle this problem, we must learn much more about Ramsey's understanding of rules and casuistry. When we see how his casuistry works, we will be in a strong position to demonstrate the underlying unity of his ethical method, and from that the unity of his political ethics. A good way to grasp Ramsey's casuistry, his view of proper analysis of action, and the importance of understanding "subsumption," is to begin with his development of the doctrine of double effect.

7

The Rule of Double Effect

Ramsey's advocacy of the rule of double effect is a bit like a sore tooth, for it continues to trouble him on and off from 1961 (in *War and the Christian Conscience*) at least until 1978 (*Doing Evil to Achieve Good*).[1] And that book hardly ties the questions up neatly. We will examine some of the decisive features of this protracted discussion later.

Before we enter the complexities of these discussions, it will be helpful to indicate their general shape and importance. The importance lies in the fact that the rule of double effect is vital to Ramsey's conception of the principle of discrimination. This, we recall, teaches us that it is never justifiable to attack noncombatants directly and deliberately. This evidently requires us to distinguish between "direct" and "indirect." As we shall see, Ramsey never had any doubt that such a distinction can and must be made. There is, however, a cluster of questions around this distinction on which Ramsey's position is not so clear.

The first is the precise definition of the principle. Like many contemporary Roman Catholic theologians, Ramsey was unhappy about the precise traditional formulation and the unsatisfactory conclusions it yields in some instances. The traditional Roman Catholic formulation is set out as follows:

> A person may licitly perform an action that he foresees will produce a good and a bad effect provided that four conditions are verified at one and the same time: 1) that the action in itself from its very object be good or at least indifferent; 2) that the good effect and not the evil effect be intended; 3) that the good effect be not produced by means of the evil effect; 4) that there be a proportionately grave reason for permitting the evil effect.[2]

The difficulty that this formulation leads to is encapsulated in a well-rehearsed test case.[3] This sets out a situation where a pregnant woman's life can only be saved by an operation involving an abortion, where the abortion is a means to saving the mother and apparently must be described as directly intended. If, however, the operation in question is a hysterectomy, the life of the fetus is taken just as surely, but the action is regarded as justifiable. This difference seems intuitively odd and unwelcome, especially as in both cases the life of the fetus is doomed one way or the other, for if the mother dies the fetus will die also. The example raises in a particularly acute fashion the difficulty involved in defining the meaning of "direct" as opposed to "indirect."

Rather than attempting a detailed revision of this tradition, Ramsey set out to give his own formulation. However, an intuitive perception in this area is not easy to articulate and defend. It took several years before he arrived at a way of expressing what seems a matter of intuitive common sense in a precise and satisfactory fashion.

Meanwhile, many Roman Catholics were also at work to remedy the apparent defects and rigidities of the traditionally accepted definition. In doing this, some in effect felt forced to abandon the principle altogether; others revised it very heavily in a consequentialist understanding of ethics in which its value and status became quite unclear.[4] Ramsey was troubled by these proposed revisions, and their implications for his own views. In his chapter on incommensurability in *Doing Evil to Achieve Good*, he set out not so much to present or expound his own position as to refute the positions of the revisionists. His complicated argument added another layer of difficulty to an already complex discussion.

We will return later in the chapter to Ramsey's debate with Richard McCormick. Now we follow through Ramsey's exploration of the principle in the 1960s. As we do this, we ourselves have a twofold aim. One aim is to expound and clarify Ramsey's views on double effect, and the other is, in the process, to gain insight into his understanding of moral analysis and his method of casuistry.

Christian love must be sovereign for all our behavior and moral thought. Reason must work to clarify and direct our fundamental commonsense moral perceptions. These two themes sometimes seem to run in different directions. Ramsey's argument is that the rule of double effect is a rational explication of love. However, as worked out and applied in traditional Roman Catholic casuistry, it leads to apparently unloving conclusions. In this context it took Ramsey some time and trouble to get out of an impasse in a discussion of justified and unjustified killing.

Ramsey pointed out from time to time that the principle of double effect is part of general moral thought, and not the exclusive property of Roman Catholic tradition. For instance, he wrote:

> The United States Supreme Court, for example, availed itself of the *flexibility* afforded by this "rule" when it declared state-action affecting religious practices to be constitutional provided the legislation had a secular legislative *purpose* and *primary effect* . . . "Double effect" was not patented by Roman Catholic theologians of the sixteenth and seventeenth centuries. It is not a teaching peculiar to Catholic morality. Instead, this explicit summary of moral wisdom belongs to the common Christian tradition. The use by military planners of the concept of "collateral damage" also shows the difference between directly intended and unavoidable direct effects must be drawn in any serious thought upon this subject. To dismiss this sort of analysis is to take the path of loose thinking. . . . the rule of double effect was the immediate result of charity forming the consciences of men.[5]

There are several significant discussions of the principle of double effect in Ramsey's work. Two key discussions center on the conflict of life with life as exemplified by the case of a mother with child where only one can live and not both.[6] These two discussions date from 1961 and 1966.[7] In 1961 Ramsey ran into a problem that he was unable to resolve satisfactorily at the time. The answer seems to have suggested itself to him when he was writing a paper on "Incapacitating Gases."[8] This paper was delivered in January 1966; it was then he first proposed the word "incapacitation" to describe the intention of the soldier in battle, and the intention of the surgeon who has to kill the fetus "directly" to save the mother. He then used the word "incapacitation" in "The Morality of Abortion" to solve the problem that was such an unsatisfactory loose end in *War and the Christian Conscience*.

This discussion points up for us two connected elements of Ramsey's casuistry: the importance of describing action correctly, and a concern with the meaning of moral rules. Our discussion of double effect leads into this central area of Ramsey's thought.

(1) 1961: The Problem Unresolved

There are two discussions of double effect in *War and the Christian Conscience*, rather different in character. In Chapter Three there is an examination of a passage in Aquinas in which the language of double effect is used. Ramsey's concern in this context is to show that noncombatant immunity has its origin in an ethic inspired by Christian love. In Chapter Eight ("A Thought Experiment: Cannot the Use of Unlimited Means of War Sometimes Be Justified?") we find the first of several discussions of abortion dilemmas with which Ramsey hoped to clarify the ethics of war. It was this latter chapter that reached only to an unsatisfactory resolution of a key problem. In 1976, Ramsey lamented the emphasis given by James Gustafson to the discussion in Chapter Eight, when he could rather have directed the attention of students to Chapter Three, on the origins of noncombatant immunity.[9]

In the earlier chapter Ramsey had examined an article from the *Summa Theologiae*, "Is It Legitimate for a Man to Kill Another in Self-Defense?"[10] In this article Aquinas employed the point he had made earlier, that an act can have two effects: "An act of self-defense may have two effects: the saving of one's own life, and the killing of the attacker." Provided then that the agent's intention is self-defense, it is legitimate for him to use sufficient force to defend himself. "It remains nevertheless that it is not legitimate for a man actually to intend to kill another in self-defense, since the taking of life is reserved to the public authorities acting for the common good, as we have seen."

Ramsey makes the following claim about this passage:

> It is not reciprocity or the standards of an equal justice alone that are here being applied in the analysis of the action. If this were so, then without doubt Aquinas would simply have said that, since it is intrinsically right to kill an unjust assailant, no guilt is to be imputed to the direct intention to do so. Profoundly at work in this line of reasoning is what justice transformed by love requires to be extended even to him who wrongfully attacks. This is what produced the original statement of double effect.[11]

Is Ramsey right to claim that Aquinas's analysis is affected by considerations of Christian love? Curran maintains that "there is no evidence that Thomas employed *agape* in his reasoning."[12] I think Curran's assertion is based on a reading of the Reply alone in Article Seven. The first two Objections are quotations from Augustine, who forbade killing in self-defense. Aquinas answered both by using the distinction between direct and indirect intention: "Augustine must be understood to be referring to a man's direct intention to kill another in order to save himself from death."[13] The importance of this is the reason Augustine had found in Christian love to forbid slaying in self-defense. This reasoning, it is clear, lies behind Aquinas's use of the distinction between direct and indirect.

Ramsey was not entirely accurate in claiming that this was the first statement of double effect. Aquinas had already used the principle in a discussion of scandal. He distinguished two kinds of "active scandal"—the direct and the indirect. "It is indirect if it is beside a man's intention (*praeter intentionem*)," but it is direct when someone "intends to draw another into sin, and then it becomes a special kind of sin on account of the man's intending a special end, because to moral acts, as we have explained, the end gives a specific character."[14]

In the case of scandal, it seems clear enough how the difference between direct and indirect is to be understood and how it is to be maintained. On the face of it, one can distinguish readily enough between the purpose of the initial action and its subsequent effect in leading another to sin. However, one may wonder whether the subsequent effect might not be so immediate as to be indistinguishable from actively leading another to sin. A similar difficulty may arise in a case of killing in self-defense. Consider two situations. In one, I am able to foil an assailant by knocking him to the ground. As a result, however, he is fatally injured. In another, I can only save my own life by using a lethal weapon, which causes his death. In the first, it was clear both to myself and to observers that I did not intend the man's death, whereas in the second perhaps neither I nor an observer could be clear what was directly or indirectly "intended." Here it is important to be clear that the word "intention" is used in a technical sense in this discussion. When used in this sense, it refers to the inherent purpose of the action, and is not necessarily to be identified with the "psychological" intention in the actor's mind. One suspects that the difficulty of this technical definition is partly responsible for the difficulties of many arguments in this field.

Later Roman Catholic interpreters shied away from using the principle of double effect to cover the case Aquinas had used it for—the killing in self-defense of an unjust assailant. Instead they specified that the unwanted evil effect must not be the means to produce the wanted good effect. Killing in self-defense was held to be justified on grounds of natural justice—the assailant is, after all, not an innocent man. Ramsey wants to base his analysis wholly on the foundation of Christian love, and therefore seeks a fresh statement of the principle.

Ramsey's continuing analysis of this question often returned to one or more of the following four cases:

1. The killing of soldiers in armed conflict.

2. The unavoidable killing of noncombatants in military action.

3. A pregnancy in which both mother and child are in danger, and in which an operation on the mother to save her (e.g., a hysterectomy) will also unavoidably take the life of the child.

4. As case 3, with the difference that the child must be killed *directly* in order to save the mother.

Ramsey's idea is to use cases 3 and 4 to clarify the main interest, namely a correct understanding of rules and double effect in cases 1 and 2. In the end it may seem rather to work the other way around. First we must just note one or two points of interest as far as 1 and 2 are concerned.

In Chapter Three of *War and the Christian Conscience*, Ramsey sketches the subsequent history of the development of the principle. Aquinas had never thought to use it to cover case 1, the killing of soldiers in war. For Aquinas (and Augustine, too, of course) the taking of human life by public authorities is permitted to be directly intended.[15] Aquinas's disallowing of the directly intended killing of an unjust assailant by the private citizen was followed by Cajetan, but after him this case was allowed as a matter of natural justice. Ramsey appeared to concur with this:

> Perhaps for good reason, then, this tradition in moral theology ceased to employ the rule of double effect in attempting to solve the problem of defense against an unjust aggressor, and to confine its use, after Aquinas and Cajetan, to the problem of the killing of an innocent person.[16]

Later on, as we shall see shortly, Ramsey was to return to this and find a way of defending the statement that all justified killing is correctly described as indirect.[17] Before we can see how and why his analysis reaches that point, we continue with case 2, the unavoidable killing of noncombatants.

Noncombatants must be held immune from direct attack. This is demanded by the moral logic of the permission to oppose the aggressor by force, but it is an inescapable feature of warfare that those who neither fight nor play any close part in assisting the fighters are bound to be caught up, and sometimes killed, in the fighting. The principle of double effect allows that where noncombatants are unavoidably, though foreseeably, killed in the conduct of war, this does not necessarily make that conduct wrong.

At the same time, the principle insists that we must never directly intend the death of noncombatants, no matter what great military or political advantages may be gained. Rather than continuing the discussion by examining examples from the field of battle, Ramsey turned to the cases of ectopic pregnancy, which we have called cases 3 and 4. This, he hoped, would help us to see whether there are any justifiable exceptions to the principle, for here is a circumstance that seems to require that we should take life directly in order to bring greater good.

We must first remind ourselves of the ground rules for this discussion, which is not without significance in its own right but which we concentrate on for theoretical reasons. It comes from the mainly (but not exclusively) Roman Catholic tradition of moral theology. We accept that the unborn child is of equal value to the mother and entitled to the full protection due to any human being. Traditional Roman Catholic analysis agreed that our case 3 may be resolved using the principle of double effect, but denied this in case 4.[18] Where the operation is directed on an organ of the mother (such as a hysterectomy, but other examples could be given) the death of the unborn child can legitimately be regarded as a side-effect. But where the mother can only be saved by directly taking the child's life, even though the child would not survive in any case, this cannot be permitted by the rule of double effect. This would be directly to aim at the death of the child—even as a means to preserving the mother's life. Ramsey wished to deny this conclusion (as of course did some contemporary Roman Catholic moralists). This denial was consistent in 1961, 1968, and 1976, but the arguments used to support it shifted in an important and revealing way.

In 1961, Ramsey failed to find any weakness in the double-effect argument, any way out of the problem. He first rejects a simple shortcut solution: "It is too weak . . . to say only that a more flexible practical wisdom should be allowed . . . to override the conclusion of a static ethics of natural law."[19] Instead, he appeals to his thesis that natural law was devised and used in the service of charity. In an apparent impasse, where the natural law rules appear clearly to contra-

dict the controlling grasp of charitable wisdom, we can appeal directly
to charity itself:

> Charity enters into a fresh determination of what is right in the given
> concrete context, and is not wholly in bondage to natural-law determina-
> tion of permitted or prohibited means. These rules are opened for review
> and radical revision in the instant *agape* controls; this was, indeed, what
> all along drove the Christian to the very act of devising them, and to
> employ them for centuries not as a reliance but as a service.[20]

A page earlier Ramsey had written: "Sometimes love acts in a quite
different way from what justice alone can enable us to discern to be
right."[21] All this is to give rather a substantial hostage to fortune, and
in applying this conclusion to noncombatant immunity in war, Ramsey
immediately backtracks. He denies that this sovereign freedom of love
can override the natural law understanding of noncombatant immunity.
There are great differences in the two cases (2 and 4); most notably in
case 4 the child was going to die anyway, while in the case of bombing
enemy cities the innocent would not otherwise die, and the gains are
much more in the balance.[22]

Ramsey concludes that, although there may be cases where "Christian love . . . *should* not be bound by the prohibition of the direct
killing of the innocent,"[23] these certainly do not include direct attack
on noncombatants in international armed combat. The latter question
was the one Ramsey had primarily in mind, but in questioning the
overly rigid Roman Catholic interpretation of double effect he raised a
new question. This question is how to explain and limit the exception
to the rule prohibiting the direct killing of the innocent. It was to this
question that Ramsey returned in 1966.

(2) 1966: The Problem Resolved

A better approach was found when Ramsey first considered the
question of abortion for its own sake in 1966. Here he comes again to
cases 3 and 4. First he states what we are calling the hypothesis: "It is
permissible, nay, it is even morally obligatory to kill the fetus directly
if, without this, both mother and child will die together."[24] It is not
sufficient, though, simply to assert this by looking merely at the end
result, for we must still ask if "direct abortion is not in every way
incompatible with . . . the sanctity of the nascent life." It is inadequate

to look merely at the motives and the ends of the action, although it is clear that as to motive this child's death is quite unwanted, and as to ends this is the best possible. It is the intention on which we must focus. Previously there seemed no escape from saying that the intention was directly to kill the child, but now Ramsey argues: "The intention of this action is not the killing, not the death of the fetus, but the incapacitation of it from carrying out the material aggression that it is effecting upon the life of the mother."

Ramsey applies this line of reasoning to the killing of enemy soldiers (case 1):

> Just so, in warfare it is not guilty aggressors but material aggression that ever warrants the taking of life to stop the action that is going on. Moreover, a proper analysis of the intentionality and direction of an act of war in killing an enemy soldier is exactly that proposed here in the case of justifiable abortion. It is the incapacitation of the soldier and not his death that is the intention of the action.[25]

Ramsey here suggests in a footnote that this analysis is close to that of Thomas Aquinas in the passage discussed earlier in *War and the Christian Conscience*, Chapter Three. We are back, then, to the difficulties of disentangling a twofold intention on effect, when both "effects" are only two ways of looking at one event or action.

In *Speak Up for Just War or Pacifism* Ramsey commented on this use of the rule of double effect. He pointed out, in discussion with Yoder, that this is only an explanation of the justification for killing enemy soldiers, it is not the main point or use of the rule of double effect. That remains the clarification of the limits of justifiable military action affecting noncombatants.[26] But for our present discussion of Ramsey's ethical methodology, the point that we need to underline now is the importance to him of correctly describing (or redescribing) what is happening in a case of justifiable killing. We will return to the importance of moral description shortly, but first we should examine Ramsey's further discussions of double effect.

Ramsey's Continuing Defense of "Double Effect"

It is hard to see that Ramsey's later and extensive defenses of his proposed revision of the rule of double effect added very much to the substance of the position he had arrived at in 1968.[27] Of these, the most notable is Ramsey's defense of his position against McCormick in *Doing Evil to Achieve Good*. It is not hard to see why Ramsey described this as a "failed book."[28] His own contribution to it is long, difficult, and unsatisfactorily presented. From our point of view here, a full account of the debate is not needed, if only because Ramsey's main concern is with attacking his adversary rather than defending and clarifying his own view. Nevertheless, it is necessary to give a sketch of the arguments, partly because one of the key issues, even if submerged for much of the time, is the principle of discrimination.[29]

Ramsey's active intervention in what had hitherto been a largely Roman Catholic discussion was sparked by McCormick's article "Ambiguity in Moral Choice." In this article McCormick had reviewed recent analysis of the principle of double effect offered by a number of writers. In it he had offered his own point of view, rejecting on the one hand a traditional defense of the principle, but wishing to maintain it on teleological grounds more fully than some of the critics (especially Schüller). Ramsey's attention was caught by this article and he quickly proposed to McCormick that they should collaborate to produce a volume of articles in response. The volume that emerged was *Doing Evil to Achieve Good*.

We can begin our brief analysis with an important observation about Ramsey, McCormick, and Schüller. Schüller had offered a clear, coherent, and powerfully argued opposition to the distinction between direct and indirect voluntariety.[30] McCormick did not agree with Schüller's account, and his own position sought to maintain the distinction in some form much more widely than had Schüller. Yet Ramsey is hardly interested in Schüller's arguments, and then only in order to pursue McCormick. The pursuit of McCormick, on the other hand, is unrelenting. Two reasons for this can be confidently surmised. One is that McCormick has gradually shifted away from a fairly traditional ethical theory toward a subtle form of consequentialism under the label "proportionate reason."[31] But it seems probable that it took more than this to sting Ramsey so painfully. The sting, surely, was the way in which McCormick wished to retain the apparently conservative conclusions he still held. He continued to defend the principle of discrimination, which he called "virtually exceptionless."[32] In other words, he appeared to offer similar conclusions to Ramsey, in identical language, but on an almost entirely different theoretical basis. Surely it was this that Ramsey found so provoking!

McCormick proposed a conservative revision of a radical new approach in Roman Catholic moral theology. This new approach, typified for us by Schüller, rejected the principle of double effect. A number of problems had been found with it, and Schüller believed that a satisfactory account could be given by teleological ethics of all the cases that double effect was supposed to cover. The problems included the unsatisfactory way the traditional doctrine was applied to certain questions of (especially) contraception, sterilization, and abortion. The precise definition of what is to be considered directly voluntary, and what indirectly, is a problem Schüller drew attention to. He concluded that the distinction is in fact superfluous, and can be replaced by teleological methods alone. These are already used, he pointed out, in the traditional doctrine (which requires "proportionate grave reason" as its fourth condition). Schüller maintained the distinction between direct and indirect only to cover "actions apt to induce other people to sin." He argued that here the distinction could be clearly and straightforwardly maintained, and derived from teleological considerations.[33]

McCormick was content for the most part to follow Schüller's account. He was, however, unhappy with Schüller's dismissal of the principle of discrimination. McCormick argued that killing noncombatants directly will have different consequences to killing them indirectly. The distinction should therefore be maintained, in this instance, at least for teleological reasons. "This leads to the suggestion . . . that where we view norms as 'virtually exceptionless,' we do so or ought to do so because of the prudential validity of . . . a law established on the presumption of common and universal danger."[34]

This is the nub of the proposal that caught Ramsey's attention. We must now examine his reply by first summarizing the main arguments of his long and difficult article. The introduction argues that it is the incommensurability of goods which makes the distinction between direct and indirect voluntariety necessary. Section One contains three main arguments.[35] The first picks up the agreement that one should never directly intend the sin of another. Ramsey suggests that this is because the value violated by such an intention is incommensurate with any other good, and he argues that one cannot separate so simply between intending the sin of another and intending other evils (especially the death of a human being). The second main argument of the section becomes very convoluted. Here Ramsey suggests a secular objector to McCormick and Schüller, who might argue that there could sometimes (even if only rarely) be occasion to violate one's moral integrity for the sake of the greatest net good overall. Ramsey's purpose here is to argue that the argument for never directly intending the sin of another is assumed, and needs justifying just as much as the argument that one should never directly intend the death of another. Both, he argues, are correct. In the third and final main argument of Section One Ramsey challenges for the first time the value language adopted by his opponents. Again the focus is on human life, and here Ramsey's suggestion is that life is not so much a value as the basis for all human values. To talk of human lives as values to be weighed against other values is misleading and dangerous.

Sections Two to Five are specifically directed against certain of McCormick's arguments and statements. Section Two looks at McCormick's account of the distinction between direct and indirect intentionality. McCormick is not clear whether he means this distinction to have moral significance in itself, i.e., whether it is morally significant how the intention stands in relation to the doing of a (nonmoral) evil or whether this distinction rests on the consequences that will follow from this psychological difference in how the evil is done. Ramsey believes that the latter interpretation is stronger in McCormick's thought, and that this line of thought is ultimately insufficient to support the distinction.

Section Three examines McCormick's use of rule-strengthening rules. McCormick makes several moves that point to the dangers of abandoning various rules, which, however, are not in themselves more than summary guides on the basis of their likely consequences, but there may be good reason to think of them as virtually exceptionless when we consider the long-term consequences of suggesting otherwise. Section Four follows through the logic of this argument in the area of euthanasia. Ramsey points out that if there is no good reason to think of certain classes of killing as wrong, as far as a proportional weighing of good and bad effects is concerned, then a clear-thinking doctor cannot be corrupted by doing the right thing. Only if he (erroneously) believed that his (direct) killing was wrong would there be any long-term evil consequences. Ramsey's argument is that McCormick's rule-strengthening rules are, in effect, parasitic upon the traditional distinction between direct and indirect intention. If McCormick really wants to maintain that distinction, then it cannot simply be based on a sophisticated long-run consequentialism, but rather must be allowed its own moral significance.

Finally, in Section Five, Ramsey considers McCormick's attempts to find a proportional basis for self-sacrificial acts of charity. He argues that McCormick's attempt to include such acts under the heading of proportionate reason "stretches the category beyond the breaking point."[36]

Does Ramsey's defense of the distinction between the directly and indirectly voluntary succeed? On the whole, I think we may conclude that it does although there are certain qualifications that must be made. Possibly the least of these is that Ramsey's language appears to slip and fall into error in at least one area.[37]

There are more serious defects in Ramsey's presentation of his case. We may suggest two difficulties in which the reader often tends to find himself. The first is bound up with the complexity of the argument, and the difficulties experienced by the protagonists in coming to grips accurately with one another's positions. The problem is simply that it is extremely difficult for the reader to discern with sufficient precision the exact aim of Ramsey's essay. The second area of difficulty is that Ramsey concentrates very largely on attacking his opponents without offering much clarification of his own alternative position. Let us take first the aim of the essay: What is Ramsey trying to do?

The heart of his essay is, unusually, to be found in the middle. Here for the first time he challenges the language of values in which the debate is conducted. He maintains in a rhetorical passage:

> Whatever we do to [our neighbor] . . ., we do to Christ. Killing Christ anew would seem to be entirely excluded from Christian volition and action. Killing may be tragically necessary in the fabric of life that restrains and sustains others for whom Christ also died.[38]

For this reason, we can never hold it to be right directly to intend the death of another—killing must always be "indirectly intended" to be morally justifiable. It seems to me that if Ramsey had allowed himself to set off more explicitly from this point, he could simply have made plain the radical nature of his disagreement with McCormick. Instead he tends to concede too much to his opponent.

This is not done by mistake. The point is, I think, that Ramsey admits from the outset that the principle he defends will not provide answers to all our moral questions. It is all too easy to overlook the vital sentence right at the beginning of the essay:

> My contention is that the rule of double effect, which is often supposed to be a program for reducing ambiguity in moral choice until there is none, has served rather to sustain acknowledgement of an actual ambiguity that characterizes much of our moral experience and many moral judgments.[39]

This admission means, of course, that Ramsey cannot claim to have a moral method that will lead with confidence in every case to the "right" moral answers. His claim is not a lesser claim than this, but it is different, and rather more subtle (and deserving of careful attention). His claim is rather that the aim of moral theory must be to do justice in language and concept to our moral experience—to the moral demands of the Christian faith and the moral intuitions of Christian love. Recognizing this aim immediately clarifies a good deal of Ramsey's argument, and also his passion. It explains why he uses the arguments he does to overthrow McCormick and Schüller, for he is not concerned (as we might be led to suppose) primarily to show that their arguments lead to wrong conclusions. Instead he wishes to demonstrate that their methods do not match up well with our moral experience, and that they too make assumptions about that experience, which are no easier to justify than the ones Ramsey himself makes. It is for this reason that Ramsey's most serious disagreements are with McCormick, from whose relatively conservative moral conclusions Ramsey differs much less than from those of, say, Schüller.

The admission Ramsey makes about moral ambiguity also goes some way to explain why he gives so little time to clarifying his own defense, preferring instead to attack the proportionalist case. Although he makes it clear why he insists on the traditional distinction in some form, he never makes clear with sufficient accuracy how this is to be done. It is not quite enough to show that the distinction is needed, for we also look for more help in seeing how it is to work and what results are to be expected from it. Ramsey's case would have been stronger had he set out his own position on this.

None of this is made any easier by Ramsey's combative style, with his concern for detail and precision. He uses the same style of argument as is his custom, attempting to find admissions and inconsistencies in his opponents, which will force them on their own premises to reconsider. The method simply becomes too complicated and cumbersome in this discussion to be tolerable.

It is not that Ramsey alone is to be held responsible for this. At the root of the problem represented in the book *Doing Evil to Achieve Good* is the fact that a very radical revision of moral language is taking place under cover of a highly technical discussion of a difficult ethical theory. One result of this is that all the technical terms being used tend to mean different things to the disputants, often in a way that is extremely difficult to disentangle. Therefore, in taking up an opponent's phrase, it is all too easy to misrepresent it, with the best will in the world. There is also, paradoxically, a sense in which each is somewhat too ready to use the language of his opponent, language that simply ought not to be admitted by the protagonist. Ramsey, for instance, cannot really afford to use the language of "values," for to do so already concedes too much. Ramsey is no doubt aware of this, but fails to give it sufficient weight.[40]

In spite of these difficulties and others, argument is definitely joined. We must ask: Does Ramsey succeed in showing McCormick's account of moral method to be unsatisfactory? I would judge that he does. At least he forces McCormick to reconsider and change his views. He also offers helpful clarification for those unsatisfied with consequentialist moral revisionism on the nature of that revision.

It may be wondered whether sheer theoretical complexity is almost sufficient for us to disqualify McCormick's as a satisfactory account of morality. Ramsey's arguments against him and his rule-strengthening account of the principle of discrimination are less forbidding than the earlier part of his essay. There is a persistent unclarity or ambiguity about McCormick's account of proportionate reason, which Ramsey correctly identifies. McCormick admits as much, if not in explicit response to Ramsey.[41] Whether McCormick's final account of his position can be considered satisfactory may be doubted. It is finally clear that he rests his argument for the principle of discrimination (which he maintains) on proportionate reason. Nevertheless, the notion of proportionate reason is still unacceptably vague.

McCormick's earlier account contained a serious circularity. He argued that the direct killing of noncombatants must be prohibited because of the grave dangers entailed in permitting it. But this, as Ramsey points out, either warrants only a merely psychological account of the distinction between direct and indirect, or assumes what it sets out to prove, namely, the moral wrongfulness of direct killing.[42] McCormick's further rule-strengthening moves do not alter this at all. He needs some other base to ground the principle of discrimination. He is not prepared to take the route offered by Schüller, who thinks it can be adequately replaced by the rule prohibiting more harm than necessary, and a prohibition of extortion (which Schüller presumably would base on teleological grounds, though he does not explain them). McCormick is quite reasonably worried that this will allow through one case in a hundred. "Hiroshima?" he remarks, pointedly enough.[43]

McCormick feels that proportionate reason must give a stronger basis than this to the principle of discrimination. He accepts that it must rely on a prohibition of extortion, which he wishes to maintain is "wrong in itself." Here is the argument he gives for this proposition:

> Extortion by definition accepts the necessity of doing nonmoral evil to get others to cease their wrongdoing. The acceptance of such a necessity is an implied denial of human freedom. But since human freedom is a basic value associated with other basic values (in this case, life), undermining it *also thereby undermines life*. In sum, extortion, as life undermining . . . is disproportionate.[44]

This quotation illustrates well the problem of handling the method of proportionate reason. It is not the apparent flexibility of McCormick's method that is worrying (although it is worrying enough) so much as the way it talks of "undermining values." I have to admit that I am unclear as to what this phrase might conceal. It seems possible that it may conceal the arguments that McCormick and others are so anxious to banish from ethics, arguments that forbid certain actions if directly intended or willed. Only so, as it seems to me, is such language capable of bearing the weight McCormick wishes to entrust to it. If, on the other hand, "undermining values" is simply a strong way of talking about the undesirable consequences, which may follow in men's minds and culture from some necessary but brutal actions, then it is very unclear to me how such consequences can render those actions "wrong in themselves."[45]

The method of proportionate reason, and the various associated forms of consequentialism, have been subjected to severe criticisms since the publication of *Doing Evil to Achieve Good*.[46] These criticisms have been made more tellingly (and more briefly) than those made by Ramsey. Nevertheless, it is not hard to see, even from that volume, that the proponents of proportionate reason have at least as many difficulties in giving a satisfactory moral account of the ethics of war as has the old rule of double effect. Ramsey at least pointed to those difficulties—and to the wide gulf separating his account from the apparently similar one of McCormick (verbally identical to Ramsey). When we come to consider critics of Ramsey's just war theory, we will be aware of that gulf, and the even wider one between Ramsey and Schüller. For now we must return to Ramsey's casuistry, starting from a point we made above in studying his earlier work on the rule of double effect.

8

The Analysis of Action

We saw at the end of Chapter Six that a difficulty with the rule of double effect is clarified by a *redescription* of the act of killing a soldier, or of operating on a mother with child. This gives us an important clue to the best way in which to grasp the theoretical aspect of Ramsey's view of correct moral analysis. It is not exactly a discovery to point to the fact that the problem of describing an action correctly is central to any moral analysis. My aim here is to suggest that Ramsey's answers to the questions clustering around this problem provide the best way of characterizing the quality of moral judgment to which his ethical theory leads. It is the clue to hold together a number of his reiterated themes—let us instance three or four major ones.

First it shows how he views casuistry as a process of understanding and clarification. Casuistry aims at finding "intrinsic principles which *anatomize* the nature of politically responsible action."[1] Principles and rules are clarified and refined as we think through the problems with which we are concerned. In the ethics of war the principles of proportion and discrimination are inherent in a correct understanding of political theory. "None of these concepts are drawn from another world and extrinsically imposed upon the political realm."[2]

Second, correctly analyzing an action is equivalent to ascertaining the intention of that act.[3] Two examples of what Ramsey means here can be cited: "Beginning in the *aiming* of an action, the intention of an act then includes the main *thrust* of it upon its immediate objectives," or when he says that the heart of an action can be found "in its intention and in the shape of its primary thrust in the world and in its immediate effects."[4] We can note here Aquinas's handling of the importance of intention in understanding human action. He asks, "Are human acts what they are by reason of their end?'' He answers this affirmatively, replying to his first two objections as follows:

> Hence: 1. The end is not altogether extrinsic to the act, but is related to it as its origin and destination, and so enters into its very nature, . . . 2. We have observed that the end affects the will as prior by intention, and in this way does it give specific character to a human or moral act.[5]

This clarification of why the effect of an action is important to its moral character is vital to any grasp of the meaning of intention. But Aquinas leaves unstated what is properly considered the "end" (*finis*) of an act. Learning to analyze an action correctly involves distinguishing between which consequences are relevant (and which irrelevant) to the characterization of the moral meaning of an act. One of Ramsey's reasons for hesitating about the word "deontological" is that this might indicate that he is not concerned at all with consequences. Far from this being the case, he holds mainly that they cannot tell us everything about morality.

Third, seeing to what kind a particular action belongs is the work of subsumption, or practical reason. To know whether a particular action is aimed at murder, or at a (justifiable) incapacitation, we have to use our practical wisdom. This cannot be determined by any general theory or "subsumption-ruling rule," but only by particular judgments of particular events.

We will now illustrate these three important themes with a simple example. Let us look at the relationship between intention and action. First we should remind ourselves that we are not concerned here either with motivation or with the final goal of an action, so it is not a justification of an act of killing an enemy soldier to say either: (a) I did it without hatred in my heart (motive), or (b) I did it for my country, to help win the war against injustice (overall aim, or final goal).[6] An action, in order to be justified, may have to pass three tests. These are of motive, of intention, and of overall aim. We say "may have to pass" because there are some actions that are good in themselves, requiring no further justification in their general consequences. Some actions may be questioned and ultimately justified or not according to the good or evil they bring, whereas there are some means that cannot be justified by any ends.

In between motive and goal there is still a great variety of possible ways of describing the same action. Consider the following sequence of descriptions of a shot fired in wartime:

1. I pulled the trigger on my gun.

2. I shot a human being.

3. I killed an enemy soldier.

4. I prevented a man from killing me (by incapacitating him).[7]

The difference between descriptions 3 and 4 was a point of some theoretical importance for Ramsey. It seemed to him that Christian love required that one should never directly intend the death of any human being, so he preferred description 4 for cases of justifiable killing in combat. This description gives the direct intention as incapacitation, and the indirect intention as the enemy's death.

David Smith challenged the consistency of this account of the meaning of "direct" and "indirect."[8] He pointed out that Ramsey was, on one hand, clear that intentions had always to be related closely to physical action. Smith cites a passage from *War and the Christian Conscience*:

Intentions alone are always open to suspicion, unless they are also controlled by some more objective determination of right *action*. Double effect cannot mean merely letting the bullet go and withholding the intention. . . .

The modern improvements of the rule [of double effect] make it clear that the good effect must not only be the formal object of the intention but also the immediate material object of the physical act. More simply, the good must be not only willed directly but also done directly, if the agent is not to be held directly accountable also for the foreknown evil consequence of his action.

Smith cites these passages to show that Ramsey makes a tight "correlation of intention and direct doing." He then points out that Ramsey elsewhere redescribed some "direct" killings as "incapacitation":

An observable, physically direct killing of an unborn child could be understood to have the function of *stopping* its lethal action upon its mother's life and not to have the objective of killing that child as such apart from its fatal function.[9]

Smith argued that these two accounts of what is directly intended are at variance with each other. If so, Ramsey would have to give up his moral acceptance of some physically direct killing (and hence his foundation for just war theory), or adopt a looser style of redescription of direct intention (which Smith felt would need to resemble the approach of McCormick et al.).

Is there a way in which Ramsey's understanding of intention can be defended? Ramsey's reply to Smith makes clear that Smith's initial difficulty lies in the two senses in which the word "direct" is used:

> I should be able to place *two* qualifying predicates—"observable, physically"—before "direct killing"; and expect then to be understood *not* to be using the word "direct" in the technical sense of traditional teachings.[10]

How can Ramsey advocate this redescription of the agent's intention and still object to other redescriptions? Can his opponents not argue that this type of redescription will become so flexible as to lead to a position very like theirs? What are the limits to redescription? Smith insists that Ramsey should explain "how one specifies the units of action which are appropriate subjects of moral judgment."[11] Ramsey's answer to this brings us, I believe, very near to the heart of his thought.

Ramsey's answer to these questions is that there can be no rules which tell us in advance how to describe action correctly in moral analysis. Moral reasoning, in the application to cases, the subsumption of cases under rules, cannot be done by theoretical reason, but by practical reason:

> There can be no "application-rules" supplanting prudence in determining those units of action. Indeed, a large part of moral discourse and ethical disagreement is about just that. The strange work of prudence in "subsuming" cases remains to be exercised, in saying, *this* so far and no further is the unit of action to be appraised, *that* is the ulterior end or conspicuous consequence in view; *this* is the intended means or the intention of the immediate human act, *that* is the motive or end. No demarcation-line can be deduced, nor a fixed one found to be applicable to all cases.[12]

To return to the example of the killing of the enemy soldier, we can say that that redescription makes sense in that type of situation because there is physical combatancy to be stopped. If killing, or threatening to kill, a man's children, will bring about great good, even the saving of many other lives, by dissuading him from his evil purposes, then in such a case the killing cannot be so redescribed as "incapacitation" or "stopping the combatancy." However evidently true this moral distinction is, it cannot be proved syllogistically. Rather, Ramsey maintained, the correct redescription flows from a love-informed reason as it is exercised on cases and types of cases.

The connection between action and moral judgment is not loosened indefinitely. It is worth exploring this a bit further as we look at another alternative account of the shot fired in battle:

5. I fired the shot that swung the course of the battle.

This statement does not so much interpret the action as describe it by including another different type of consequence. It refers to the wider consequences that followed that one death—which could of course be traced out in all directions, thinking of all those connected to the enemy soldier quite apart from the more immediate consequences on the field of battle. In the strict sense, though, the relevant consequence of my pulling the trigger is the death of this one man. Only if the action is correctly describable as incapacitation should one then consider (in moral analysis) the wider aims and consequences. At the same time the wider context is by no means irrelevant, for only some good end can justify this killing as a means, however tragic, to that end.

With this example, we have continued to explore the principle of twofold intentionality (double effect), but focusing on the limits of what is to be considered legitimate description and redescription in this discussion. I have aimed to show that the problem of correctly interpreting human action in order to describe it is a central problem in moral analysis. Describing an action means claiming that it is of a certain kind—that one killing is properly to be understood as a (justifiable) incapacitation, whereas another is not. This leads us to suggest that the assessment of the action proposed in statement 4 could be similarly expressed as follows:

4a. I killed a man, but I did not murder him.

This is to approach the same problem by asking the meaning of the forbidden killing. Rather than talk of a general rule against killing, with certain specified exceptions, Ramsey prefers to ask the meaning of the prohibition:

[Christians] have asked: what is the meaning of the forbidden theft, what is the meaning of truth-telling, what is the forbidden murder? They have explored or deepened or restricted the moral meaning of these categories or rules of conduct.[13]

Either way, the question turns on the extent to which any correct description must include an element of interpretation; it cannot be a bare account of physical actions. Here we reach the heart of Ramsey's casuistry.

Ramsey's approach thus differs subtly but importantly from what may crudely be called ethical literalism. Direct-action rules are not to be sought (such as, for example, "any telling of verbally inaccurate statements is forbidden" or "sexual intercourse is only permitted between a man and a woman possessing a valid marriage certificate"). Any positivism of this kind has to be rejected. What Ramsey would rather say is "All unfaithfulness is wrong." Then at least two tasks remain: one theoretical, one practical. The meaning of faithfulness has to be inquired into—what are the features of a faithful or unfaithful act? And the practical determination of any specific act also remains to be done—is this truly a case of unfaithfulness or not?

Act-description provides us with a convenient vantage point for some of Ramsey's leading themes in moral theory. It has also highlighted for us the central importance of understanding the nature of an action in order to interpret and describe it correctly.

The Interpretation of Action and the Meaning of Rules

How are we to interpret and describe actions? This would be one way of expressing one of the questions that Ramsey set out to answer in "The Case of the Curious Exception."[14] We can now see how this article expresses in theoretical terms the point we have illustrated in our discussion of justifiable killing. Let us briefly review some of the main steps of its argument.

Ramsey's argument defends the case for the existence of exceptionless moral rules. Rules are here distinguished from principles in being more specific, as "directives" rather than "directions," for instance, though it should be noted that Ramsey sees this as only a relative distinction. In the first section Ramsey argues that finding and specifying qualifications, or exceptions, to principles and rules, does not destroy those principles or rules but actually clarifies them. In the second section he examines how definite and specific rules can be. Here he points out that the moralist can never escape dependence on what he calls the work of prudence in applying rules to actual situations, in subsuming actions under the relevant rules. In the third and fourth sections Ramsey argues against holding every rule open to future possible revision in the light of new exceptions. He does this first by arguing that people need rule-strengthening rules in some areas of life, as it were to compensate for the weakness of human reasoning when under pressure, and, more significantly, by appealing to the significance of covenant faithfulness for Christian ethics. The concern to be faithful will lead us to consider some moral rules to be significantly closed, not open to future possible exceptions.

Our present concern for understanding the shape of Ramsey's casuistry prompts us to concentrate on the first section.[15] Ramsey is asking what it means for rules to have exceptions. He points out that one can only talk of justifiable exceptions to rules or principles by giving reasons for them. These reasons cannot be of the form "except when it would be better not to keep the rule," for this is to give up the work of moral reasoning. For instance, suppose the situationist were to say, "We should not commit adultery except when it would do more good on the whole to do so." This kind of exception-making criterion has the effect of destroying the principle of marriage:

> The attachment of an exception-making criterion to the marriage-principle has already destroyed that principle and set it aside, whether the decision in a present instance is to abide by it or actually to depart from it for the sake of doing good.[16]

Moral reason demands that an exception must be justified for reasons that have to do with the features of that exception. Analyzing those features can then permit us to apply the rule more definitely when those excepting features are not present: "If anything, a justifiable exception fixes the application of a principle or rule more firmly and definitely in all cases to which it continues to apply."[17]

Casuistry has to do with understanding the morally relevant features of actions. This can be done in one of two ways. Either we can formulate a moral classification of principles, rules, feature-dependent exceptions, and so on, or we can learn to understand the meaning of the principle or rule in question more thoroughly. Both of these ways offer the possibility of understanding the nature of an apparent exception to a rule. The first admits that a certain case is an exception, and considers whether the factors that make it so constitute a sufficient exempting-condition to justify an exception. The second way, rather than admitting an exception to a principle, sees the exceptional case as illuminating the meaning of the principle in some way. By considering this case, we come to a better understanding of the meaning that was all along implicit in the principle. Ramsey's exposition of these methods of casuistry centers on the case of Mrs. Bergmeier (a woman in a Russian prison in wartime, who got herself pregnant by a prison guard in order to gain her freedom and return to her family). Ramsey offers two ways in which (we may decide) her "adultery" was justified.[18] Either we can say that she committed adultery, but was justified in the exceptional circumstances; or we can say that her action was not the forbidden adultery, but expressed the true meaning of marital fidelity. Ramsey concedes: "It may be questionable whether the latter line of reasoning can be carried through in the matter of 'adultery.' "[19]

To explore the implications of this choice, let us follow up one of the instances Ramsey gives. Suppose we are considering whether a lie may be told to save life, perhaps to save a victim from a would-be murderer. We could say, "Never tell a lie except to save life." Or we could say, "Never withhold the truth from someone to whom it is due." The advantages of the second formulation are clear. On the one hand, the first formulation still needs to be expressed much more clearly and specifically. There are occasions when we would not think it right to lie in order to save life (to provide a false alibi for a guilty man to save him from execution, perhaps), so we need to specify the exception "to save life" more carefully, which may well prove very difficult to do satisfactorily, let alone simply. On the other hand, the second formulation helps us to understand the prohibition of lying as something intended to safeguard our relationships, and trust within them.

This is brought out by another classic example, this time of an unjustified lie. Suppose this time a lie might be told to a gravely sick person, perhaps to avoid giving her bad news (say, about her own illness, or the death of a close relative). Here the formulation "Never tell a lie except to save life" is inadequate to reach the heart of the dilemma we face, for this lie might well be a betrayal of the sick person. The second formulation, on the other hand, points us clearly to the considerations we must bear in mind. Why might the truth not be due to this person? And how can we give her the truth that is due to her in a way that most fully respects her frailty and weakness? Whatever we decide, our attention is directed to a key area of moral concern, namely, our faithful care of the sick person.

Ramsey complicates this central point by going one step further. Wherever possible, he wants us to redefine lying as "withholding the truth from one to whom it is due." Thus every "lie" defined in this way will be a forbidden lie. He also attempts to do the same for other principles of conduct, and, if possible, redefine theft, forgery, and adultery (although he concedes that this is probably impossible in the case of adultery), so we would never need to say that there was an instance of "justified theft" in the same way that one cannot have an instance of "justified murder."

Ramsey has substantial reason for wanting to insist that we should be ready to redefine our use of moral terms in this way. He sees the moral life as a unity springing from its basis in the nature of Christian love. The prohibition of theft is an expression of our love-formed respect for others, embodied in our respect for their material goods. But love may require of us that respect for others, in some circumstances, be embodied in some other way. We will, in this situation, find that we gain a fuller understanding of the basis and meaning of property, its nature, and its purposes. It is this understanding, not the common use of language, that should govern our grasp and expression of moral truth.

Evans thinks that this attempt to redefine language is unhelpful:

Consider, for example, Ramsey's claim that "there could be no good charitable reason for saying that picking someone else's apples to save life belongs among the meanings of 'theft,' or for saying that mere verbal inaccuracies of speech to save life belong among the meanings of 'lying.' These were extensions and explanatory principles 'conditioned' by principle itself."[20]

Evans further argues that:

. . . charity does not require us to give such an elastic meaning to "theft" or "lying." And the demands of clarity, rather than charity, would be operative—in the reverse direction. The clear and straightforward thing is to say that theft and lying are prohibited *except to save life*.[21]

Although Evans rejects Ramsey's attempt to redefine words, he thoroughly agrees with the main point, which is the importance of focusing "on the deeper meaning of traditional moral rules."[22] All that is at issue at this point is the best way of using language, and the extent to which it can be reshaped. Ramsey generally tends to want to reshape moral language "since the ingredients in the moral situation are not altered by the language we use (but our language should rather be perfected in order adequately to sort out the true nature of the ingredients)."[23]

Our moral theory, perhaps even more than our moral language, needs to be helpful for sorting out moral situations. Ramsey's theory is a theory of love in action. It takes its shape primarily from its theological basis in covenant love, *agape*, but *agape* also needs to pay close attention to the realities of the world in which it acts. We have suggested here that a good way of appropriating Ramsey's thought at this point is to see how he interprets and describes action from a moral point of view. This has brought several things into focus.

First, it reminds us that there is a moral reality that is there to be grasped. Morality is not something that is imposed upon the world by human thought and language. Second, it insists that it is possible to understand, to grasp that reality intellectually, for the most part with a reasonable degree of confidence. (This is not to say, of course, that this is an easy task all the time.) Third, it draws our attention to the shape of moral thought, which in a real sense must follow the shape of reality. We cannot overlook the fact that we are actors, and our actions have a definite place in the world. We are required to be faithful to our neighbors, those to whom our actions are immediately directed. Our actions also may have wider consequences for many people. We have to pay attention to at least these features of our actions. (There are other possibly relevant kinds of features also.) But in the nature of the case, our faithfulness to our immediate, near neighbor must be the first thing we attend to before we think about the wider consequences for many other more distant neighbors. Ramsey's ethic is therefore a unity, but it is an articulated unity, not a uniform one. To defend the thesis that Ramsey's ethical theory is not only self-consistent, but also unified, we turn to some critics who have maintained otherwise.

9

The Unity of Christian Ethics

Does Ramsey's ethics give us a divided approach? Are there some things on which we can have certainty or near certainty, morally speaking, while on other questions there is nothing moral to say? Is it so with regard to discrimination and proportion in just war theory? Here we approach these questions from the theoretical end, bearing in mind that they will return even more pointedly in the discussions of the morality of war.

One attempt to characterize Ramsey's theory as a twofold system is that of David Little. Little's essay is in some ways unsatisfactory; he appears to find some difficulty in reading Ramsey straightforwardly. However, he argues merely that his interpretation, or "reconstruction," is "at least plausible." Essentially, this goes as follows: "The basic concept of agape has two sides or dimensions for Ramsey: a *discretionary* and a *formalistic* side. Everything in Ramsey's system is keyed directly to this distinction."[1] This distinction seems to have been suggested to Little by the principles of discrimination and proportion, and when we come to consider these more fully, we will meet similar analyses with particular respect to just war theory. Such an analysis of the morality of war should perhaps expect to find the roots of the distinction in Ramsey's general ethics. This is what Little attempts to expose.

Little's formalistic category contains principles and rules, which are "rationally" applicable. The discretionary category refers to the "indeterminate and incalculable" aspects of *agape*, subject to no fixed law or principle. In this way Little's analysis of Ramsey divides his moral theory in two distinct halves. The two categories are linked as follows. The "formalistically determined requirements of agape" set "fixed or determinate outer limits of agape. But within the limits set by these requirements, the teleological task is 'systematically indeterminate' and incalculable.''[2] This seems promising enough if one thinks only of exceptionless rules, but the interpretation runs immediately into a difficulty.

We note first that Little puts act-agapism and summary rule-agapism in the discretionary category. There are situations in which *agape* must make its own fresh determinations of what is right in the situation, possibly with the guidance of maxims, guides, or summary rules. We can observe that Ramsey showed these to be the same, formally speaking. A summary rule is always ready to be set aside in any circumstance, so that in principle it never yields a different answer to a moral question from that given by act-agapism.[3]

The problem for Little is how to understand some of Ramsey's political principles. Are they to be considered as part of the formalistic category, or the discretionary? Little plumps for seeing them as formalist: "The formalist side of agape yields certain principles and rules—like order, justice, and law—that are of special significance for guiding political behavior." Although Little is puzzled by Ramsey's vagueness in defining these principles (e.g., "Ramsey defines justice in a bewildering way") and fails to see that they are deliberately left open-ended to be as flexible and useful as possible, still he insists that they specify a range of actions "that have a certain definite and unmistakable form." Now clearly these three principles do not specify the same actions, or ranges of actions. How does Ramsey hold the principles together? According to Little, "the configuring of these principles in concrete political situations is achieved *in a discretionary way.*"[4] Surely this should have convinced Little that his sharp division of Ramsey's thought into the two categories "formalistic" and "discretionary" is unsatisfactory. Earlier he had related the two categories by saying that a systematically indeterminate discretion is free to operate within certain outer limits. Now, on the other hand, he is saying that the actor's discretion is determined by rules, or perhaps that the supposedly fixed rules are subject to discretion.

Could Little not have maintained his analysis of Ramsey's "system" by regarding justice, order, and law as summary rules, within the discretionary category? No, for to do so would have shown immediately that Ramsey's "discretion" (or principle of proportion) is by no means "indeterminate" or "transrational." The two sides begin to blur together. There is, I hope, no need to show that they blur from the "formal" side also; this can be seen in the importance of interpreting and applying any exceptionless moral rule.

No other critic divides Ramsey's theory in such a severe way, but many critics emphasize Ramsey's pure rules so heavily that it becomes almost impossible to grasp the unity of his thought. One such critic is James Gustafson. He begins by calling Ramsey's ethic a "love monism":

> A love monism does not in and of itself lead to the kind of ethics that Ramsey expounds. It is the knitting of love to a deontological method that shapes his particular moral judgments and prescriptions.[5]

Gustafson makes Ramsey's "deontological method" a key to his account, talking of "Ramsey's intention to be as rigorously deontological as possible." Gustafson is not the only one to label Ramsey in this way, although he probably makes more of it than most others.[6]

Ramsey himself is much more hesitant about the term, recognizing that its meaning needs to be carefully specified in each discussion.

> The word "deontological" is empty until a conversation partner tells us what he means by it. Until then it designates any norm "that evaluates an act by a characteristic that cannot be gathered from its consequences."[7]

In virtually all the (comparatively few) places where Ramsey himself uses the word, there is a hesitation (such as "what we may call," or the use of quotes, or a hypothetical "if we have to choose between deontological and teleological").

Gustafson regards Ramsey's ethical method as made up of two components—a "love monism" and a deontological approach. In failing to see how Ramsey's method is derived from the theological understanding of love, Gustafson arbitrarily divides Ramsey into two aspects. It also leads him to allege that much of Ramsey's ethics is actually controlled by the supposed methodological presupposition:

> One of the features of Ramsey's work, in comparison to the ethics that follow from my theocentric perspective, is that the description of the morally relevant circumstances is much more limited. Those limits follow reasonably from the ways he has developed a Christian ethics of love in a deontological mode.

and

> . . . the description of the relevant circumstances of the moral act is stringent, and this follows from the method.[8]

Gustafson's point about the limitations Ramsey puts on the range of circumstances to be considered may be misleading. Ramsey was always ready to consider the relevance of circumstances and consequences, though in the end he often limited the decisive considerations more narrowly than Gustafson would wish. It is only in the moral decision itself that the description of the act is limited in the way Gustafson supposes. What cannot be accepted is Gustafson's charge that this limitation follows from some prior methodological choice. For instance, in discussions of abortion, it is not a prior commitment to a deontological method that leads Ramsey to defend the claims of the fetus. It is, rather, his concern with the given realities of human life and medical action, and the duty of faithfulness to any human life. In other words we are led to the doctrines of covenant and creation, to which we will return in a moment.

For a third critic of Ramsey's ethical method we turn to Paul Camenisch.[9] In this case, the detailed analysis is basically correct, but Camenisch seems to be misled by Ramsey's championship of rules into thinking that this comprises the whole of Ramsey's ethical theory.

Camenisch sees that Ramsey's concern is commonly with opposing various modern secular trends, such as "momentalism" or the "atomistic individualism of secular thought in the modern period."[10] Ramsey replies with a "varied group of antidotes." But, says Camenisch, Ramsey then concentrated so much on rules that there is a danger that other continuities "recede to the background so that now rules properly so-called must carry the entire load of continuity once shared by these other elements." He continues with analysis of "The Case of the Curious Exception" and concludes as follows:

> Thus, if I can summarize without caricaturing, all of Ramsey's impressive argumentation on behalf of exceptionless principles and rules has resulted in giving us the *possibility* of *negative* rules and principles which require a *continuing interpretation* to discern what they forbid, are to be held to as exceptionless only in the absence of love-violating counter-instances, and are prohibited by the inviolable rights of prudence from making pronouncements in individual cases. *That* is not much in the way of positive rule making as a means to continuity.[11]

We can accept the first sentence, without accepting the second.[12] In following out Ramsey's detailed argument so carefully, Camenisch has perhaps lost sight of the bases of the argument. Ramsey's aim is not only to show that there can be exceptionless moral rules, and what this means, it is also to defend a confident kind of moral thought, in basic continuity with the Christian tradition. This arises from Christian faith, and shares its qualities:

> We mean and should mean in Christian ethics to say that there are correlative performative understandings of moral acts, relations and situations that arise from our faith-commitment or acknowledgement of God's performatives and his mandates. . . . This we express when we say "I look on all men as brothers whom God made to be one."[13]

Camenisch, like Gustafson, has mistaken the part for the whole. Neither "a deontological method" nor exceptionless moral rules are the whole of Ramsey's concern. Rather they are an important part. In contrast to all these widely different understandings of Ramsey's ethical method, we have tried to analyze and expose his thought as an articulated unity.

Here we can follow up the two doctrines already noticed—creation and covenant. The doctrine of creation is never very far below the surface in these discussions. Principles and rules are possible because there are created continuities in the world. There are features that are common to human lives. Marriage, illness, mortality, speech, economics, politics—all these have a character that depends on the created order as it is. It is in this created world, not in some creation of our minds, that we are called to love our neighbor faithfully. For instance:

> Starting with persons in all the actuality of their concrete beings (but without the blinkers of momentalism on his eyes), a Christian with unswerving compassion asks: What does love require?
>   There are structures of life into which we are called; and practices into which every man was born who ever was born.[14]

The fact that we are embodied beings in a structured world means that the principles and rules of morality are articulated and structured. They form a unity, but it is not a uniform unity, it is a differentiated one.

There is a range of confidence in the guidance offered by the moralist from the definiteness of "Never torture your wife to death while giving her to believe that you hate her" [!] through a range of principles and rules to more or less confident judgments of particular situations, where love must, with prudence, decide on grounds of proportion and consequences. This theory then offers us a flexibility appropriate to the complex realities we often have to face. Making moral decisions involves a grasp of these realities, which may also help us to clarify the moral understanding with which we began. This is absolutely vital to the political theory, where it is commonly supposed that morality is in some way extrinsic to political reality.

The doctrine of creation is thus an essential basis for Ramsey's ethics. There are given realities and continuities in the world of human action. Correctly describing that world and its actions involves understanding and interpreting it correctly. We have seen that there is work to be done to grasp and describe human action. We have noticed that this is possible partly because the intentions of an action can relate to quite limited aspects of the relationships and the consequences surrounding a particular action.

But the indispensable key to the doctrine of creation is the doctrine of covenant. It is God's covenant love which is the inner meaning of his creation. God's covenant love is faithful, so our love is to be faithful. We need hardly emphasize this, but we can give one example from the heart of the argument about exceptions:

> In the Christian life we are driven deeper and deeper into the meaning of covenant obligations, to specify as aptly as possible the meaning of the faithfulness to other men required by the particular covenants or causes between us. The relevant moral features which this understanding of the moral law uncovers in every action, moral relation, or situation are primarily the claims and occasions of faithfulness.[15]

Faithfulness is the key to Ramsey's priorities. These priorities are shaped and formed as love goes about its work in the real world of flesh and blood people. We have seen that actions can be grasped as having an immediate aim and purpose. They may also have wider repercussions and consequences. In trying to estimate the latter, however great the future gains may be, it is never right for the actor to overlook the actual effects of his actions on those who are the immediate target. At the same time, in the wider context as well as in the immediate act, there are regular features that can be discerned and analyzed, yielding rules and principles of various kinds. The principle of discrimination draws our attention sharply to the targets of our attacks, while the doctrines of political thought help us to assess the nature of politics and act for the best in that sphere.

It is impossible to think that at root the obligations of love are in any fundamental way divided. As we have tried to explore the quality of moral demands, we have seen that they are best visualized as an articulated unity, varying from confidence to perplexity, from a firm objectivity to a prudent weighing of pros and cons. The demands all spring fundamentally from the same source, but at the heart of that source is the model of God's faithful covenant love for his people. Expressing faithfulness patterned on that love means that a basic protection of the neighbor will take precedence over a general concern for his welfare. This does not mean that the two can be sharply separated.

So, despite some appearances, there is no dichotomy in this moral theory. Concern for the other's inherent worth, for the sanctity of life, lies at the root not only of exceptionless moral rules. The same love lies also at the root of all moral judgments involving a weighing of more or less good.

At the back of our minds in this discussion all along has been Ramsey's just war theory, with its use of the twin principles of discrimination and proportion, and their application to vexing contemporary issues. The next two chapters turn to the justification of the use of force in Christian ethics, and the working out of this in the morality of nuclear deterrence.

Part Three: The Wrestle with Pacifism

10

A Christian Ethic of Resistance

It is now time to examine the proposition that force is sometimes justified in the service of love. At the outset of *War and the Christian Conscience*, Ramsey admitted that the early church was pacifist for two centuries. His outline of early church pacifism appears to follow that of R. Bainton.[1] Ramsey in fact stated the case for early church pacifism more strongly than Bainton, who was more cautious with his historical assertions:

> From the end of the New Testament period to the decade A.D. 170–180 there is no evidence whatever of Christians in the army. The subject of military service obviously was not at that time controverted. The reason may have been either that participation was assumed or that abstention was taken for granted. The latter was more probable.[2]

There is evidence of Christian soldiers from A.D. 173 onwards, and from this same period explicit condemnations of Christians in military service are to be found. Ramsey also accepted Bainton's argument that the heart of the condemnations of military service was an aversion to killing. While there can be no doubt that there were a number of reasons for Christians to avoid military service (e.g., avoidance of idolatry, opposition to Roman imperialism, general disengagement from social involvement), still Ramsey agreed with Bainton's conclusion, saying:

> Yet there can be no doubt that early Christian pacifism was in the main a consistent deduction from the new foundation laid by Christ in the lives of men for a new kind of exercise, in intention and practice, of love for every man for whom Christ died. How could anyone, who knew himself

111

to be classed with transgressors and the enemies of God whom Christ
came to die to save, love his own life and seek to save it more than that
of his own enemy or murderer?[3]

Ramsey's wrestle with pacifism was begun in *Basic Christian Ethics*,
continued in *War and the Christian Conscience*, carried on throughout
the 1960s in *The Just War*, and resumed in a major discussion of J. H.
Yoder and others in *Speak Up for Just War or Pacifism*.[4] From
beginning to end, his analysis gained strength from his earlier pacifist
convictions,[5] and his view of this divergence at the heart of Christian
political ethics was perceptive of the implications of Christian faith on
both sides of the question.

From the beginning Ramsey argued that the change from pacifism to
just war thinking is not a capitulation to social or historical forces, and
not a fall from purity. It is rather a change of tactics, as Christian love
reconsiders how the neighbor may best be served. "The basic strategy
remained the same: responsible love and service of one's neighbors in
the texture of the common life."[6]

The use of force is sometimes a duty for the Christian, and when it
is commanded, it is of course then justified and legitimate. Morally
speaking, it is never merely an option. In the final analysis it is either
commanded or forbidden. This is not in contradiction with the strenuous ethic that Jesus taught; in fact, it is a fulfillment of Christian love,
not a denial of it. Force is necessary in order to fulfill the concern of
Christian love to protect the weak and the unjustly oppressed. The
duty of using force arises from the concern of love to protect the
innocent in the harsh necessities of a sinful world. This means that the
justification of force is both permission and command. The command
is limited in two ways: first, in that its use must be both "discriminate"
and "proportionate," and, second, in that the ends that justify its use
are themselves limited. Both the command and its twofold limitation
must be grasped correctly.

In this part we are mainly concerned with the permission and the
moral limits of the use of force. In Part Four we will consider the way
Ramsey applied his theory of just war to the vexed and vexing question
of nuclear deterrence. Here it seems that the command to protect the
weak by means of force clashes with the moral limits on the use of
force, placing us in a genuine moral dilemma. At least it is widely
perceived to be a dilemma. Ramsey did not believe that it is insoluble,
but he does not want to weaken the claims either of security or of

justice in the conduct of war. In order to get hold of his approach to nuclear deterrence, a thorough understanding of the principles of discrimination and proportion is essential. We now trace the way in which Ramsey derived these principles.

Although Ramsey first dealt explicitly with the question of war in *War and the Christian Conscience*, he had laid the foundations for this in *Basic Christian Ethics*, especially in Chapter Five. This is where we must start.

Chapter Five of *Basic Christian Ethics* is divided into five sections, the first and the last of which we shall regard as introduction and conclusion to the main argument in the three central sections. Section Two concerns the nature of Christian love—"Non-Preferential Love and Duties to Oneself"; Section Three attempts to find roots in the gospels for the rightness of protecting the weak by resisting evil; and Section Four exposes the main themes of "A Christian Ethic of Resistance." Sections Two and Three are to be seen as ground-clearing and foundational exercises, preparing the way for the argument of Section Four.

Section Two tackles the themes of self-love, preference among neighbors, mutual love, self-sacrifice, enlightened unselfishness, and vocation. The key to the section is the consideration of what is truly unselfish when properly enlightened. It is no good simply being "unselfish" or "sacrificial." There are hints here of Ramsey's later criticism of Reinhold Niebuhr's distinction between mutual love and self-sacrificial love, which plays a central role in his analysis of Christian love.[7]

There are two prongs to Ramsey's attack. The first is that external observations of action do not provide a safe test of the presence of Christian love. Turning away a beggar may be an act of selfishness, or it may be an enlightened work of love. It may be selfish to refuse to intervene to prevent injustice, and unselfish to resist evil, preferring one neighbor to another. Human action cannot be considered apart from its context. To make a moral judgment one has to know about the actor's motivation and intention, and one has also to know the social context of his action in its relevant features.[8]

Two important characteristics of Ramsey's argument should be noted. One is the constant emphasis on proximate neighbor love, and the particular way he views it here. Ramsey believes that we have definite duties to those who are in a significant way near to us—those for whom we have responsibility, in family or neighborhood or state or other office. This was later to be expressed (in a somewhat different emphasis) in the notion of "covenants of life with life."[9] Along with this goes the element of love as relational. Love is always love for individuals, whether one or many; love is in this sense always personal or relational. This is so basic that it almost seems to drop out of sight for some critics. As Paul Camenisch points out, a concern for the individual is an "absolutely necessary starting point" in all Ramsey's thought.[10]

Even more important for Ramsey's politics is the theme of love's special concern to protect the weak. This theme is clear here, and fundamental. It is often explicit in many different areas of his writings, not least the political. Protecting the weak is a theme traced back to the Old Testament. It is both a key motivation for the use of force and a vital limit on it. This is also expressed as concern for the innocent, for example,

> Love not itself self-defensive, which would rather suffer any deprivation than go to law against a brother, nevertheless will impel men to develop an ethic of protection lest injustice be done to innocent third parties.[11]

By "innocent" in this context we are clearly meant to understand "defenseless" or "innocent of aggression," and not that the "innocent" are blameless in every respect. It is important not to misunderstand this.[12]

The first prong of Ramsey's attack on "unenlightened unselfishness" is, then, that some truly unselfish actions may appear to the onlooker closely to resemble the same or similar actions undertaken for merely selfish reasons. But the vocation of love may mean that these actions were really performed for love, for protection of another (threatened) neighbor. The second prong of his attack is to analyze what it means for love to be prudent, to be enlightened.

The argument here starts by saying that it is necessary to care for oneself, to love oneself so that one may fulfill one's love for the neighbor. It may be right to abstain from action for the sake of future loving actions. Prudent love also means that sometimes, where one ought not to resist a neighbor's unjust claims, if he were the *only* neighbor, still one ought to resist his claims for the sake of *other* neighbors. Taking these two considerations together, it may also be right to resist another for the sake of one's future love for others.

Here is the heart of Ramsey's just war thought at its divergence from Christian pacifism: an ethic of resisting evil, using power, and if need be force, can be the way of love in action. Such an ethic may also spring from other roots (e.g., natural law, or an enlightened selfishness perhaps), but that does not alter its derivation from Christian love. To do what is necessary in the service of one's neighbor is the calling of Christian love. This opens the door to a variety of possibilities being the true expression of love.

Ramsey laid great stress on the point that love is never directly concerned for the self. His emphasis that just war theory should be derived from other-regarding love marks out his theory at many points from others, though he liked to claim to be in the center of the tradition. For instance, "Just-war theorists did not first adopt an ethic that intrinsically justifies self-defense in general, and then simply apply this general principle to the just defense of the nation."[13]

His concern perhaps led him to build his own theory more or less without any reference to just war theory as it developed in the later medieval period.[14] It also predisposed him to be more ready to consider interventionary wars as possibly just than the typically Western attitude does, and by the same token to be much more suspicious of defense as an automatic justification of any war.

Although Ramsey continued to treat questions relating to the justice of going to war (*jus ad bellum*), it does not appear as a major explicit theme until *Speak Up for Just War or Pacifism*.[15] One of the important concerns of that book is the accurate location of the divergence of pacifism and just war. Ramsey was troubled by the view that both share the same, or a similar "presumption against violence."[16] He accepted this only in the sense that there is a burden of proof to be borne by those who would resist evil by force:

> But the point of just-war tradition is that this is a burden of proof that can be borne. Indeed, in this world—and not some other—there are situations of injustices so massive and concentrated and threats so overwhelming that the "presumption" shifts against anyone who continues to believe that nonviolent means are our reasonable service.[17]

In place of a presumption against violence, Ramsey continued to argue that a presumption against injustice is the implication of Christian love, and that "protective violent or nonviolent *resistance* is an 'alien' work of love that for one's own life alone would not resist evil."[18]

It is important, then, to get a good grasp of the flexibility of Ramsey's view of the calling of Christian love. This foreshadows and provides the theological roots for the important insistence that true morality is never extrinsically imposed on its subject matter.[19] "The Reformation doctrine of vocation recognizes a large area of relativity in ethics, disclaiming any hard-and-fast absolute principles or rigid laws.''[20]

Sometimes this restricts what may be done in any situation, and sometimes it makes it clear that love has a wider field of choice and freedom than is apparent at first sight. Ramsey's concern is to pursue as rigorously as possible what the enlightened unselfishness of Christian love requires us to do in order to protect the neighbor, to be faithful to him in political situations where no easy choices are possible. When the work of the moralist is done, responsibility will always remain with the political decision maker (great or small), who has to apply his understanding of Christian doctrine as prudently as he may to the political task at hand.[21]

The Ethics of Jesus

We continue exposition of Chapter Five of *Basic Christian Ethics* with its account of the teachings of Jesus. Section Three picks up the conclusions of an earlier section that tackled the question of the validity of the ethics of Jesus.[22]

On the surface, it almost seems that Ramsey finds the strenuous ethic of Jesus an embarrassment, and after dealing with it in these two chapters of *Basic Christian Ethics* (Chapters One and Five), it by and large appears to be considered done, and then put out of the way. But, as we shall see, Ramsey considered the strenuous ethic of Jesus a vital inspiration of the teaching of Ambrose and Augustine, and thus part of the true foundation of the just war tradition in the ethics of Christian love. The change from pacifism to just war thinking is one of tactics and not actually of fundamental moral substance. It is in the strenuous aspect of this teaching that Ramsey finds the root of the prohibition of direct attack on noncombatants.

This analysis we now have to follow through carefully. As we do this, it will be worth bearing in mind the claim that Ramsey believed that he was following out the logic of Jesus' radical and strenuous ethical teaching. He claimed despite appearances to the contrary that it was his pacifist opponents, or those who confuse the tests of discrimination and proportion, or those who aspire to banish the use of force from the world, who had most deeply abandoned the true meaning of the rigorous demands of Jesus.[23]

In *Basic Christian Ethics*, Chapter One, Ramsey argued that Jesus' ethic is not an ethic of passive, or nonviolent, resistance. It is rather an ethic of nonresistance. In its eschatological context it shows the relation of one man to another, without thought of any others, their needs or demands. In this context the Christian is not to resist evil. However, we do not share with Jesus an apocalyptic eschatology that expected God to intervene shortly to overcome evil with divine power.

If we realize that Jesus' teaching was only intended in the context of the apocalyptic expectation of God's intervention to defeat the forces of evil, then we will not make the mistake of thinking that he thought all evil could be overcome by nonresisting love. Not sharing his apocalyptic, we ourselves should interpret love as sometimes requiring us to resist evil.

O'Connor has objected that Ramsey justifies violence in a way inconsistent with love, and that it would be better to leave these in unresolved tension or dialectic. We will consider O'Connor's general objections to Ramsey's position later. At this point we must note one of the ways in which he supported his objections. He objected, rightly, to the view that human violence in preventing evil should take the place of the divine violence that will overcome evil according to the apocalyptic thought of Jesus. O'Connor believed that Ramsey attempted to justify political violence in this way. He quoted the following passage from *Basic Christian Ethics*:

The other alternative is to justify the employment of force in dealing with tyrannical structures of evil. This involves the substitution of human power-controls for divine power and, it may be, humanly directed violence for the divine violence entailed literally in Jesus' eschatological expectation.

O'Connor adds: "Ramsey prefers this second alternative, although he admits that it goes beyond the explicit teaching and example of Jesus."[24]

On this we must make two comments. First, it appears that this was a plain misreading, for Ramsey clearly says that this is "guilty of departing from the mind of Jesus," for it has lifted his teachings from their eschatological context. Second, and decisively, Ramsey held that only limited goals are possible or right in politics. Evil cannot be simply defeated in this age, but at best, it can be held in check.

We have now to ask whether there is any basis in the gospels for saying that Jesus also taught that one should resist evil-doers for the sake of those they oppress. Ramsey considers three things.

The major point is that Jesus certainly resisted the religious leaders of Judaism. He denounced them fiercely, and even acted physically if not violently during the cleansing of the Temple. E. P. Sanders, in his recent elegant study *Jesus and Judaism*, has challenged the traditional understanding of the cleansing of the Temple with which Ramsey worked. In detail, Sanders's critique of the popular view would no doubt force Ramsey to rephrase what he writes on this.[25] (It would also require Ramsey to rewrite completely, with the benefit of hindsight, his material on Jesus' objection to Jewish legalism. But we are safe enough in supposing that Ramsey would not have written this in the same form in the 1960s, let alone the 1980s. Ramsey would rather have found a good deal of support for his own concern for in-principled love in the fresh understandings of first-century Palestinian Judaism, and in Sanders's rejection of its supposed legalism.) Sanders has persuasively advanced the thesis that:

> Jesus publicly predicted or threatened the destruction of the temple, that the statement was shaped by his expectation of the arrival of the eschaton, that he probably also expected a new temple to be given by God from heaven, and that he made a demonstration which prophetically symbolized the coming event.[26]

He objects strongly to the idea that there was "a huge burden of fossilized religion fastened upon the people of the land"[27] from which Jesus promised liberation. Sanders sees the overthrow of the tables in the Temple as symbolically foreshadowing destruction. Ramsey's argument assumes that Jesus' "resistance" was somewhat more interested in temporal change than this. But the point—that Jesus adapted the style of his actions to make the point he wished to make with a display of symbolic violence—will perhaps still hold. In any case, his way here can hardly be described as nonresistance.

There follows a brief and inconclusive look at the parable of the Good Samaritan—asking the question "What would Jesus have made the Samaritan do if he had come upon the thieves robbing the traveler?" Ramsey quotes opposing opinions (that Jesus would not have had the Samaritan resist the thieves with a sword—or that he *might* have approved such resistance) without supporting either very fully. Finally he cites the parable of the Unforgiving Servant by drawing attention to the behavior of the king (rather than the servant). The king forgave the servant his debt, but changed his decision when the servant began to oppress others. Ramsey wants to point out more than that the king acted with severity in punishment. It is also clear "that love which for itself claims nothing may yet for the sake of another claim every-thing."[28]

In this section, Ramsey makes the point that there are clear signs that Jesus would have reacted differently in more complex situations than the ones he pictured. John Knox (Ramsey's contemporary) is quoted: "Jesus did not say: 'If any man smite one of your friends, lead him to another friend that he may smite *him* also.' " Neighbor-centered love must sometimes take the form of severity. In the account of Jesus' strenuous teaching, then, the same logic is to be found: concern for the unjustly oppressed makes an overriding claim.

Since the publication of *Basic Christian Ethics* in 1951, the debate over pacifism, and its relation to Jesus, to Christology, and to theolog-ical thought generally, has moved on considerably, but even in these pages Ramsey indicated clearly enough the outline of his position. The points that stand out are these: Ramsey's just war theory is determined to be faithful to Jesus, and to the strenuous character of the moral demands of love. At the same time we need to be careful to interpret those demands intelligently in a fallen world, noticing that the eschat-ological setting of Jesus' life and teaching is not precisely ours. His relation to the kingdom of God is not identical to the relation of his followers to the kingdom. To support the contention that Christians should adopt a policy of resistance in order to serve their neighbors, Ramsey points to some important gospel evidence leading in that direction.

It was not, however, until the challenge raised by Yoder and Hauer-was that Ramsey came under any pressure to elaborate and defend his approach. As it turned out, in the discussion crystallized for us in *Speak Up for Just War or Pacifism*, Ramsey's challenge to Christian pacifism was a powerful one, and needed to adjust very little (if at all in substance) the position he had indicated in *Basic Christian Ethics*. Before we consider that challenge fully, we need to follow the argu-ment of Chapter Five in *Basic Christian Ethics* a bit further.

Ambrose and Augustine

The important distinction between self-defense and the defense of others is taken up in Section Four. Here we first encounter Ambrose and Augustine. Ramsey also discussed the same passages from these two church fathers in *War and the Christian Conscience*, Chapter Three, "The Genesis of Non-Combatant Immunity." The second discussion has a different direction, and leads on to consideration of Aquinas on self-defense.

Here is the essence of the passages quoted by Ramsey. The key sentence of Ambrose is:

> Yet I do not think that a Christian, a just and wise man, ought to save his life by the death of another; just as when he meets with an armed robber he cannot return his blows, *lest in defending his life he should stain his love towards his neighbor.*[29]

Then Augustine is quoted drawing a distinction between the legal permission of killing in self-defense, or at the state's command, and the moral wrong of killing to defend one's own life or possessions:

> As to killing others in order to defend one's own life, I do not approve of this, unless one happen to be a soldier or public functionary acting, not for himself, but in defense of others or of the city in which he resides, if he act according to the commission lawfully given him, and in the manner becoming his office.[30]

From this Ramsey seeks to learn various points.[31] First, a Christian ethic of resistance is not based on the notion that self-defense is justified, nor does it provide a justification for it. This is seen in their analysis of self-defense against a lone assassin, or of whether one should take a plank from an ignorant sailor after shipwreck. This point has several implications for the path Ramsey will travel. It means that he will not find notions of natural justice at all appropriate for analysis of the ethics of war, for this would lead in quite another direction. Rooting ethics in Christian love means that the idea of self-defense cannot be the key justification for a just war, as a natural justice ethic would seem to indicate. And in quite another direction, Ambrose and Augustine are quite clearly in diametrical opposition to many modern pacifists who display a general tendency to justify self-defense and simultaneously reject the collective defense of society in war. On the contrary, "for Christian ethics generally *self-defense is the worst of all possible excuses for war or for any other form of resistance or any sort of preference among other people.*"[32] This is to form one part of Ramsey's later rejection of the "aggressor-defender" doctrine of the just war.

Second, this rejection of self-defense places a strong and essential limitation on what may be legitimate in defending others. This thesis does not become explicit until *War and the Christian Conscience*, but the ground for this is prepared already: "This combination of ideas, which seems strange to men today, is clear proof that non-resisting love was still the groundwork of all reasoning about Christian participation in conflict of arms."[33]

Third, then, we can see both the closeness of Ramsey's position to pacifism, and in another sense the width of the gulf between them. On the one hand, his serious consideration of the strenuous character of Jesus' ethic means that pacifism is in some sense an option. For instance, writing in 1968 about Mennonite pacifism, Ramsey said:

> I have never seen how I as a Christian ethicist could require more of this point of view than *consistency*: if this be the meaning of the Christian life, let all who believe so . . . have nothing to do . . . with any actual use of armed force . . . [or] with any means of *resisting* evil (violently or non-violently); let them rather specialize in overcoming evil with good, while other men to the end of history must needs do otherwise.[34]

At the same time, Ramsey has a robust approach to violence, bloodshed, and suffering:

> The word "unlovely" has in Christian ethics a mainly spiritual not a merely physical meaning. A selfish act is the most unlovely thing, and an unselfish motive may lead the Christian to perform necessary responsibilities which prove not so "nice" in terms of physical contamination.[35]

We have here the basis for a continued wrestling with the claims of Christian pacifism. Ramsey has endeavored to show that an (Augustinian) ethic of involvement does justice to certain basic Christian moral themes—to an interpretation of Christian love, and to the true meaning of the eschatological ethic of Jesus. When life conflicts with life, the Christian's duty out of love may be to conclude that he is necessarily and legitimately required to act violently, even to take life to protect the lives of others. The use of force may be legitimate, though its justification is narrow, and it is not to be avoided out of sentimentality, nor engaged in merely for reasons of self-defense, for neither of these is at the heart of a true love for the neighbor.

Just War or Pacifism

Before continuing with our exposition of Ramsey's just war theory, we may now bring together the key themes in Ramsey's critique of pacifism. Perhaps we should say, in his critique of inaccurate pacifist arguments. Ramsey's ability to grasp the arguments of his opponents is most clearly displayed in his account of pacifism; this is very striking in the remarkable conclusion to his account in *Speak Up for Just War or Pacifism*.

The most prominent theme of Ramsey's critique is his insistence that moral evil is not to be proved from the existence of bloodshed, nor from its scale. Douglass, for instance, charged that Ramsey has "escalated the nuclear age meaning of 'discrimination.' " Ramsey replies that it is "Douglass who thinks it comes down to quantitative increments of destruction."[36] Pacifist objection to just war thought cannot complain that it justifies "too much killing" without considering the just war account of the importance of intention in morality. A pacifist may consistently hold, argues Ramsey, that no killing may be justified, but he must hold this consistently, and not argue, for instance, that whereas killing may be justified in some circumstances, it cannot be in others simply because of its quantity. If distinctions are to be made between the morality of different sorts of killings, then those distinctions cannot be made on grounds of quantity alone. Nor can they be made woodenly, as if, for instance, it was supposed that all killing of noncombatants was wrong.

Ramsey's concern with the tendency to see all killing or violence as wrong, confusing *evil* with *moral evil*, and overlooking the indispensable centrality of intention in moral analysis, fueled many of his critiques in *Speak Up for Just War or Pacifism*. Ramsey believed that this confusion lay behind Yoder's critique of the just war tradition.[37] That much is clear. But a similar concern may also undergird his analysis of the shape of just war theory presented in *The Challenge of Peace*.[38] Ramsey found a degree of ambiguity in the Pastoral Letter's foundations for just war. The Pastoral Letter elevated the status of pacifism and nonviolence in Catholic tradition. Ramsey traces this to the alternative presumptions at the beginning of just war theory offered by the Catholic bishops.[39] On one hand, there is the presumption against injustice: "Faced with the fact of attack on the innocent, the presumption that we do no harm, even to our enemy, yielded to the command of love understood as the need to restrain an enemy who would injure the innocent."[40] On the other hand, the Pastoral Letter spoke also (and more frequently) of "the presumption *in favor of peace* and *against* war." Ramsey feared that the elevation of this presumption to the head of just war principles, rather than correctly locating it at the end of them, tends seriously to distort the use of just war theory. The presumption against violence is correctly located, that is, when it is seen as the proportionate weighing of consequences to see whether more destruction is caused by action designed to oppose injustice.[41] If a presumption against violence or killing is given the wrong priority, it may be expressing the view that "war is evil" in an unacceptably loose way. In answer to that Ramsey quotes the Pastoral Letter quoting Augustine:

> "Augustine called it a Manichaean heresy to assert that war is intrinsically evil and contrary to Christian charity." Indeed it is a *dualistic* or *spiritualistic* heresy to say that there is for Christians a *principled* (in contrast to properly prudential) presumption against killing and in favor of violence *in a fallen world.* Instead, *the presumption is to restrain evil and protect the innocent.*"[42]

Ramsey also pressed hard on the distinction pacifists are prone to make between violence and nonviolence. His point is that the example of Jesus does not straightforwardly warrant nonviolence, but rather nonresistance. Ramsey learned this theme from Reinhold Niebuhr.[43] In contrast to nonresistance, nonviolence can encompass the attempt to use political power, to resist, and so on. In this sense nonviolence is a proper part of political life, and must be used and morally limited under the same conditions as the use of force.[44] But nonviolence is also often used as a synonym for pacifism. Ramsey comments, for instance, on "the systematic equivocation in the use of 'nonviolent resistance' and nonresistant love of the enemy that afflicts current Christian discussion of pacifism." This confusion makes it hard to know which of these positions is being adopted.[45] Ramsey's characteristic appeal to pacifists is that they should "clean up" their language, and clearly adopt a consistent theological position, but he points a way forward when he notes that one of the pressures causing this problem is the charge made against pacifists that their stance is politically ineffective. To be ambiguous about the meaning of nonviolence appears to provide an escape from this charge.

This ambiguity is more serious than we might suppose if we took it merely as a certain indeterminacy. By asking for clarification Ramsey is asking pacifists to make good their theological position. If a pacifist opts for the politics of nonviolence as an effective political choice, then Ramsey asks whether this is not merely a legalistic reading (for instance of the command "Thou shalt not kill"). This is a choice to be involved in politics, and Ramsey questions the rationale of drawing an absolute line at nonviolent resistance. He then asks whether this approach should not be considered as one political option within a just war understanding of political action. On the other hand, if a pacifist is identifying nonviolence with nonresistance, Ramsey asks whether this is not merely a superficial objection to bloodshed and physical violence and suffering.

Neither of these Ramsey understands to be true Christian pacifism. Both of them reckon insufficiently with the realities of political life in a fallen world, and have too weak a hold on the transience and provisionality of the earthly city. On both counts and in various ways, many forms of pacifism tend to identify too closely the two cities, the present age with the one to come. Here is the heart of Ramsey's criticism of the theological substance of both *The Challenge of Peace* and *In Defense of Creation*:

> If in the U.S. Catholic Bishops' pastoral letter there is too little tension between the "already" and the "not yet" of the gospel, in the Methodist pastoral there is still less.
> There is more than a slash between the words "already/not yet." There is more than a *momentous* slash. The slash is *aeonic*.[46]

What then is true Christian pacifism? We have seen that Ramsey believes this may be a possible response of Christian discipleship. In *Speak Up for Just War or Pacifism* he asked Hauerwas (and Yoder) for further elaboration of their Christological and eschatological views in relation to their pacifism.[47] He asked them whether their account of the unity of disciples and the church with Jesus does not assume "the cast of a 'realized eschatology' to be faithfully lived by a large empirical denomination, without taut tension with the Kingdom not yet a presence to the church."[48] In place of their Christology Ramsey advocated the classic Reformation (and traditional Catholic) view of Christology, which has seen Christ as Savior and Judge as well as Pattern and Example. This classic Christology does not overlook Christ's example, but offers an equally serious way of following it, of taking up the cross.

> I would not say that in taking up *his* or *her* cross (which cannot be the once-only cross of Jesus Christ or a repetition of it) the pacifist leaves to his brother or sister in Christ a more *or* a less difficult cross to bear in resisting injustice to relieve the oppressed. I say only that both are *our* crosses, and that the difference between these vocations likely stems from different fundamental accounts of Jesus Christ *pro nobis*.[49]

This brings us to a remarkable passage in *Speak Up for Just War or Pacifism*. Here Ramsey concluded his account of the difference between pacifism and just war thinking. The charge that pacifists are "irresponsible" or "ineffective" needs to be withdrawn by nonpacifists as does the countercharge that pacifists are obedient witnesses to Christ, while just war is trying to take control of the future in its assumption of responsibility. Ramsey makes clear that his disagreement with pacifism is not that it is irresponsible, nor is his advocacy of just war because he believes it will "make history turn out right." Both are ways of witnessing to Christ; both intend in fundamentally similar ways also to be effective, without depending on their effectiveness for justification. The pacifist witnesses first for peace, the just warrior for justice (to put it much more simply than Ramsey ever would). Ramsey writes:

> Niebuhr's sense of the transiency of every human achievement of a somewhat more just order, or the prevention of a worse one, suggests that effective action and witnessing action are not greatly different from one another. *The future is radically unpredictable*, for pacifist and just warrior alike. We need to withdraw Niebuhr's somewhat condescending tribute to the peace churches. We need to affirm the coeval, equally worthy, irreducible parting of the ways of Christian pacifism and justified war Christians. Neither is able to *depend* on the consequences in the whole of their activities, or discount the effectiveness of the other's witness. All this can be said, I believe, while holding that in the divine economy for this world just war is the meaning of statecraft, and that pacifism cannot be addressed to States.[50]

This point is the biggest single contribution of *Speak Up for Just War or Pacifism*. It advances the debate between pacifists and their opponents a large step forward. Ramsey insists that both are to be obedient witnesses to Christ—but that their witnesses to church and world are distinctively different, and cannot be confused and mingled to give the same advice.[51] Not only does it illuminate the debate, but more importantly, it sheds an invaluable light on the nature of both pacifist and nonpacifist witness to Christ.

11

The Twin Principles of Just War

The requirement of love to resist the evil-doer provides the foundation for Ramsey's just war thought. The implications of this were pursued in *War and the Christian Conscience*, especially in Chapter Three. In this chapter, Ramsey used the same texts from Ambrose and Augustine to draw out explicitly the limitation on the use of force required by this analysis. We saw the argument that Christian love rather than natural justice is rightly at the heart of just war thought. If this is true, what motivates and requires resistance must also control its action in detail. If opposition to enemy force is justified, then Christian love will also require that it respect the enemy innocent just as it is trying to protect its own. This, Ramsey contends, is the root of the principle of noncombatant immunity, and it is implicit in the thought of Ambrose and Augustine.

This thesis is easily stated, but questions are left in the reader's mind that concern the origin of the principle, for it seems clear enough that Augustine did not approach anything like the principle of noncombatant immunity. Rather it was developed much later, in a combination of various strands of thought in the Sixteenth Century. J.T. Johnson has analyzed three main types of source: there is development within the natural law tradition following Thomas Aquinas; there is the influence of the chivalric code of conduct; and there is the work of international law, building on the notion of *jus gentium*.[1] How can we support Ramsey here? In the first place we should recognize that Ramsey was still in the process of clarifying his understanding of the place of natural law in Christian ethics, and the relationships between it and Christian love, and of love to principles and rules. (At this time, 1961, the key motif was that of "love transforming natural law.") Furthermore, the failure of his historical thesis (if such it is) does not

127

affect the logic of his contention. It is best to conclude that Ramsey was using the thought of Ambrose and Augustine to clarify and advance his own constructive discussion.

These two thinkers were decisive theologians in the church's change from pacifism to military involvement. This change, governed by the law of Christian love, is at the heart of a Christian theory of the just war. Love sometimes takes shape for action in necessary though tragic bloodshed; when it does so, it must limit its force and direct it only at those who are aggressors, and always refrain from attacking the innocent bystander. This is the inner moral logic of Augustine's moral theology at this point, and of true just war thinking.

The basic shape of Ramsey's political ethic, we have said, is that the possible use of force is at the heart of politics. We are both permitted and required to resist injustice, sometimes physically. We must carefully limit the use of force, and we may strive only for limited goals. We have examined the tragic necessity of human life which underlies this requirement of Christian love, and how the inner logic of love also limits the force we may use. We must now sketch out more fully the basic shape of those limits.

The Principle of Discrimination

In Chapter Eight we looked at the way actions are described from a moral point of view. We took as an example the shooting of an enemy soldier in time of war, and we arrived at that by examining Ramsey's analyses of double effect. In other words, the problems, which must now be tackled in their own right, have already been used as examples of general ethical method.

One of the main points we showed was that Ramsey considered both the motive and the wider consequences of any action to be of possible moral significance. However, in between those there is the intention, or aim or thrust of an action, which may not simply be conflated with either motive or overall goal. It is this contention about the nature of morality that is essential to a correct grasp of the principle of discrimination. This principle insists that military action may only be aimed at military opposition. Its intention is the incapacitation of the opposing forces, to prevent them achieving their unjust aims by force. Even when force is used, its intention is not the destruction of enemy forces, but their disablement or incapacitation as forces.

This summarizes the heart of Ramsey's thought here, and it provides the basis on which to hold together the various concepts and distinctions that he employs. These he spelled out most fully and carefully in a paper first delivered in 1960, "The Case for Making 'Just War' Possible."[2] A further clarification, on incapacitation, was made in 1966.[3] Apart from this refinement, it is remarkable how much of Ramsey's writing from 1961 to 1968 was already present in essence in this short paper.

This chapter spelled out the concepts necessary to the principle of discrimination, in contrast with various prevalent misunderstandings.[4] The first section gives the analysis that we have already encountered in the progress from *Basic Christian Ethics* through *War and the Christian Conscience.* Christian love does not allow us to stand by in situations of conflict when people are being unjustly oppressed or attacked.

> In this world and not some other, faithfulness to all our fellow men, and not only to the enemy, must somehow be enacted. Jesus did not teach that his disciples should lift up the face of another oppressed man to be struck again on the other cheek.[5]

We may be in a position to defend the cause of justice, and if we are, our love for the oppressed will lead us to resist the attacker:

> . . . forces should be repelled and the bearers and close cooperators in military force should be directly repressed, by violent means if necessary, lest many more of God's little ones should be irresponsibly forsaken and lest they suffer more harm than need be.[6]

At the same time, those who are not engaged in fighting, on the enemy side just as much as anywhere else, are also neighbors. Our love for them demands that we do not directly attack them, whether to undermine enemy resolve or for whatever reason: "If combatants may and should be resisted directly by violent means to secure a desired and desirable victory, this also requires that non-combatants be never directly assaulted even to that same end."[7]

What does the phrase "that non-combatants be never directly assaulted" mean in practice? In the second section this is spelled out in contrast to various objections and misunderstandings. There are two major areas of concern (though these are subdivided here), namely, the meaning of "non-combatant" and the meaning of "direct assault."

The first point is to define noncombatancy. Objections to this con-

cept come from various quarters. One objection is that not all who
fight are formally guilty, since they act under orders; another is that it
is not possible in modern war to separate combatants from noncombatants; and another is that all are involved in modern warfare, for all
national resources are mobilized for war, and all share responsibility
for their nation's actions.

Against each of these objections Ramsey always insisted that it is
material, or actual, cooperation in military force that determines the
distinction. There are degrees of cooperation with the military effort,
but in almost any society there are those who are not involved in it.
These may well be contributing indirectly to a nation's military
strength by maintaining the social fabric, etc., but this does not make
such people legitimate targets of attack.

Two points of importance need to be emphasized here. The question
of noncombatancy in any given case must depend on the organization
of the society in question. For instance, some methods of insurgency
warfare tend to make most people into combatants or close coopera-
tors in the war effort. (Some military policies also have the effect of
enlarging the target in such a way that noncombatants are inevitably
involved and at risk on a large scale. As examples, Ramsey sometimes
cited the location of nuclear missile bases near large cities, as well as
some forms of insurgency.[8])

On the other hand, there are always those who are noncombatants
in any society. Merely knowing this is significant: "One only needs to
know *that* there are non-combatants . . . to know that he should limit
his targeting to *known* legitimate military targets while limiting circum-
ambient damage as much as possible."[9]

One specific example is of particular interest, both to illuminate
Ramsey's use of the principle, and because it is an unusual example of
a very specific and unhesitating moral judgment from his pen. He
spoke out strongly against a particular bombing raid on North Vietnam. This was the bombing of an iron and steel factory at Thainguygen, on March 10, 1967. What provoked Ramsey to this specific
denunciation is clear from his understanding of the U.S. aim in this
raid:

> The first reports of this action from Saigon described the raid as the first
> in which the United States aircraft had bombed a target that was not
> directly involved in infiltration of men and supplies into South Vietnam.
> This was an attack upon North Vietnam itself, upon that society directly.[10]

Ramsey comments that although there are legitimate industrial targets in war, this factory was not such a target. There was little benefit to the military aims and prosecution of the war, rather,

> this was an incidental and purely collateral benefit to our actual aim in striking the steel complex. War products constituted only a small percentage of the plant's output. We aimed to destroy not only that. This was a blow against North Vietnamese society and against the will of that country's rulers by striking its people's stake in their future economic development.[11]

In this case, it was the military aim that was secondary and indirect; the primary aim was to strike at the fabric of North Vietnam.

The distinction between direct and indirect aims is the second main point to be clarified and defended in this concept of discrimination. This distinction also follows from the conviction that the intention of an action is something that can be grasped. Provided that the action is intended against legitimate military targets, other effects of the action may also be permitted, but these indirect effects may well be both inevitable and foreseen:

> The "permitted" killing of non-combatants does not just happen to take place. It is foreknown and foreknown to result as a necessary effect of the same action that causes the death of political leaders or military personnel who are its legitimate targets.[12]

Determining what constitutes the intention of an action is a matter of subsumption. It means, of course, having access to all the relevant information as it is available to the decision maker, in order to understand the true nature of the action. This means having an appreciation of the likely consequences, but it is not simply determined by them. Both justified and unjustified acts may cause great destruction:

> There is a significant moral difference between the destruction in obliteration warfare which is deliberately wanton and murderous, and the destruction and death that is among the tragic consequences of counter-*forces* warfare. This distinction is not determined by the amount of the devastation or the number of deaths, but by the direction of the action itself, i.e. by what is deliberately intended and directly done.[13]

Ramsey concludes the section we have examined by lamenting the loss of understanding of the moral immunity of noncombatants in contemporary discussion. It is the loss of this concept, and of the necessary distinctions involved, which has meant that war is now thought of as total, involving everyone.

Thus, the traditional analysis of the morality of war has been thoughtlessly rejected, and the necessary totality of modern war largely conceded.

This, then, is the reason we are prey to the illusion that modern industrial society has completely changed the nature of warfare, and not simply that mass defection from sound moral reasoning has rendered wholly inapplicable or indeed senseless any attempt to conduct war in accordance with the carefully constructed concepts of traditional Christian morality.[14]

The Principle of Proportion

Although the test of discrimination is indispensable, that is not to say that it is sufficient. It is not enough merely to determine that an act of war is justly aimed, for in the end it can only be justified if it aims at a balance of good over evil effects. Only the ends in view can justify the means; only good consequences are worth the losses that will be involved. We quote Ramsey's 1960 essay again:

Therefore, after having permitted and prohibited actions by an analysis of the intrinsic nature of each, it has yet to be determined whether military action lawful in itself should actually be done. This requires . . . a prudential estimate of the consequences to see whether there is in the good effect sufficiently grave reason for also producing the evil effect. Thus, the traditional morality of war locates in the last place a calculus of probability and a morality of the ends in view. In the end, proper place should be given to sitting down to count the costs of a proposed action. While an effect cannot justify any means, one effect can justify another effect because of the greater good or "lesser evil" in one than in the other.[15]

These few lines contain the germ of all Ramsey's later expressions of the principle of proportion and its meaning. It is necessary to spell these out rather more fully.

The principle of proportion is closely allied to political reason in action. It requires that the political actor should aim at a net benefit of gains over costs in any action he takes. He should seek to leave the

world a better place for his action. However there are two key difficulties in reckoning on this basis. Not only are there all sorts of gains and
costs to be reckoned in all sorts of ways, and on different time-scales,
but these things cannot simply be added and subtracted by a straightforward arithmetic calculus. Whether one outcome is better than
another is not always clear, even with the benefit of hindsight. And, of
course, the politician does not have that benefit; he cannot tell how his
action will work out. This is the second difficulty. Decisions and
actions have to be ventured; in politics they cannot be guaranteed.

The term "proportion" has a wide range of meaning. To satisfy this
principle, we have only to answer positively the question "Is this
action a reasonable one?" This does not make it an empty principle,
but it does make clear its flexibility. On this flexibility Ramsey hangs a
very great deal. Let us illustrate some of the difficulties and possible
ambiguities of what are "gains" and "costs" in order to show how
wide the principle is. Many different understandings of it would be
possible if one sense alone were to be specified as "the meaning."
Ramsey, however, means to include them all.

The goals of politics are frequently in tension with each other. We
can mention the main ones again briefly. There is a tension between
the national common good and the international common good. The
statesman must have regard to both of these, aiming to do as much
good as possible, although he can never achieve all the good that might
be achievable. This tension is often related to the tension between
order and justice. Both of these go to make up the common good.
They are related to each other, and are mutually supportive, but not
every action can bring about gains in both these terms at the same
time.

The decisions that have to be made here are indeterminate. Although
the goods to be aimed at are moral goods (preserving the social order,
putting right injustice, etc.), the choices between them are political
rather than moral. A statesman cannot be faulted morally simply for
preferring order to justice, or vice versa. Of course there may be some
such decisions that are clearly disproportionate, and therefore immoral. More often, though, there can be no clear judgment on questions such as "How many lives are worth a smaller or greater social
good?"

In purely military terms (although these can never be wholly ab-
stracted from politics), there are various costs and gains to be considered. Most obviously, any wise general will aim at the use of minimum
force and the greatest military gains with the minimum costs to his

own forces. But the costs in view must not, of course, be limited only to those likely to be suffered by one's own side. They must include all the costs to be inflicted as well as those to be suffered, as it were. Again, the point here is that any action may have a variety of effects, all of which must be considered in principle.

This means that it is not possible to weigh two effects, for instance, simply by counting heads. As we have already seen in the example of the attack on one soldier involving the death of a thousand noncombatants, such a calculus is not the meaning of the principle of proportion or the rule of double effect. This is not a usage that Ramsey would allow, unrelated as it is to the wider context. He argued that the indirect effects can only be weighed in the light of the whole situation, the overall aims, costs, and consequences.

> We [Ramsey's opponents] have spoken of disproportionate destruction as if that means the ratio of civilian to combatant deaths, and not the proportion of the entire evil of war's destructiveness *to what is at stake* in arbitrament of arms.[16]

One of the strengths of the principle of proportion is that it follows the grain of politics: "It is precisely a worth of the principle of proportion that this enables no man to bring against statecraft an extrinsic norm."[17]

These considerations shed light on Ramsey's analysis of the special responsibility of the "magistrate," and at the nature of political action. Ramsey drew on Aristotle's distinction between "doing" and "making." For instance, Ramsey says: "Politics is a kind of *doing*. It is not a kind of *making*—like building a tower."[18]

A political actor cannot control the outcomes of his action. He must let his act go, in a world of action and interaction, never sure of the result or that his intention of bringing about a balance of good will succeed. Even after the event he cannot be sure, for costs and benefits are not easy to count in politics. Indeed, in one sense they cannot be *counted,* for we are always weighing things which are incommensurable with each other. Rather than counting, we "take counsel":

> Decision as to whether a very great evil must be chosen in order to prevent still greater evil, or as to whether a higher level of violence for possibly a shorter time may not be better than a lower level of counter-insurgency warfare for a longer time . . . these are precisely the decisions that must come from "taking political counsel."

Here again only the extremes on one side and on the other can be ruled out from the conduct of statecraft; and in between no man can fault the conscience of another, or the government's course of action, with which he may disagree; and no man has ground for exacerbating public debate by calling the views he opposes "immoral."[19]

The principle of proportion is a summary rule, or guide, which tries to help any political decision maker weigh up how political action may bring about the greatest overall good. There can rarely be moral certainty about such decisions. Let us summarize why this is so. Even with the benefit of hindsight, there is a variety of competing goods at which to aim. Even if we could know precisely what our actions would achieve, we could not always say how much cost is worth a particular gain. In fact, we cannot know what our actions will bring about. We can only aim at certain goods. In making judgments of proportion, we should consider all the goods at which we aim, and not merely the immediate effects of our action.

We have here a moral framework for action, but many of the choices to be made within it are political choices, not moral choices, for we do not have grounds to say that they are disproportionate. The moralist must be especially wary about venturing onto such ground, for in the nature of politics the circumstances of decisions are more obscure than the circumstances of other kinds of choice and action.

Summary

The principles of discrimination and proportion form the heart of Ramsey's just war ethic. In fact, a full grasp of these principles is virtually the whole of it. It should by now be clear how they articulate the moral demands of politics. They are by no means extrinsic to the nature of political action, but they are not reducible to mere political realism, let alone to *realpolitik*.

There is a proper flexibility and rigor in both principles. The principle of discrimination is exceptionless, but it is not a rigid external norm that takes no account of the circumstances. As with the application of any moral rule, and the subsumption of cases under it, there is no substitute for the work of practical reason in determining particular cases. We shall see how Ramsey began this work in his analysis of counterinsurgency warfare, and in thinking about nuclear weapons.

The principle of proportion, on the other hand, is very much more flexible, as we have just seen. This does not mean that it ceases to be a moral principle, for all that many of the decisions to be made under its guidance are morally indeterminate choices. Ramsey feared that he may have misled others with the way he had expressed this point:

> I myself have sometimes spoken of the *moral* economy governing the use of force (non-combatant immunity) and of an *economy* governing the use of force (the principle of proportion). . . .
> My language stressed that non-combatant immunity is intrinsic to the action itself with no prudential reference as yet to the totality of the consequences of the act, while the principle of proportion takes all the effects from the first time into account. . . . [I]t is gravely *wrong* to act in violation of the requirement that force be proportioned to greater good effects (or greater evil prevented).[20]

At this point, we can see how Ramsey's just war theory of political ethics is founded on his moral analysis of human action. Moral analysis takes its shape from the shape of human action. This requires that we pay careful attention to the understanding of the intention of an act. This means taking careful note of the relation of an action to its immediate effects, while allowing the wider context to help us understand the meaning of the act. Intention cannot be sundered from the physical structure of the action, but neither can it be simply understood merely by external observation. Human intentionality has its own complexities and ambiguities, and it is the business of moral analysis to penetrate these as far as possible. The correct description of human action also requires distinctions to be made between motivation and intention. Motivation is related to the overall goal of the actor, his final or ulterior aims, while intention is related to the immediate shape of the action. Moral analysis of any action is not complete without a consideration of both these aspects. In particular, in just war ethics, it is vital that these are kept separate and that the analysis of action is not overwhelmed by the analysis of motivation. A good motive does not thereby justify an act. This underlies Ramsey's continued insistence that the principles of discrimination and proportion must be applied separately in lexical order. Any act must pass the test of discrimination before it can apply, so to speak, for the test of proportion.

Ramsey's account of the morality of politics and of war has been repeatedly challenged. We leave the arguments over nuclear deterrence for another chapter. Other challenges are made to Ramsey's ethical methodology as he used it in just war thinking. Others again challenged his account of political morality. Responding to some of these challenges was often enough the spur which prompted Ramsey to write. For that reason the answers to many of Ramsey's critics are already contained in his expositions. Before we review the points made by his critics, we first give some time to considering one of Ramsey's most controversial analyses. In his account of the morality of the conduct of the Vietnam war, Ramsey made himself as unpopular as in all his other controversies put together.

12

Just War in Debate

Ramsey's opposition to the arguments of much of the antiwar protest at the time of Vietnam was taken by many as support for the war. It is clear that he opposed the tone, the moral self-confidence, and many of the arguments of the prevailing church opposition to the war, but he never believed himself to be advocating support of the war, or advancing the view that the war was a just war. In the unpublished "Apologia Pro Vita Sua—One Decade, That Is," he wrote:

> To my consternation, it is widely believed that I have extrapolated from the "just war" principles of vindication of our Vietnam action as a just war, that I affirm an application of these tests to be productive of a particular war decision having the same moral certitude as the criteria themselves.[1]

The "Apologia" attempts to correct this misunderstanding. Our examination of Ramsey's Vietnam writings will return to this question after looking at them as an example of his handling of the principles as he reshaped them.

The Morality of the Vietnam War

Ramsey's writings on Vietnam span a period of less than two years. The first, and most substantial paper, was presented to the American Society of Christian Ethics in January 1966. Chapter Twenty-Three of *The Just War*, "The Miami 'Appeal to the Churches Concerning Vietnam,' " was not published before its appearance in that volume in 1968, but all the other chapters were previously published, mostly by

139

June 1967.[2] Most of the material written after January 1966 shows little advance from that; there are a few fresh applications of the arguments originally advanced. If anything, the statements and questions leading toward a negative verdict on the justice of the war grow less frequent (presumably as Ramsey reacted against the increasingly emotional and heated tone of the debate).

By the time Ramsey wrote in January 1966, U.S. troops in substantial numbers had been in Vietnam only a few months. American military personnel increased from around 20,000 "advisers" in early 1965 to 184,000 within a year.[3] Student protests against the war began in 1965 (in a major way), but the United States remained largely in support of the war at least through 1966. As for church opposition to the war, this was by no means unanimous in 1966. In the summer of 1966, the World Council of Churches condemned "the American military presence in Vietnam and the long-continued bombing of villages in the South and of targets a few miles from cities in the North."[4] However, the American Roman Catholic bishops "mildly endorsed U.S. policy in Vietnam" in 1966 and 1967. In 1966 one Catholic journal, *America*, argued in favor of the war, while another, *Commonweal*, argued against it.[5] It is important to set the scene for Ramsey's assertions that there were costs and benefits on both sides, either of withdrawing from Vietnam or staying there. Such was also the general perception (not only the judgment of the U.S. administration) at the time Ramsey was writing.[6]

Ramsey's comments fall, as always, under the heading of discrimination and proportion. In his major article "How Shall Counter-Insurgency War Be Conducted Justly?"[7] Ramsey begins by outlining the principles for determining the justice of war (Section II). He then considers the application of the principle of discrimination in Section III. He argues that the main direction of insurgency is always indiscriminate, based as it is on terrorizing civilian populations, and that the terror is selective does not make it any more justifiable. At the same time, insurgency war enlarges the target of a counterinsurgency force. Both by hiding among the population, and by using it as a shield, the insurgents themselves render the population morally liable to attack. He quotes Mao Tse-Tung: " 'There is no profound difference between the farmer and the soldier,' wrote Mao Tse-Tung; and so saying made it so."[8]

This makes counterinsurgency war inevitably more destructive, greatly increasing the collateral damage entailed in discriminate fighting, as well as enlarging the target (to farmers who are also, or who may also be, soldiers). This means that political and military decisions may very largely be limited by the principle of proportion.

What does this application of the principle of discrimination teach us about its meaning? It may help us to understand why it is preferable that the principle be described rather as "exceptionless" than as "absolute."[9] The application of the principle to counterinsurgency warfare reminds us that each new situation may require that we think back again to the roots of the principle, to its basic meaning. For instance, the normal conventions of war teach us that a farmer, not in uniform and without close connection to the means of war, is always to be treated as immune from direct attack. If, however, he is in fact a soldier by night, or acting as part of the shield for the action of the soldier, then it may not necessarily be indiscriminate to attack him. (Of course, even if it is discriminate, that does not yet justify the action.) The decision as to what is prohibited and what is permitted by the principle of discrimination, which may never be breached but must always be understood and applied, can only be made with as full a knowledge of the facts and situation as possible. In the end, of course, whether one course of action or another is discriminate is a judgment that cannot *necessarily* be made by an external or distant observer (but only by one with the agent's knowledge of the relevant facts). That a farmer who is believed to be a soldier proves, tragically, only to have been a farmer does not thereby render his killing indiscriminate. Neither the precise meaning, nor the particular applications of the principle, can be determined by the moralist alone. This means that the church should be careful not to speak too hastily.

> But even in connection with the principle of discrimination, members of ecclesiastical councils should listen to experts in the political and military sectors and learn from them the new shape war may have assumed in any age, and thus learn to know the meaning of a present application of the principle of discrimination. Churchmen cannot, because *the principle* cannot, determine the cases to be subsumed under it.[10]

The word "absolute" seems not to allow for this point, with its implication that the principle is derived from elsewhere than the shape of the realities with which it is concerned, and has its validity independently of them.

In discussing the principle of proportion (Section IV), Ramsey sets out a series of possible political alternatives. These range from the possibility of withdrawing and negotiating "some sort of settlement," to the possibilities of continuing escalation of the war. He discusses whether continuing to fight the war is not a bit like striking at the fleas on a dog, bruising him to death, while the dog might prefer to die of exhaustion from scratching at the fleas.[11] However, there is not Vietnam alone to be considered, but the whole future stability of Southeast Asia (Ramsey was particularly concerned about the possibility of insurgency in Thailand).[12] He argues that although there may be different forms of communism, and that nationalistic forms of communism may not be so bad as Chinese communism, still communism ought to be resisted:

> No Christian and no man who loves an ordered liberty should conspire with communism in coming to power. . . . Then there arises an obligation to assist others in resistance to communism, even in its more "liberal" forms, if there are actual alternatives.[13]

This, he points out, does not create an obligation supreme over all others, but one to be weighed as one of the goals of policy. He points out the realities of some of the proposals for negotiation, considering the weakness of the 1954 Geneva Accords, and pointing out that a determination to end the fighting by negotiation means accepting victory by the North. This last is an argument he develops more fully in later articles.[14]

Ramsey's treatment of the principle of proportion here exemplifies many of the characteristics of his theoretical discussions on the subject. One of these is the insistence that all the costs and benefits of an action must be weighed together. Therefore, the wider perspective may justify military action that, taken on its own, might well appear disproportionate. In Vietnam, the wider perspective included the possible progress of communism throughout Southeast Asia. An allied theme is that it is all too easy for churchmen to overlook the costs that are attached to a course of action, especially if they have absorbed the modern liberal notion that there is always a better alternative to the use of force.

In contrast to those who were confident that they knew the best course of action for America, Ramsey continued to suggest alternative courses of action. It is not possible, he argued, to be sure that one course of action is better than another, or will assuredly lead to the best results. The principle of proportion attempts to give guidance for wise political decisions, which weigh up the costs against the benefits in terms of justice, order, the common good, etc.

Apart from these theoretical points, which in themselves have large implications for the way he thought about Vietnam, there is one substantial theme of Ramsey's just war thought that also contributed to his outlook. This he exprssed in *Speak Up for Just War or Pacifism* as a presumption against injustice. This reaches right back to his foundational argument for Christian involvement in war, namely, the duty of love to protect the oppressed. The structure of Ramsey's just war ethic is at heart an interventionary rather than an isolationist approach. Of course the duty to intervene is subject to the ability to intervene, and to the principle of proportion that more good can on balance be done by intervening. But merely to stand by in times and places of conflict, in an isolationist spirit, is to fail to fulfill the claims of Christian love.

In the concluding sections of the article, Ramsey discusses the nature of political action, the duties of a statesman, and the relation of this to the role of the church in political debate (Section V); and he discusses the possibility of a just revolution, denying that his theory is necessarily or in practice always opposed to revolutions.

We are now in a position to consider more fully the accusation of those who read Ramsey as supporting the Vietnam war. Is there any justice in that accusation? Ramsey's first, and main, defense against this charge was that his concern in what he had written was to clarify the meaning of just war theory in application to the Vietnam war, and to consider the ways in which the possible justice of that war should be considered. It is not an indictment of Ramsey to say that the atmosphere at the time was too heated to permit such theoretical analysis (though clearly in one sense, alas, it was). Ramsey attacked the language and moral argument of those who claimed that the war was clearly immoral. As to the charge that it was indiscriminate, Ramsey argued that the bombing of villages that covered Vietcong strongholds, and the bombing of military targets in the North, could not clearly be said to violate this test. As for the test of proportion, Ramsey's point was not that he knew the war to be politically wise (or proportionate), but that it was not clear whether it was or was not. Even if it was, in hindsight, a mistaken policy, it still could not be described on that ground as immoral.[15] That Ramsey was right in this point is surely borne out by the division of opinion in the country and in the churches at the time he was writing in early 1966.

There is more that can be said in defense of Ramsey's writing on Vietnam. Although he is correct to claim that he himself made no judgment for or against the war, he certainly raised some important moral questions about it. As we have seen, he raised the point that the defense of South Vietnam could do it more harm than good, and that one alternative was to lose the war and negotiate as good a settlement as could be obtained.[16] In considering the decision of President Johnson to escalate the war in 1965, Ramsey argues that decisions of this kind can only be ventured, they cannot be assured of success. He cites the view of President Kennedy, who was reported to have felt "that there was a reasonable chance of making a go of it." He also cites one of his favorite examples of this kind of decision, the decision of Churchill to fight on against Germany in 1940. But in respect of Vietnam, Ramsey remarks, "This is not to contend that these decisions were not tragically mistaken."[17]

Ramsey also admits that though the main direction of the war is discriminate, there still may well have been immoral acts committed:

Peripheral to the "central war" against the insurgents there may be taking place many intrinsically wrong actions in this confused and bloody war. (I only say that this is not proved by reference to the bombing of villages, etc., that may in fact lie within a vast Vietcong stronghold.)[18]

In his first paper he had already worried about the bombing of villages:

Still the least that can be said, and I think the most, is that the question whether the bombing of "stabilized" Vietcong "strongholds" is discriminating enough raises initially grave doubts about the morality of this action.[19]

Ramsey's doubts on this point were not strong enough to lead him to condemn that particular military conduct, but the attacks on the North in 1967 did cause him to speak out. In the article "Over the Slope to Total War,"[20] Ramsey condemned the March 10, 1967 bombing raid of the Thainguygen iron and steel factory complex. This was the first bombing, Ramsey argued, that could clearly be shown to be indiscriminate. Earlier bombing had been directed against the infiltration from the North; this attack was directed against the society of North Vietnam itself. Ramsey complains, however, that the church protests against earlier actions meant that there was now no way of indicating the line that had been crossed. Truly indiscriminate acts of war could not be identified as such, because of the way earlier, probably discriminate, action had already been described as immoral and intrinsically wrong. Ramsey's complaint is a version of the complaint of Anscombe against pacifism "that it teaches people to make no distinction between the shedding of innocent blood and the shedding of any human blood." Ramsey argues that a failure to grasp and use the true sense of the prohibition of direct attack on noncombatants means that such attack cannot be discerned when it does happen.

In any correct use of moral language, this has been a limited war whose conduct has been held within the test of discrimination determining the justice of acts of war. But liberal religious and academic opinion has screamed bloody "murder" or "indiscriminate" war, as if that could ever be proved by the *amount* of the destruction or by the fact that it is not possible to *separate* civilians from combatants, so often that we now have nothing to say when our government may have let loose a real *counter-society* strike in destroying the steel complex on March 10. We have wasted our substance in riotous moralizing.[21]

We can see in this quotation that Ramsey's verdict on the U.S. conduct of the war up to March 1967 is clear. Gone are the earlier hesitations that "initially grave doubts" were raised. It is, I think, clear that Ramsey reacted against calls that all church people should oppose the war.[22] It is surely also true that Ramsey was more confident than he should, or need, have been in pronouncing the bombing of villages to be definitely discriminate acts of war. By his own criteria, this could surely not be wholly apparent to a distant observer. Ramsey's protest on this point against the antiwar protest lent some substance to the perception that he supported the war.

An equally serious difficulty in discerning Ramsey's views may have arisen from changes made by editors to titles of articles (without consultation). One of these in particular illustrates the difficulty Ramsey had in being heard clearly.[23] The article "Is Vietnam a Just War?" was entitled by Ramsey "How Shall the Vietnam War Be Justified?" Under the title actually over the article, and reading it alone of Ramsey's works, it would be hard to reach any other conclusion than that the author thought Vietnam a just war. The original title would instead have alerted any reasonably careful reader to the main concern of the article, namely, how to think through the just war criteria to see how a true verdict should be reached. But in the charged atmosphere of 1967, such a reading would have needed a cooler mind than most possess.

The paper presented in January 1966 also contained an essay on "Incapacitating Gases."[24] Ramsey took up an article by Julian Pleasants on gas warfare, which had argued that the use of gases in war is not simply to be dismissed from a moral point of view. Ramsey gives examples of military encounters in which the use of incapacitating gases could save much life and much bloodshed as compared with the use of guns, explosives, etc. Nor, Ramsey argues, would gases only be properly used where it was possible to confine their use only to affecting combatants. That gases are foreseeably and inevitably likely to affect noncombatants does not make their use necessarily unjust, any more than the inevitable effects of other weapons of war. Indeed, there could well be occasions when the use of incapacitating gases could mean less destruction of noncombatants as well as of combatants.

Nevertheless Ramsey concluded against the revision of the presently accepted rules banning chemical warfare. He considered the argument that allowing chemical weapons to be used would be to cross a threshold or firebreak. It would breach a barrier that prevents the much greater evil of widespread, escalating use of such weapons. He saw that it would be difficult to replace the general prohibition of chemical weapons, a clear threshold, with other boundaries between one kind of chemical and another. It should be possible to create firebreaks between one kind of weapon and another, and the possible gains of using weapons, which merely incapacitate rather than destroy, are a strong incentive for attempting this. On the other hand:

> There is danger that war would move rapidly through the class names, chemical and biological, the lethal as well as the non-lethal; and that these weapons might be directed at mass casualties sooner than weapons we are used to.[25]

Ramsey left the matter, finally, without completely settling it. This, of course, is because he saw it as a matter of proportion. Not all incapacitating gases are indiscriminate in use, and their use could save life. On the other hand, breaching the accepted threshold of their complete moral and legal prohibition could lead to much greater evil in the long run. But the work of charity may find ways of replacing the blanket prohibition with others more flexible:

> A charitable reason may be able to find a way to think through the problem of imposing further limits and enforcing other rules upon warfare

when the prohibition of incapacitants is breached in the direction of
humanization.[26]

Some Objections

Ramsey observed in "Some Rejoinders" that he could get his
commentators (in *Love and Society*) into argument with each other, so
that their criticisms might cancel out and leave him unscathed. Of
course, he enjoyed the argument too much to let that happen. What he
enjoyed more was proving that his opponents to right and left really
shared the same premises or conclusions. He claimed this of pacifists
and deterrentists, but perhaps a greater coup was to establish "that
the conservative Catholic philosopher Grisez is willing to lie down in
the same Procrustean bed with the liberal Judith Thompson!"[27] We
might with justice quite easily attempt either of these games with
regard to the pacifist and realist opponents of Ramsey. They do indeed
make diametrically opposite comments about the same thing. At the
same time one might easily try to say that, for the most part, they
make the same assertion about the morality of killing. In almost all
critics is the assumption that bloodshed is wrong in itself. The pacifists
conclude that no Christian may ever kill, while the realists conclude
that minimizing bloodshed is a key determinant of morality. These
oversimplifications would cover too many varieties of approach, and
fail to do justice to the strength of opposition Ramsey faces.

One of the clearest pairs of opposing views is to be found in the
comments of Laarman and O'Brien. This will provide a helpful place
to start. One of Laarman's main criticisms of Ramsey is that his
account of the principle of discrimination is too loose. He bases this
charge on a number of points. First is the vagueness of Ramsey's view
of the greatest size of nuclear weapon whose use could be discriminate,
nor does he place sufficient limit on the numbers of weapons that could
be justified. In addition, he is "rather casual in his assessment of actual
Western targeting." Ramsey would allow military bases near cities to
be legitimate targets in spite of the extensive collateral damage inevitable in such targeting. Laarman also quibbles over the euphemism of
"collateral damage" for the deaths of thousands or millions, reminding
us of the meaning of the word "damage" as it is used in this context.
Laarman therefore complains that although the principle of discrimination might "save millions of lives in a nuclear war," Ramsey "has

used the criterion so loosely that in many cases it would make little or no difference."[28]

Surely Laarman gives himself away with this last remark, if he has not already done so. His concern is not finally with the morality of action, but with the actual results to be obtained. Of course no one would deny that it is good to save millions of lives, if possible, but the question at issue is not how to do this, but what moral means may be used to attempt to do it. Laarman, like so many pacifists or nuclear pacifists, jumps too easily from the threats involved in contemporary nuclear deterrence to the (possible) actuality of the great horrors that may be considered or envisaged in those threats.[29] However, there are other pacifists who give a more careful account of the morality of their position than Laarman manages.

We can contrast the opposite complaint that the criterion is too restrictive. This is the charge made by O'Brien. Based on his considerable work on strategy, morality, and law, he writes:

> Moreover, in my view, Ramsey's principle of discrimination is inconsistent with the requirements of adequate deterrence and defense, as recognized by international law. This principle is an obstacle to the proper exercise of the moral rights of deterrence and defense indispensable to political life. Ramsey's use of discrimination likewise appears to preclude meaningful exercise of the right of revolution, a fundamental human right.[30]

O'Brien claims to find the arguments of Ramsey for the foundation of the principle of discrimination unconvincing. He claims to adhere to the traditional Catholic view of natural justice rather than love-informed reason as founding the just war theory. However, O'Brien's account of just war is hardly traditional, for he offers his own basis for *jus in bello* in the principle of proportion. His underlying aim is "to produce a more reasonable balance between moral limitation and military necessity." It is surely a correct reading of O'Brien that his view of *raison d'état* and military necessity is what underwrites his account of just war theory. This is justified by the phrases "moral rights of deterrence and defense" and "the right of revolution, a fundamental human right." It is these rights, for O'Brien, which are conclusive in considering the morality of war and politics. Whatever is genuinely necessary to protect them may be held legitimate.[31]

O'Brien offers us a typical example of what we can call the realist objection to Ramsey. On the other hand, Laarman's critique is typical enough of the pacifist objection. Neither of these two gives us a very full account of how they think Ramsey's theory is wrongly drawn.

We have already sketched something of Ramsey's relation to pacifism, and we will examine his debate with nuclear pacifism in the next chapter. We conclude this chapter by examining some realist critics of Ramsey.

O'Connor's is the most interesting full-length study devoted to Ramsey's just war theory. He is very critical of Ramsey from a Niebuhrian standpoint. His main criticisms (maintained and applied throughout his study) are that Ramsey moves too easily from a love ethic to just war, and that his principle of discrimination is both legalistic and formalistic. He illustrates these criticisms with particular reference to nuclear deterrence, and insurgency in Vietnam. O'Connor prefers Niebuhr's love-justice dialectic to Ramsey's ethical method. Consistently with this, he regrets that Ramsey moved away from the "love transforming natural law" motif.[32]

At the heart of O'Connor's criticisms seems to lie a difficulty in grasping Ramsey's presentation of Christian love and the way it is embodied in principles and rules. Ramsey "has an overly *exclusive* view of *agape in theory*," he writes. *Agape* is understood as selfless love, and Ramsey's Christocentric ethic of love is too divorced from human experience. It loses touch with the doctrine of creation. But, O'Connor recognizes, this contrasts with what Ramsey also writes about preferential neighbor love. While meaningful in family and community life, this "cannot be applied to the nation-state without kindling a dangerous spirit of nationalism." Thus, O'Connor is able to conclude that Ramsey "has an overly *inclusive* view of *agape in practice*."[33] O'Connor is at a loss to see how these two views are to be reconciled, and resorts instead to Niebuhr's dialectic of sacrificial love, mutual love, justice, etc.

In the foregoing paragraph, I reversed the order of O'Connor's account of what he calls the theoretical and practical side of *agape*. If he had understood that the point of describing love as selfless is to provide the correct motivation and perspective for action, and that the point of characterizing love as preferential is to help embody love in the realities of human life, all O'Connor's problems could be solved. This makes the connection with creation plain, at least in principle, and, for instance, demonstrates the resources Ramsey has for criticizing nationalism in pointing to love as selfless. Another way of making O'Connor's mistake clear would be to refer to the first section of

Ramsey's essay on Niebuhr. Ramsey contrasts Niebuhr with Kierke-gaard, and concludes:

> No more should be written on the subject of Christian ethics unless it is right to separate the material from the subjective problem of love and law. If we persist without this distinction Augustine's *On the Spirit and the Letter* will haunt our dreams.[34]

It is probably O'Connor's failure to grasp Ramsey's doctrine of Christian love that leads him to his other major criticisms. Clearly he is in no position to appreciate Ramsey's argument for a love-based ethic of resistance, so we can leave on one side the charge that Ramsey too easily reconciles love with involvement in war. It will be more helpful to examine for a moment the charges that Ramsey is both legalistic and formalistic.

O'Connor's charge of legalism is somewhat oddly made out, and in fact turns out to be circular. It concerns Ramsey's treatment of nuclear deterrence. (We can give the structure of O'Connor's charge without anticipating the substance of the next chapter.) The argument runs as follows. O'Connor claims that Ramsey wants to apply "an absolute principle of noncombatant immunity" to the practicalities of nuclear deterrence. Here he assumes what he mistakenly takes for Ramsey's conclusion, which it will become clear he wishes to share. This he identifies as "granting approval to the present deterrence strategy of the United States."[35] O'Connor proceeds to an exposition of Ramsey's views, and to the crucial debate between Ramsey and Stein. He concludes that "Stein is thus correct" (on the interpretation of the rule of double effect) and that Ramsey's argument for justifiable nuclear deterrence fails. Ramsey must either give up the principle of noncombatant immunity, or the strategy of deterrence. O'Connor follows this with an argument that Ramsey's advocacy of counterforce strategy is inadequate, and, indeed, that the traditional understanding of war on which Ramsey draws is outdated. O'Connor's arguments would seem to lead either to a critique of Ramsey's moral method, or to the conclusion that Ramsey should become a nuclear pacifist. Even if we were to grant the detail of O'Connor's arguments, the second conclusion is the more natural one on their grounds, but all O'Connor will allow is the former: "These criticisms all point to the fundamental problem in Ramsey's position: his commitment to a legalistic and formalistic approach to the question of war."[36] The problem is always assumed; it is never demonstrated. That Ramsey's view of nuclear deterrence does not in fact justify the mainstream Western strategy, which O'Connor espouses, appears to be the problem. This is merely to beg the question.

Something worse than question-begging, I fear, takes place in O'Connor's account of Ramsey on Vietnam. Here again, his charge is similar. Ramsey's absolute principle forbids too much, and is unable to relate properly to the particular realities of the question. Ramsey takes the principle of discrimination to disallow all forms of terrorism, whether selective or not.[37] O'Connor is unhappy with this, thinking that Ramsey moves too quickly to condemnation of Vietcong policy. He writes:

> Since by Ramsey's own admission, combatants are largely defined by their *function*, some selective terror may be justified against public officials of the Saigon government without violating the principle of discrimination.[38]

This seems to be a very doubtful argument, but we must accept that it claims precisely to be an interpretation of the principle of discrimination. However, O'Connor also wishes to take issue with Ramsey's interpretation of that principle as applied to counterinsurgency: "If, as Ramsey himself argues, the guerrilla achieves his goals by terrorizing villages of innocent, frightened peasants, why should these noncombatants be sacrificed in order to get at the bullying insurgents?"[39]

O'Connor has entirely overlooked Ramsey's careful consideration of who is a noncombatant in these circumstances.[40] We may make three brief points. First, the peasants have been caught up in fighting, and are materially part of the aggression. Second, this is not what is meant by the word "innocent" in the principle of discrimination since "innocence" refers to material lack of cooperation in the fighting, not to moral innocence. Third, Ramsey's point is, of course, that it is the insurgents who have enlarged the aggression, and hence the target. The counterinsurgency force is still bound to avoid attack on noncombatants, but it may be very difficult to identify them as such. This may be tragic and disproportionately destructive, but it is not indiscriminate.

O'Connor's willingness to justify some forms of terrorism goes awkwardly with the stringent requirements he places on counterinsurgency. We must leave that problem on one side in order to point to the same failure in argument that we observed in analyzing nuclear deterrence. We have seen that O'Connor's arguments center on interpretation of the principle of discrimination, yet his charge is that that principle is in itself inadequate. O'Connor writes: "His conclusions appear so arbitrary and so unrelated to special conditions existing in this troubled area, that the validity of Ramsey's entire ethical methodology is again called into question."[41] Sadly, again we are forced to conclude that it is O'Connor's own political conclusions that have led him to dismiss Ramsey's moral methodology.

In order to make a charge such as legalism or formalism stick, it is necessary to challenge the roots of Ramsey's ethics more radically, and give greater attention to his careful arguments. Were he writing today, we may speculate that O'Connor might have found support in the critique offered by Gustafson, which we have already examined.[42] At the same time, he need not have waited for that, as the analysis of R.W. Tucker was already in print.[43] Tucker offers a largely careful and correct appreciation of Ramsey's position, while radically rejecting his moral account of politics.

Like O'Brien, Tucker regards military necessity, or the principle of statecraft, as providing the overriding moral obligations of politics. Like O'Connor, he thinks (1) that Ramsey fails to justify nuclear deterrence on his own moral grounds, and (2) that the proposal for nuclear deterrence Ramsey thinks justified would in any case be ineffective. Unlike both, he enters into detailed argument with the substance of Ramsey's writings, and reaches to the heart of the argument.

The heart of Tucker's critique is the view that morality and military necessity are irreconcilably opposed:

> If the injunction against doing evil that good may come is taken seriously the price is political irrelevance. If *bellum justum* is to remain politically relevant, the price is the erosion of the significance of "doing evil."[44]

To demonstrate this, Tucker examines the principle of noncombatant immunity, to which he says the just war theory gives "an absolute and unconditioned character." This is, of course, Tucker's characterization. He has two ways to show that such an absolute rule must clash with military necessity. In the first place he examines the definition of noncombatancy. He observes, correctly, that the meaning of noncombatancy must depend on the nature of warfare (we might say, combatancy). This, he concludes, gives the principle "a relative and contingent character."[45] Its effective scope can be reduced in practice "almost to a vanishing point" by belligerents. This argument only shows the problem in defining the principle as "absolute" in the first place; it would be much clearer if the "absolute" character of the principle were referred to as "exceptionless."[46]

Tucker's second challenge concerns the principle of double effect, for he undertakes to show that the notion of indirect effect, or indirect intent, is implausible, indeed that it is a mere sophistry. Tucker's account here is difficult to follow. He uses the word "means" in a confusing way, arguing that the unwanted, indirect effects of an act are still means to the desired end. In effect, he appears to deny altogether any meaning to the distinction between direct and indirect, although he (almost) reinstates it a page later. Such arguments, we have already observed, can take a great deal of work to clarify. Ramsey duly undertook this task at length, with considerable success.[47] In his refutation he clarifies the meaning of "intention," distinguishing it carefully from motivation and final aim or goal. Here we can only refer directly back to Chapter Two, where the exposition depended to a large extent on this essay of Ramsey's.

Tucker also attempts to argue that an effective deterrent "will continue to rest largely on what is interpreted as a threat to do evil." This is so even if that threat is not actually made immorally, which Tucker almost concedes as a possibility. Quite where the immorality rests here is not clear. Here, as elsewhere, one is left with the impression that Tucker assumes what he sets out to prove, namely the irreconcilability of morality with politics. That this is in fact the case is surely made clear by his short account of retribution, "the constituent principle of statecraft." He argues, "Yet it is precisely this principle that *bellum justum* must reject if it is to set limits to the necessities of state."[48] Tucker's assertion that retribution is the constituent principle of statecraft sheds a good deal of light on his approach to politics. It reveals a narrow "realism" (or cynicism?) that overlooks a wide area of political reality and a large part of the tradition of political theory. In any case, we are forced to the view that Tucker believes morality is only moral if it sets unacceptable limits to statecraft. He sets out from his conclusion, which we can perhaps paraphrase over-simply, but not in the end unfairly, as the statement that politics is a tough and bloody business, and as such, immoral.

Our analysis of O'Connor and Tucker has revealed some of the typical arguments which are apt to be brought against Ramsey. It would be impossible to tackle all of the possible ways of leaving the road along which Ramsey travels. However, many of them would no doubt also show how seriously meant is the joke of Maritain that Ramsey quotes at the head of his reply to Tucker:

Moralists are unhappy people. When they insist on the immutability of moral principles, they are reproached for imposing unlivable require-ments on us. When they explain the way in which those immutable principles are to be put into force, they are reproached for making morality relative. In both cases, however, they are only upholding the claims of reason to direct life.[49]

If Tucker's attack on the principle of double effect is comparatively unsophisticated, that deficit is more than made up for by the Roman Catholic proportionalists whose theoretical debate with Ramsey we have already surveyed. It is surely no accident that these writers characteristically have little to say about nuclear deterrence, for a consequentialist methodology can equally plausibly lead to pacifist and realist positions. Still, it would seem that they are bound either to reject the principle of discrimination or to override it in some circum-stances. It is therefore appropriate to enter them in the list of realists.

Langendörfer's essay offers a useful account of Ramsey's proposal for nuclear deterrence, together with the views of Michael Walzer.[50] His attention is largely on the ethical arguments, and so it can be tackled here. Langendörfer summarizes Ramsey's position, and then considers the critique offered by Walzer. He concludes that as to "the correctness of his ethical argumentation Ramsey seems to be unassail-able as far as the points in question are concerned. One can, of course, dispute the correctness of his analytical assumptions."[51] It is Ramsey's assumptions that Langendörfer is unhappy with—he repeatedly de-scribes Ramsey's principle of discrimination as "absolute."[52] Langen-dörfer himself follows Schüller in giving a proportionately based ac-count of this principle. This leads Ramsey to talk about deterrence almost exclusively in terms of counterforce conduct of war.[53] This is true, but hardly does justice to the subtleties of Ramsey's account, of which Langendörfer otherwise gives a fair summary. More seriously, Langendörfer considers that Ramsey's concern with the principle of discrimination prevents him from considering the principle of propor-tion. To misread Ramsey as ignoring the principle of proportion is surprising—all the more so in the face of Ramsey's repeated reiteration of the twofold nature of *jus in bello*.

That Langendörfer (like others) is unable to give an accurate account of Ramsey at precisely this point is interesting. It strongly suggests a failure to grasp the basic outline of Ramsey's casuistry, fundamental to his account of just war theory. The failure is twofold. As regards the principle of discrimination, it persistently sees this as an absolute rule, and fails to consider how it is both exceptionless, and at the same time flexibly and intelligently (not woodenly) applied to differing circumstances. As to the principle of proportion, the realist viewpoint is accustomed to seeing this as the whole of morality. Understandably, it looks for something rather more definite and detailed than Ramsey is prepared to offer. Ramsey's principle of proportion is very loosely and widely drawn, though this does not make it empty. He is much more agnostic than many of his critics when it comes to answering the imponderable questions of political goals. "How much justice is worth how many lives?" and so on. Answers to these questions, for Ramsey, can rarely on their own yield moral imperatives. Of course, he says, it is wrong to act foolishly or unthinkingly, and there is much thought to be taken over the nature of political goals. But these goals do not alone define the morality of action, and can leave us many hard choices. Partly because the ends of action are incommensurate with each other in such political choices, there is all the more need to pay very close attention to the means employed.

Part Four: Nuclear Weapons and Nuclear Deterrence

13

Rational Nuclear Armament?

Ramsey's remarkable defense of the possible morality of a policy of nuclear deterrence needs some clarification. This defense began in 1963, with *The Limits of Nuclear War*, and continued through 1965 with two long articles, "More Unsolicited Advice to Vatican Council II" and *Again, the Justice of Deterrence*.[1] Throughout all this, and subsequently, there are clarities and continuities, but there are also explicit changes. There is also one substantially difficult phrase, the wording of which Ramsey defended to the end.

The basic continuity of thought is this: that a just policy of nuclear deterrence must be based on a just policy for fighting a nuclear war; that there are some nuclear weapons for which a just use could be envisaged; and that there can be no justification for a deterrence based on threats to destroy entire populations (whether only implied or conditional) "no matter how much peace-by-deterrence results from it."[2] Ramsey's arguments did not vary from these propositions, and, notwithstanding the varying discussions of bluff, there is no serious obscurity about them.

Within these broad outlines, there are a number of changes both of substance and of emphasis. Between 1961 and 1963 Ramsey changed his mind significantly about the possibility for a just nuclear deterrent, as he admits in the introduction to *The Just War*.[3] In 1963 he allowed the morality of deterrence by bluff, which he then subsequently disallowed. His withdrawal on this point was, however, rather guarded; it only became clear and unmistakable as late as 1982. In the 1965 articles Ramsey introduced a recalcitrant phrase about disproportionate threats, which forces one to reexamine the 1963 essay. The obscurity of this phrase is somewhat reduced by later discussion and defense, but it remains problematic, and Ramsey stood staunchly by it.

Our task now is to retrace this progress, to try to establish a coherent position and then evaluate it. In this there is bound to be some circularity, for Ramsey's theory of the just war has to perform two tasks for us. Without denying the possibility of inconsistency, we have to read the obscurer passages on nuclear deterrence in the light of his firm and clear basic convictions. At the same time, it is those basic convictions that also largely provide the standard by which the later writings must be judged. In the end, whether or not we find Ramsey clear and consistent, he has provided us with the materials to fashion our own view of the contemporary moral dilemma.

In 1961, Ramsey did not defend a policy for nuclear deterrence, although he did defend the possible morality of some nuclear weapons. We turn now to the discussions in the closing chapters of *War and the Christian Conscience*.

Rational Nuclear Armament?

Ramsey discussed the moral defensibility of different kinds of nuclear weapons in Chapter Twelve of *War and the Christian Conscience*, entitled "Rational, Politically Beneficial Armament." Ramsey allows himself to be instructed by an expert, and in doing so he draws to a conclusion and application some of the key themes of the book. The chapter takes the form of an extended exposition of, and commentary on, a book by Thomas E. Murray, *Nuclear Policy for War and Peace*. Murray was a civil servant, prominent in the nuclear weapons field in the 1950s, and approaches the moral problems of politics (and nuclear weapons in particular) from a political point of view.

Ramsey calls Murray's analysis "the just-war theory completely intact."[4] He then goes on to quote two paragraphs on the distinction between force and violence, which seem so important that it is worth repeating them in full at this point:

> This is a political distinction, based on a moral premise. By violence I mean the use of military power in such an extensive, undiscriminating, or even unlimited, measure and manner that it becomes useless for the rational purposes of politics, which are always limited. By force I mean the use of power in such a proportionate measure and in such a discriminating manner as to constitute an apt means for the achievement of legitimate political goals.

Given the nature of man, the art of international politics cannot dispense with the use, or at least the threat, of force, any more than human society can dispense with the law, which requires force to back it up. On the other hand, international politics perishes as an art if power is allowed to suffer moral debasement and become mere violence, which is destructive of the very idea of force and of law, too. . . . For the last decades, we Americans have subscribed to a strategy not of force but of violence—excessive, incredible, and politically irrelevant.[5]

In these few lines are implicit not only the basic thesis which we earlier identified as the heart of Ramsey's thought, but more besides. There is the threefold equation "correct political thought = rational thought = true moral thought." There is an indication of the limited objectives of political life, i.e., a stable legal and justly ordered peace. There is the twofold moral test of means in war—discrimination and proportion.

It is from this basis that Ramsey began to develop his view of nuclear weapons. This is so obviously an important subject, and one on which Ramsey's conclusions and applications were adjusted and worked out at length in *The Just War*, that it is worth making sure we have his position in 1961 quite clear before us. There is a slight elusiveness of expression, and a tendency to speak as it were via Thomas Murray, but the point of view expressed is clear, and equally clearly it is Ramsey's own view at this point. First we examine (with Murray all the time) the deficiencies of massive *violent* nuclear deterrence and see how these move us toward rethinking the truth of the moral limits in just war theory.[6] The heart of this discussion is an examination of the range of nuclear weapons.[7] This range takes us from multimegaton weapons down to nuclear weapons, which are indistinguishable in their destructive power from certain "chemical" explosive bombs ("conventional" as we now say). Following this discussion the chapter looks at nuclear testing and at Murray's specific proposal for disarmament. Ramsey's own statements (as always) are very carefully and specifically phrased. To sum up at the outset the position he holds may help us to trace its exposition as he puts it side by side with the views of Thomas Murray. We must first be clear that he only intends to illustrate the principles which have been clearly and definitely enunciated. We have just seen that in principle it is not within the moralist's competence to apply these principles either to particular weapons or to particular actions. Rather "it is the task of strategists and tacticians to determine how to apply [these principles]."[8]

We will now follow Ramsey's discussion of the range from multimegaton weapons to fractional kiloton weapons. Ramsey thinks that it
has yet to be shown that multimegaton weapons have any rational
moral political purpose; that it is at least an open question whether
some nuclear weapons in the lower kiloton range may not be rational
and right weapons for military and political use; and that although the
widely accepted distinction between nuclear and other weapons may
be important and valuable, this distinction is not unshakable. The
pressure to disarmament at the high end of the range is pressure to
unilateral disarmament, for if the weapons are purposeless it makes
little sense in moral terms to keep them even for any purpose of
negotiation. At the lower end of the scale, Ramsey implies that he
thinks "small" nuclear weapons can be rational weapons in political
and military terms and that they ought to be retained if necessary. It is
worth getting Ramsey's argument in *War and the Christian Conscience*
accurately documented here.[9] Then, when we come to the discussion
of nuclear deterrence in *The Just War*, we may see as accurately as
possible what changes are made, to what extent these are of substance
or detail, and where the same position is merely refined or elaborated.

The question is "What is the nature of 'rational, politically beneficial
armament' today?" We begin by examining multimegaton bombs.[10]
Murray refuses to condemn these weapons outright, but he points out
that they can be used against very few targets, and that there is no
conceivable need to have a large number of these weapons. Making
the weapons cleaner, less contaminating, is not to alter their destructive character or the essential morality of their use or threatened use.
Ramsey points out that Murray has given as the only example of
proper use that against a fleet at sea, and wonders whether Murray is
consistent in not pressing the case against these weapons rather
harder.[11]

The questions of kiloton weapons and of nuclear testing are considered together.[12] These weapons and their testing above ground leads to
limited and controllable fallout. The needs of national defense, Murray
argues, require the testing and use of weapons of this order. This is to
control the technology and make it subservient to the proper needs of
political and military doctrine. This is the important point, both politically and morally, and it is a prior issue to debates about the desir-
ability of ending nuclear tests. Ramsey comments: "I do not know
whether Murray is correct in his belief that rational, politically beneficial armament means rational *nuclear* armament. Moreover, I do not
see how the moralist, alone, can know this." He then goes on to ask

that some evidence for the proper usefulness of megaton weapons, and also of "kiloton weapons, at least in their upper ranges" be brought forward. He comments: "I tend to think that rational nuclear armament would need to be confined more to the lower range in such firepower, i.e. closer to the conventional weapons they will replace."[13] This distinction is then discussed. Ramsey makes the important concession that this distinction is of great practical value, for "the nations cannot afford to let go of even irrational limits upon the conduct of war." Is this distinction or limit then an irrational one? In principle it cannot be automatic: "I see no reason *a priori* for a radical distinction between nuclear and chemical [i.e., 'conventional'] bombs."[14]

At the same time, it is possible that the distinction between just use and unjust use of weapons in war may turn out to follow "exactly the distinction between chemical and nuclear explosions."[15] Of course it may well be that the reason that the threshold before the use of nuclear weapons is so well respected is the fear that nuclear weapons once used may lead to all-out nuclear war. The doctrine and policy of nuclear deterrence thus tends to confuse policy at lower levels: "Because of the fear that inept force may be used we are deterred from the use of apt force, and from vigorous thought about what apt force may be in this age."[16]

From this it is a short step to a consideration of proposals for nuclear disarmament. In the analysis of Murray's specific proposal for mutual and equal disarmament at the top end of the range, Ramsey's own views emerge. He argues that questions or quibbles about precise equality or mutuality are not to the point, and neither is the question of inspection. In fact, "the case for unilateral rational armament and disarmament is sufficiently demonstrated, politically, militarily, and morally." Any opposition to this point, this proposal, simply has not thought through the meaning and implications of the test of discrimination in the conduct of war.

The importance of this discussion of the morality of nuclear weapons rests on the conclusions of the previous chapter.[17] Ramsey there examines and contrasts two versions of a nuclear deterrence policy, those offered by Morgenstern and Kahn. The former offers a version of deterrence based on the infeasibility of ever using the unlimited power of nuclear weapons. Kahn by contrast argues that deterrence can only be based on the capability actually to fight a war. With this Ramsey agrees, but in following Kahn's proposals for deterrence he concludes that Kahn also rests these on infeasible and incredible policies for fighting. For instance, examining Kahn's view that single cities may now and then be destroyed, Ramsey says:

> Yet it is as much as admitted that we can decide to make ourselves objectively capable of fighting a nuclear war, and firmly resolved to do so, only by a dint of a large measure of belief that deterrence will work and that we will never have to do any such thing.[18]

Ramsey's objection to nuclear deterrence in 1961 is chiefly an opposition to the deterrence of massive nuclear destruction. His target is the "central war" with its threats and fears of massive destruction of cities and populations:

> We shall soon all live in a great desert, whose wells are all poisoned, unless the people of the world are plainly told by their leaders that no political or human good can come from doing anything so essentially wrong (because so stupid) or anything so essentially irrational (because so immoral). Warfare is not feasible, deterrence is not feasible, and what is more, politics is no longer feasible, unless this central war, with intrinsically unjust means, is abolished.[19]

In contrast to this kind of deterrence, Ramsey argues that the only truly moral deterrence is that based on weapons whose use could itself be moral. It is this very close link that is loosened in 1963, and then seems to be loosened even further in 1965. Before we look at how this is done, we should just see how he handles the problem that will trouble him so much in 1963—how to deter an opponent who threatens massive nuclear destruction. Ramsey, in the end, does not take such a threat seriously:

> In the face of brandished missiles with megaton warheads, there is in no case any other recourse than to stand firm in the right as God gives us to see the right and to stand firm with arms that are the arms of a national purpose. . . . The courage to defy blackmail is the main ingredient needed.

Indeed, we already have to do just this: "This [courage] must in fact be exercised beneath the so-called umbrella of nuclear deterrence."[20]

The Limits of Nuclear War

The 1963 essay starts from a very similar critique of nuclear deterrence to that offered in 1961.[21] Ramsey criticizes "rationality of irrationality" policies, and other unthinkable and undoable policies involving, e.g, "counter-value" attacks, or city-exchanges. Deterrence based on plans such as these is both immoral and irrational. These plans have their roots in contemporary American voluntarism, which sees war solely as a conflict of wills, a test of resolve. There are no limits to what we may do to prove our resolution:

> War as a test of the limitlessly variable "strength" of resolve may go as high as city-exchanges. War as a test of real strength to defend or effect objectives can and will go no higher than counter-forces warfare. A nation determined to play a game of wills to the end, and resolved to win in accord with the internal "rationality" of a radical voluntarism, never will discover that there are any limits in resolutely willing to win this game of hostile wills in conflict.[22]

Ramsey then puts forward "with a great degree of reluctance" a series of policy proposals for the United States and the West.[23] He says little here about the size of nuclear weapons (in contrast to 1961). Instead he concentrates on a particular strategic question, namely the problem of deterring a Russian attack on Western Europe. How is this to be done justly in a nuclear age?

Ramsey sets out his policy proposals in six steps:

1. Strengthening of conventional forces to "match the mythical Russian 'hordes.' "

2. No first use of nuclear weapons, except against enemy forces which have actually invaded and crossed a national boundary, and then only over one's own territory.

3. Consideration whether the United States should work toward a complete renunciation of the first use of nuclear weapons. This means, again, the strengthening of conventional forces in order that the only reason for retaining nuclear weapons would be to deter their use by an enemy. This, it must be realized, is more a matter of action than of words.

4. Retention of nuclear weapons for tactical use against enemy forces on enemy territory. This is necessary to enforce the ban on the offensive use of nuclear weapons, by punishment and deterrence.

5. Retention of strategic nuclear forces in order to deter tactical nuclear fighting. The possibility of "no-city" strategic warfare exists in order to keep war limited and to enforce the limits proposed (and communicated) in points 2 and 4.

One must have the ability to carry limited counterforce warfare to the enemy's own territory in order to bargain effectively about the limits and rules by which war is to be fought.

6. This point is not so much a proposal as an introduction to the question: "How is the threat of city destruction to be deterred?" It seems that city destruction can only be deterred by the threat of city destruction. This question leads into the two final sections of the essay, on "Reprisals" and "The Justice of Deterrence."[24]

Ramsey rejects the doctrine of reprisal vehemently, especially in this context. It cannot make a wrong action right to perform it as a reprisal against someone, even if they have done that wrong thing, nor can this approach possibly be justified on the basis of Christian love. Finally, it is also inconceivable, for it would be a purposeless act to destroy an enemy society in retaliation.

This then brings us to the question of formulating a just deterrent:

It remains only to be asked whether actually *carrying out* this reprisal in kind is really necessary in order to "provide a sanction" for the lesser laws and rules of warfare which it is urgently necessary for the nations of the world to impose on themselves and one another.[25]

The answer to this is provided in three stages in addition to the counterforce capabilities already proposed. It is these that form the basis of the debate in *Peace, the Churches and the Bomb* in 1965. Before going on to that debate, we should first look at the major change of emphasis between 1961 and 1963. There seem to be two main shifts.

Most importantly, Ramsey is obviously impressed by the need to deter an enemy from nuclear threats and destruction. He no longer feels that weapons which are close in power to the maximum size of conventional arms will be sufficient for this task. The sense of this necessity, though, goes hand in hand with a fuller examination of the link between the use of weapons and the deterrence to be obtained from their possession. In 1961 Ramsey assumed that this was a tight link; in arguing against the "nuclear umbrella" and the threat of the "central war" he showed that these were immoral because they rested ultimately on the willingness to use nuclear weapons indiscriminately. What he overlooked (he now claims in 1963) was that nuclear weapons designed and intended for counterforce use will also deter in other ways than by simply threatening enemy forces. A further shift in perspective seems to be gained also by considering strategy (e.g., how to deter an enemy) rather than armament policy more or less in the abstract.

Ramsey himself summarized this change of view in the Introduction to *The Just War*:

> In concluding that no sort of force could be retained for deterrence's sake which it would be immoral ever to use, I had not paid careful enough attention either to some of the findings of fact or to some of the findings of moral law that are necessary to show how a *possible* deterrence posture and governing moral principles mesh together.[26]

14

The Justice of Deterrence

There are three ways, Ramsey suggests, in which deterrence can be obtained without involving the direct intention to cause the destruction the prospect of which deters.

In the first place, any fighting (not only in the nuclear age) is likely to have indirect effects on civilians. Nuclear war will cause great collateral civilian damage, and the prospect of such damage will deter anyone from nuclear warfare.[1] Second, the existence and possession of nuclear weapons is in itself a deterrent, whatever our real or declared intentions about the use of them. No nation can safely assume that an opponent would never resort to their use against cities and populations, even if it is his declared intention not to do so: "No matter how often we declare, and quite sincerely declare, that our targets are an enemy's forces, he can never be quite *certain* that in the fury or the fog of war his cities may not be destroyed." Third, and only if enough deterrence, so to speak, is not yielded by the two points just outlined, we come to the proposal for deterrence by bluff. Ramsey words this as follows:

> The distinction between the *appearance* and the *actuality* of being partially or totally committed to go to city exchanges may have to be employed in deterrence policy. In that case, only the appearance should be cultivated.[2]

Ramsey defends this proposal, albeit reluctantly, against the charge that it is immoral because it intends to deceive an enemy. This, however, overlooks the much more serious moral charges that can be brought against such a policy, which in the end forced Ramsey to withdraw the bluff argument outlined here.

These three points form the basis of the debate in 1965. During that

169

debate, Ramsey greatly complicates his position by introducing a new phrase: "A threat of something disproportionate is not necessarily a disproportionate threat." It is not immediately clear how this is related to these first three elements, and, indeed, this new phrase is loaded with obscurity and ambiguity.

This shift to advocating the possible morality of a realistic nuclear deterrent is but the first of a number of shifts and complexities that appear in the course of the discussion in 1965. As we will see, a complicated position is harder to appreciate when presented in debate.

The 1965 Debate

This debate was collected together in *Peace, the Churches and the Bomb*, which needs to be read in conjunction with Ramsey's papers, *The Limits of Nuclear War* and *Again, the Justice of Deterrence*.[3] This debate has attracted comments from, among others, Charles Curran, Richard McCormick, and Michael Walzer. Walzer surely voices a common reaction, when he says that Ramsey's analysis

> involves him in a highly sophisticated application of just war theory to the problems of nuclear strategy. In the best sense of the word, Ramsey is engaged with the realities of his world. But the realities in this case are intractable, and his way around them is finally too complex and too devious to provide a plausible account of our moral judgments. He multiplies distinctions like a Ptolemaic astronomer with his epicycles and comes very close at the end to what G.E.M. Anscombe has called "double-think about double-effect." But his work is important; it suggests the outer limits of the just war and the dangers of trying to extend those limits.[4]

Although Walzer finds Ramsey both "complex" and "devious," he goes on to offer a substantially accurate, clear, and concise account of Ramsey's position. He does not, however, quite do justice to the meaning of two crucial terms in the discussion. These are the use of the word "collateral" in the analysis of double effect, and the problem of proportion and disproportion in war and deterrence. In fact it may well be that Ramsey's wording on these points has misled many as to his actual position on nuclear deterrence. Walzer's comment about the "outer limits" is a significant one; Ramsey himself used the same phrase in 1973: "I am a moralist whose business it is to try to indicate the *outer* limits of a possible moral deterrent if one has to go that far to find a feasible way effectively to limit war in a nuclear age."[5]

The arguments concern the moral character of bluff, the application of the principle of proportion to the making of threats, and the correct use to be made of the principle of double effect. On bluff, Ramsey reluctantly withdrew his argument. On the questions concerning double effect and the principle of proportion, Ramsey, in my view, withstood his opponents, but his formulations need to be read with great caution and might appear at a casual glance to justify rather more deterrence than they actually do.

The agenda for our survey of the debate is best taken from our outline of the concluding section of *The Limits of Nuclear War*. To the three (or four) points presented there we add the question over proportion and disproportion.

It may help if we briefly headline Ramsey's position. There are five ways in which it may be justified to deter an enemy from threatening or using nuclear weapons against our cities and populations:

1. Deterrence arising from the threat of massive destruction of military targets.

2. Deterrence arising from the threat of massive collateral civilian destruction.

3. Deterrence flowing from the mere possession of nuclear weapons.

4. Deterrence from threatening to use nuclear weapons directly against civilians, while not intending to (deterrence of bluff).

5. Deterrence from threats of disproportionate action.[6]

Many of the main points are argued between Ramsey and Stein, so we will take their arguments as controlling the flow of our exposition, while drawing in the others at appropriate junctures. Before we embark on this, we must establish what precisely is the common ground between the protagonists.

First there are some points of moral philosophy. Ramsey and Stein are in no doubt that it is immoral to intend to do an immoral act, and immoral to threaten to do one, if that involves the intention. This remains true no matter how hypothetical or conditional the threat may be. (Ramsey, as we will see, wants to make an exception where a threat is not really or seriously intended, but bluff of one kind or another. This exception does not weaken his allegiance to the general moral truth in most circumstances.) We can also be clear that the word "immoral" is intended by both in a strong sense. There can be no "trading-off" of immorality for the sake of greater benefits or desirable consequences—even if the immorality is "theoretical" in nature and the consequences of global significance. That Ramsey has a different view of the necessity of nuclear deterrence does not allow him to soften his observance of moral principle.

Then there is also general agreement on some substantial matters of the morality of war. Both hold a very similar understanding of the just war tradition, in particular the principle of noncombatant immunity.

Stein is willing to accept in theory that there may be nuclear weapons which can be discriminately aimed.[7] This theoretical concession is enough for further argument to proceed, although Stein is unwilling to grant that it is of any significance, for he wishes to make a forthright condemnation of the present state of affairs: "The underlying moral fact [is that present deterrence] involves massively murderous commitments *in its total structure—here and now.*"[8]

For the moment, we should just note this commitment of Stein's. The main burden of Ramsey's arguments is not to defend current policy against such charges; it is rather to explore the theoretical questions about whether and how it is possible to mount an effective moral deterrent in the nuclear age. We will return later to the question of how close Ramsey himself believes U.S. policy to be to such a deterrent.

Later in the debate Ramsey questions whether Stein will allow that there can be any just war,[9] and indeed Stein's nuclear pacifism does sometimes veer very close to full-blown pacifism. For instance, one might cite the introductory chapter in *Nuclear Weapons and Christian Conscience*. Nevertheless, the two argue with each other within a clearly definable tradition. Ramsey says of Stein at one point: "His premises and categories of analysis are close to my own."[10] We are now ready, I think, to begin the survey of the debate itself. The first point need not detain us long.

(1) Deterrence Arising from the Threat of Massive Destruction of Military Targets

This point does not form the basis for any lengthy moral discussion for the simple reason that this is relatively uncontroversial, especially in comparison with the other points at issue. (It may be, however, as we will see, that Ramsey means us to read "disproportionate" for "massive" here, but this we can pass over now, assuming that only justified counterforce fighting is in view.)

Here we should note that Ramsey would prefer to see this as the basic and only component of deterrence if possible: "I'd be happy, also, if strategic thinkers could come up with models or arrangements that do not need the other elements of my scheme of graduated deterrent."[11]

Here seems to be the main shift that took place in Ramsey's thinking on deterrence between 1961 and 1963. In 1961 he believed that the only credible way to deter a nuclear armed enemy threatening massive destruction was by responding in kind (i.e., threatening thermonuclear war with the planned general destruction of cities[12]). By 1963 he came to be convinced that a credible deterrent could be mounted by just war means.

But this type of deterrence must be considered along with the inevitable side-effects on civilians and civilian life. It is not possible to attack combatants and military forces without causing collateral civilian damage. This leads to a point much contested by Stein: whether the collateral effects, which are unwanted and unaimed at, can still be wanted for purposes of deterrence. Stein argues that they must not be wanted in any sense.

We turn, then, to the question of the civilian damage associated with discriminate nuclear warfare. Our aim is to clarify Ramsey's point and defend it against the charges brought by Stein and McCormick.

(2) Deterrence Arising from the Threat of Massive Collateral Civilian Destruction

Both Stein and Ramsey get into verbal tangles in discussing this point, stemming partly from Ramsey's first expression of it. His first phrasing was, "The deterrent effect . . . is then, as it were, an indirect effect of the foreseeable indirect effects of legitimate military conduct." However, the way in which he wished he had phrased it was: "[the deterrent effect is] a *direct* and *wanted* effect of the unwanted, indirect, collateral consequences of even a just use of nuclear weapons." And again:

It is entirely moral to intend to derive deterrence as, in the objective order, a *direct* effect flowing from the mutual prospect of the indirect

consequences of acts of war planned and intended to be properly placed
in a nuclear age.[13]

Ramsey is making the simple point that although counterforce nuclear war may be discriminating, it will have a vast and unwanted
destructive effect on civilian populations ("collateral damage" or
"indirect consequences"). This is collateral damage resulting from war
between military forces only. The prospect of this damage deters us
from undertaking even discriminate military struggle, so we are morally correct to want this prospect of enormous destruction in order that
we and our enemies may be mutually deterred from fighting. Stein's
objection to this is the obvious question: Is it legitimate to want the
prospect of something which is in itself radically unwanted, namely,
the side-effect of our warring acts?

Stein's objection to "collateral deterrence" is that we are depending
on deterrence for the unwanted secondary effect—in other words that
we must want what we ought not to want. Stein calls this a "radical
abuse of double-effect categories," linking his criticism with the well-
known remark of Anscombe on "double-think about double-effect."[14]
However, a reading of Anscombe's article makes clear that her criticism is of the abuse of double effect whereby, for instance, a bomber
of a city "directs his intention" to the killing of troops, with any
innocent bloodshed being "accidental." This is merely to equivocate
about one's intention. Subjective intention cannot be separated from
the structure of the act—one cannot let go of the bomb and at the same
time make a little speech to oneself about "What I mean to be doing."[15]
Stein knows that Ramsey knows this, but he still argues that to "want"
the collateral damage for purposes of deterrence proves that the
"collateral" damage was never really collateral, but actually wanted
and intended.

But this is to miss Ramsey's point altogether. It is the *prospect* of
damage that deters, not the damage itself. The damage in question is
unavoidably attached to justified war fighting, and by contemplating it
we and the enemy are made all the more reluctant to fight. Since we
are deterred by the prospect of damage, it is not wrong to want (in one
sense) that prospect for the sake of deterrence, although we certainly
do not want the damage itself. At the same time, there is a sense in
which the prospect is neither wanted nor unwanted, it is simply there,
unavoidably attached to any just war.

Ramsey attempts to clarify this by analogy with some medical
research. He outlines a research program carried out by a Dr. Rock in

conjunction with medical hysterectomies.[16] Dr. Rock's aim was to examine the development of the fertilized human ovum over the first seventeen days from fertilization. To obtain these ova, Dr. Rock performed his hysterectomies at the best times in the ovulation cycle. The analogy with collateral deterrence arises out of a consideration of the way in which records were kept, and the way in which women were asked to avoid or facilitate pregnancy. Ramsey argues that if the women knew nothing of the experimental purpose, then the deaths of these embryos could properly be described as "incidental," brought about indirectly. If, on the other hand, the women had been encouraged to get themselves pregnant, then the deaths of the ova would no longer be properly describable as incidental, because they would be actually intended (at least by the doctors, perhaps also by the mothers).

It has to be questioned whether this analogy substantially clarifies the point Ramsey wishes to make about nuclear deterrence. Whether the reader finds it clarifies the issues, or rather hinders one from obtaining a clearer view of them, there is a more serious problem. The weakness of Ramsey's analogy is that it compares the prospect of civilian damage with the actual death of the fetus (as a result of which it is available for research). The wanted deterrence is quite compatible with minimizing the unwanted side-effects, while the wanted research is incompatible with minimizing the unwanted deaths of fetuses. This weakness in the analogy opens the way for McCormick's objection.

McCormick takes up this analogy and introduces a new idea to it. He argues that the doctors should have actively discouraged the women from becoming pregnant in view of the forthcoming hysterectomy. He deduces from Ramsey's failure to consider this point that Ramsey is not sufficiently concerned to avoid civilian destruction:

> The point is important; for otherwise Ramsey is equivalently saying that there is no duty to try to avoid collateral civilian damage by warning the civilian population to evacuate areas around legitimate target sites. I believe there is such a duty whenever this is compatible with achievement of the military objective. This reflection points to the fact that use of collateral damage as a deterrent, while it is perfectly justifiable on paper, is or can be a very dangerous way of thinking in practice.[17]

Perhaps McCormick is right to say that Dr. Rock should have warned his patients to avoid conception before their operation, but he uses Ramsey's silence on this point (or rather his defense of what is

assumed to be Dr. Rock's procedure) to infer that Ramsey's allegiance
to a policy of avoiding collateral civilian destruction is not quite
wholehearted. We must read McCormick here carefully, for all McCormick will say is that Ramsey's argument is "perfectly justifiable on
paper" but that it "can be a very dangerous way of thinking in
practice."[18] We might reply to McCormick that this is indeed a dangerous world.

However, if McCormick fears that Ramsey is too relaxed about the
extent of civilian damage, his point is quite unfair, for Ramsey is at
pains to point out elsewhere that we must always try to avoid collateral
damage as much as possible. Our concern is with the unavoidable. If
we could avoid it, we certainly should:

> We are speaking of the unavoidable and radically unwanted damage that
> will take place in a policy of "counter-force plus *avoidance*" of as much
> civil destruction as it is possible to avoid. It is the prospect of *this* that
> deters. We are not speaking of any measure of additional, purposefully
> essential, radically wanted or indispensable civil destruction such as
> would be entailed in "counter-force plus *bonus* civil damage."[19]

Suppose, however, that a politician understanding this point feared
that strategies justified by this argument were still insufficient to
provide a credible deterrent. McCormick here points out that Ramsey's talk of collateral civilian damage may mislead our hypothetical
politician into failing to take steps to avoid the prospect of civilian
damage. Walzer's comment that "the word 'collateral' seems to have
lost most of its meaning" bears this out.[20] Walzer's main objection is
very similar to that of Stein. Walzer argues that Ramsey's argument is
undermined because he "relies so heavily on the deaths he supposedly
doesn't intend." This would seem to support McCormick's contention
that Ramsey's formulation might be read to imply that we should
design strategies to cause the greatest collateral damage, and hence
the strongest possible deterrent.[21] Does this lead us into a dilemma?
We may be pulled in two directions.

On the one hand, we make the most of the destructive power of our
new weapons, for we believe that by this an enemy is deterred and war
prevented. On the other hand, we are morally bound to take every step
to reduce the destructive power of those weapons, as to their side-
effects, and to generally avoid the extent of "collateral civilian damage" in the event of their use. Does this avoidance of prospective
damage not lessen the deterrent effect, by reducing the possible scale

of destruction? Ramsey may sometimes give the impression that this could perhaps be a real dilemma for his moral theory, but it cannot really be a dilemma at all.

The moral instruction which Ramsey himself has given us (not to speak of other arguments) makes this quite plain. There is an overriding moral duty to find counterforce weapons with minimum side-effects. (In 1973, in fact, Ramsey went further and argued that we should aspire not so much to a counterforce policy as to a countercombatant policy.[22]) The weapons must be "cleaned up," made more accurate, less destructive, with the minimum of civilian damage in prospect. Ramsey strongly criticized the siting of missiles and associated military bases in and near cities rather than in wide desert spaces. Such siting exposes those cities to the possibility of legitimate military attack.[23]

In the end, then, even if Ramsey's formulation is misleading to the careless reader, and after allowing that the debate with Stein does become verbally intricate, and difficult to follow at times, the main point is both clear and accurate.[24] Is it not also true that it has been the prospect of widespread damage that has contributed to the nonuse of any nuclear weapons since World War II?[25] Given, then, that there may be just counterforce uses for nuclear weapons, we are right to deter and be deterred by thinking of the damage their actual use could cause.

In this discussion, the question of proportion or disproportion has not arisen. But we should put the reader on notice that it remains a question whether Ramsey thinks that we may deter with threats of disproportionate, but still discriminate, destruction of military targets and the associated civilian destruction. When discussing deterrence of military destruction, we postponed this question, and we must now do the same again here.

There are two more elements in Ramsey's proposal. One of these has to do with the mere possession of nuclear weapons. Once possessed, they are an irremovable deterrent, no matter what we declare about our intentions. It is clear that this can only be held legitimate by someone who already thinks that these weapons could have some legitimate use. The fourth and final element is the deterrence of bluff. This Ramsey first suggested, unhappily, and then in the end he withdrew it.

(3) Deterrence Flowing from the Mere Possession of Nuclear Weapons

Any possession of nuclear weapons carries with it the inherent possibility that they could be used against an enemy city. However much it is declared and intended that one side will not resort to countercity warfare, no other nation can or should take the risk of assuming this to be an absolute guarantee—in "the fury or fog of war" who knows what might happen? It should be noted that such deterrence depends on the legitimacy of possessing these weapons in the first place. If there can be no legitimate ground for discriminating and moral use of nuclear weapons, there can be no morality in the threat of their use, and no morality in their possession. On the other hand, anyone who possesses these weapons must devise a policy for their possible use. If they are merely kept, unready, in stockpiles, then there can be no serious threat in their possession. It needs to be noticed that this is not an argument from bluff—in some ways it is the very reverse of that.[26]

Stein does not accept Ramsey's argument here. In the first place, he uses Ramsey's point about inherent uncertainty to argue that this unpredictable aspect of nuclear weapons in itself renders their possession and possible use "gravely immoral." In response to Stein here we need only point to Ramsey's condemnations of being out of control and of policies that depend on "the rationality of irrationality." The uncertainty is inherent; it is neither planned nor wanted in itself. Second, Stein argues that this undesirable "side-effect" of nuclear weapons is open to the same objections as the "collateral deterrence" argument—in other words an *unwanted* secondary effect which is really *wanted* for the purpose of deterrence. Again Stein misses Ramsey's point. Here we are talking of the inbuilt dangers of nuclear weapons in a dangerous and unpredictable international community (especially in time of war). The very fact of the existence and possession of nuclear weapons is a deterrent; in a sense their use is neither wanted nor unwanted in this connection. The things are simply there.

This is made clear when Ramsey confronts the objection that his scheme of graduated deterrence will not be sufficient against threats of ultimate destruction. In answer to this, he first remarks that threatening this very thing is not a certain way of preventing it, but he recognizes that even this irrational threat needs to be deterred:

> Deterrence of the *ultimate* threat of destruction had better be left to the simple philosophic consequence of the possession of nuclear weapons (Kahn), the subjectively unintended consequence of the mere possession of these weapons[27]

The importance of this kind of deterrence, which Ramsey learned from Kahn and others, has been taken up by Kenny in *The Logic of Deterrence*.[28]

(4) Deterrence from Threatening to Use Nuclear Weapons Directly Against Civilians, While Not Intending to (Deterrence of Bluff)

Bluff is the deterrence that comes from our ambiguity and equivocation about our possible use of weapons, which, however, we secretly resolve we never will use.

This sort of deterrence we can also deal with quite briefly. Rather reluctantly Ramsey did advance this in *The Limits of Nuclear War*, but he later withdrew it. This withdrawal of the argument was not as clear or unequivocal or well published as the initial argument, but in the end it was definite enough.

The argument is put in terms of a distinction "between the *appearance* and the *actuality* of being partially or totally committed to go to city exchanges."[29] Ramsey first argues that a deception of this nature against an enemy might either not be wrong (as certain forms of deceit and secrecy are legitimate in war), or if morally objectionable, then less so than the intention to commit murder, and ultimately justified by the necessity to save life. Even given this argument about deception, Ramsey still hopes "that the first two types of deterrence must, if at all possible, be made to work." It was in the first place because he was assured that the first two types of deterrence (collateral deterrence and inherent deterrence) were in fact sufficient that he stopped advocating deterrence by bluff. However, he only admitted "some shift of emphasis," while still arguing that bluff, or *ambiguity*, is a legitimate policy from a moral point of view. The position put forward in *The Limits of Nuclear War* is still maintained in *Again, The Justice of Deterrence*; that is to say, Ramsey still wishes to justify *the deception* practiced against an enemy of pretending to be ready to use force immorally.[30]

But he did not attempt to justify it against a more serious charge. In a later section of *Again, The Justice of Deterrence*, he admits:

> I am personally most troubled by Walter Stein's contention that a government cannot maintain nuclear deterrence from which *its own* murderous intention to use nuclear weapons against a whole society has been removed without still "authoritatively leading its own subjects into a gravely sinful consent."[31]

While not accepting that this argument is sufficient to fault all nuclear deterrence, Ramsey does admit its force. The problem is that though the top authorities know that they will never directly attack

cities, they wish to leave the enemy fearing that they may. In order to
do this, the ordinary soldiers and citizens also believe that this is a
possibility that may be intended. This is something that they ought to
know to be unjust, and so to require or lead them to such an intention,
even as only a conditional possibility, is to lead them into "murderous
thinking":

> If this element of deterrence is practiced, can a government avoid leading
> its people into gravely immoral motives? How in fact can it shield them
> from murderous thinking and from genocidal commitments out of hatred
> and mortal despair?[32]

At this point, Ramsey's acceptance of the objection does not appear
to be complete. He only "hesitatingly or subjunctively" wishes to
argue that deterrence of bluff is justifiable. It has only "probable
morality." But at this stage he is unwilling to withdraw it altogether:

> It is possible, however, to begin to unpack an average citizen's relation to
> his government's deterrence from ambiguous willingness so as not to
> leave him so indiscriminately black in his intentions as the objection
> supposes. I have only a few questions to raise in this connection, without
> asserting that the points I will make, which I believe are valid, add up to
> the entire removal of the objection.[33]

The question that Ramsey has at this point concerns the extent to
which the average citizen actually believes in his government's policies, or can be held responsible and guilty in complicity with them. Of
course, this does not touch the heart of the problem which is that,
insofar as the citizen does wish to identify with his country's policies
and support them, he is actually being led into sinful consent. It does
Ramsey's case no good either, to allege, as he does, that many others
than political leaders speak wrongly in this sphere:

> I cannot . . . exculpate publicists and leaders of opinion of all sorts,
> editors, teachers, churchmen, moralists, etc., who often seek to save the
> world by inciting extremes of fear and extremes in moral condemnation
> that responsible leaders know better than to share or inculcate.[34]

So, even though Ramsey's original defense of a policy of deliberate
ambiguity about a willingness to bomb cities was reluctant, his abandonment of this aspect of a graduated moral deterrent is still less than

straightforward in *The Just War*. Fortunately he makes his position clearer in later writings.

In two articles, published in 1972 and 1973, he makes a statement that more or less amounts to a definite withdrawal of the argument on moral grounds:

> . . . and, finally, deterrence from a "bluffing" manner in which these weapons are possessed. I now think that an input of deliberate ambiguity about the counter-people use of nuclear weapons is not possible unless it is (immorally) meant, and not a very good idea in the first place. But, again, I was marking off the outer limits of justice in deterrence, if this final ingredient were needed in crisis to prevent holocaust. But I gather that few experts today think it a feasible "performance."[35]

There is here no mention of the argument put forward by Stein and partly conceded by Ramsey, namely, that this policy of bluff must lead the citizens into a sinful consent. Fortunately an article published in *Newsweek* in June 1982, which summarized Ramsey's just war thought, drew a definite response from him. In this article, Walter Goodman wrote:

> Ramsey defended nuclear deterrence as "bluff." Deterrence is moral, he argued, if a nuclear nation is resolved never to use the weapon to strike at a foe's cities, even though this is not announced to the potential foe.[36]

In a letter to the magazine Ramsey made quite clear for the first time in print that he had renounced this:

> Those arguments [sc. defending "bluff"] were insufficient, indeed disturbingly insufficient, within the year. The "bluff" was withdrawn from my analysis of a possibly moral deterrence. Again, my reasons were two: (1) one's *real* intentions (*not* to go to such use) will be found out; the "bluff" must fail to deter; and (2) even if our top political and military leaders were pure in heart, they *must* count on thousands of men in missile silos, planes and submarines to be conditionally willing, under some circumstances, to become murderers. One should never occasion mortal sin in another, tempt them to it, or enlist them for it.[37]

In this same letter Ramsey continued to maintain and defend his statement about disproportionate threats, to which we now turn.

15

Deterrence, Threats, and Disproportion

A shadow is thrown over the view of nuclear deterrence apparently put forward in *The Limits of Nuclear War* by a later assertion that it may be justified to threaten to act disproportionately. We must now try to untangle the reasons Ramsey has for claiming this, and the implications for his theory as a whole.

That any nuclear warfare is soon likely to become disproportionate to any political or military goals is a point first made in this debate by O'Brien:

> Finally, of critical importance, the just war doctrine does not deal with modern deterrence wherein *disproportionate* (in terms of traditional military utility) threats are seemingly the indispensable means of avoiding general war.[1]

Ramsey replies with a statement that proves alarmingly recalcitrant to careful analysis. It is a statement confusing in its epigrammatic simplicity:

> A threat of something disproportionate is not necessarily a disproportionate threat.

and again:

> One ought not to say that, just as a real threat or intention to do murder is a murderous threat, so also to threaten something disproportionate is a disproportionate threat.[2]

(For the sake of convenience, we will refer to the first of these two sentences as "the Proposition.")

There are at least three possible glosses, or interpretations, of the Proposition that we could make.³ To arrive at these, to see which of them may correctly be held, and which Ramsey meant, is the task in front of us. We will tackle this by considering to which of the four types of deterrence the Proposition should be attached.

We note that for our present analysis we may bracket together threats of combatant damage with the associated deterrence arising from the prospect of collateral civilian damage. In this interpretation, we should read "disproportionate military destruction" for "massive military destruction," etc. Alternatively, we might consider that making disproportionate threats is a species of bluff, and consider the Proposition under this heading. Finally, of course, it has to be considered whether more than one of the possible readings should be understood simultaneously. We shall see that this was probably what Ramsey himself thought.

We consider first the possibility that this is a version of deterrence by bluff. In this case we should gloss the Proposition as follows:

(a) A threat of something disproportionate is not necessarily a disproportionate threat, because a threat is not always fully intended, it may be partly or wholly a bluff.

This way of reading the Proposition supposes that what is meant is that threats are not necessarily made with the full and defined intention of carrying them out. Threats can be made that are firmly intended, or at the other extreme, as pure bluff. In between, no doubt most threats are made in some uncertainty or indecision, hoping never actually to come to the question of execution—"Will we really do this?"

In considering this interpretation we may first ask whether this is what Ramsey himself intended. There are some indications that it is. In two of the explanations Ramsey gave of what he meant, he certainly included this idea as part of his meaning:

Threats that would if carried out have disproportionate military utility may well have proportionate military utility so long as they are unemployed, and are intended to be unemployed, or so long as they are employed for deterrent effect, to enforce shared limits upon actual fighting, and to keep war itself proportionate to political purposes. There is disproportion here only when done, not when merely threatened; and the threat is well ordered to the prevention of disproportionate evil in actuality.

In 1972 he offered three points in defense of threatening disproportionate damage in deterrence. The third was: "that, of course, there is an obligation never to mean to do and accept damage disproportionate to political goals; but I suppose no military commander would actually calculate on doing any such thing."[4]

Ramsey is here trading on the real vagueness involved in the business of threatening, and of a potential gap between a threat and the clearly formed intention. He points out that deterrent threats, especially in war, often have the nature of bluff. There are, after all, different kinds of bluff. There is the simple bluff, when we are not at all prepared to do what we threaten. At the other extreme there is a different gap between threat and intention (which we would hardly call "bluff"), in which the threat is unspoken, and the intention unformed. This is rather close to the deterrence inherent in the mere possession of weapons. In between these two is no doubt a range of preparation and threat, spoken, hinted and unspoken, but all designed to leave the enemy in uncertainty and dissuade him from injustice and aggression.

To all of these the same truth continues to apply, "that it is immoral to intend anything it would be immoral to do." We must continue to combine this with the fact that it is immoral to threaten an immoral action (whether or not it is truly intended) if this leads soldiers and citizens into holding that immoral intention. Both of these truths were things which Ramsey himself held and taught.[5] It is for this reason we must argue that this is not an acceptable interpretation of Ramsey's Proposition, and one that he could not consistently have held, for he continued to advance the proposition that "A threat of something disproportionate is not necessarily a disproportionate threat" long after he had abandoned the argument for deterrence by ambiguous countercity bluffing.[6] At the same time, we must remember that Ramsey believed that there are things which are disproportionate in such a way that they should never be intended. They would include, for instance, policies which built in inevitable escalation of military action: "It is possible to define, for the instruction of the consciences of political leaders, what would be intrinsically immoral because it is already intrinsically disproportionate in this matter of deterrence."

He gives as an example:

> It is wrong to be resolved at any point to put oneself out of control, no matter how much peace-by-deterrence results from it. To *commit* oneself to "rationality of irrationality" policies would be the epitome of irrationality and political immorality.

If this is what deterrence means, "then deterrence would be intrinsically and irremediably disproportionate, and most wicked."[7]

There are things that are disproportionate in such a way that they may never be threatened, whether seriously or in a bluffing fashion. This draws our attention to the point that we need to investigate different kinds of disproportion, and the potential ambiguities of the word "disproportionate" rather than concentrate on the ambiguities of threatening.

That deterrence by bluff is not the point on which we should hang too much here is supported by a remark of O'Brien, which Ramsey appears to agree with in a footnote. O'Brien argues:

In so subjective and sensitive an area of human interaction I think there is much to be said for bone dry honesty to oneself and to one's enemies (not to mention one's friends) when it comes to making threats. In other words, it seems better to threaten and, to the extent that this is practical, to *seem* to threaten only what one is actually prepared to do if the deterrent fails.[8]

We can now summarize the discussion of our first gloss (a) of the Proposition. We have asked whether the Proposition is a version of deterrence of bluff, and answered that this should not have been Ramsey's meaning. If there is any moral truth in gloss (a) of the Proposition, it is that it may well be right to hold a *capability* to inflict disproportionate damage, while avoiding and disowning the intention ever to use it. This interpretation is a restatement of deterrence of possession; it exploits the ambiguity in the word "threat." However, it does not appear to be the main sense that Ramsey had in mind in his Proposition.

In order to understand whether Ramsey's Proposition has a defensible point to make, we must inquire further about the kind of disproportionate damage he had in mind. When we reexamine Ramsey's advocacy of deterrence arising from the threats of military destruction and collateral civilian damage, points (1) and (2) above, we find that he had disproportionate damage in mind all along.

Let us remind ourselves of the formulations in *The Limits of Nuclear War*. There Ramsey wrote: "The collateral civilian damage that would result from counter-forces warfare in its maximum form may itself be quite sufficient to deter."[9] In examining this point earlier we assumed that this meant not only discriminate, but also proportionate, warfare. However, a question now arises whether it was all along meant that we should here understand "maximum" to read "discriminate but possibly disproportionate." And when we come to later discussions, we find that this is indeed how Ramsey and his contemporaries construed it.

Let us take Ramsey first. In *Again, the Justice of Deterrence,* he wrote: "In addition to deterrence from disproportionate combatant damage with its associated deterrence from the prospect of extensive collateral damage, I analyzed two additional respects."[10]

That this is not a verbal slip is shown by a repetition on the following page, and other instances. Let us just take "Can a Pacifist Tell a Just War?"—an article written in 1968.[11] Here Ramsey takes up the criticisms of James Douglass, who analyzed his claims to have put forward a theory of justified nuclear deterrence. Ramsey admits to espousing the morality of "deterrence from the expectation of disproportionate collateral damage accompanying legitimate strikes and in the case of shared deterrence stemming from the ambiguous uses modern weapons have in themselves."[12]

Stein picks up the phrase quite early in the debate. He sets out a summary of the proposals in *The Limits of Nuclear War* that includes:

(A) Deterrence from "disproportionate 'combatant' damage."

(B) Deterrence from "the prospect of extensive damage collateral even in 'justly targeted' nuclear war."[13]

We accept then that this is the right way to approach the construing of our Proposition. Ramsey offers slightly varying explanations in two or three places. From these it is possible to identify two main points, each offering us a way of reading the Proposition.

(b) The threat of an apparently disproportionate act is not necessarily a disproportionate threat, until made in a specific well-defined situation.

This interpretation has to do with the principle of proportion, drawing attention to its breadth and flexibility. A judgment under this principle can only be made with an eye to all the surrounding circumstances and context at the time of a specific action. There are many things that would be disproportionate under most conceivable circumstances, but not under all.

This is the first point Ramsey makes in his first discussion of disproportionate threats. He points out: "The disproportion 'in terms of traditional military utility' of which O'Brien speaks is a disproportionate act *when done* and only when done or when very concretely contemplated."[14]

There is a distinction then between the apparently and the definitely disproportionate. The kind of disproportion Ramsey wants to permit to be threatened is limited to the kind that might not be disproportionate under some circumstances. In one other place Ramsey makes clear that this is what is in his mind, among other things. He offers a variety of conditions in which a citizen would be justified in objecting to policies of deterrence resting on threats of disproportionate damage. He may object "if he is soberly convinced that he knows that the use of weapons planned to meet any eventuality is *actually* disproportionate."[15]

To spell out interpretation (b), we may recall our earlier analysis of the principle of proportion, covering some of the salient points of Ramsey's understanding.[16] This is the principle that anatomizes the nature of political reason and political realism. It tells us only to try to do good, to bring about a balance of good effects, greater gains than costs. This is often a very difficult matter to judge, even with hindsight. Who is to say, for instance, that Russia's national identity was or was not worth the many millions of lives spent for it in World War II?[17] If Britain had failed to retake the Falkland Islands in 1982, and the Task Force had come limping home at the cost of many lives, who could have condemned the decision to fight if they had supported it both prospectively, and in the event retrospectively also?[18]

Ramsey also points out that political decisions never have the luxury of hindsight. They have always to be ventured; they can never be taken in complete certainty of success. Even a reasonable probability of success may be too much to ask on occasion. In support of this, Ramsey is fond of the example of Britain's defiance in 1940, when there was little prospect of success.[19]

Both of these considerations must mean, then, that it may be very difficult to make the charge of disproportion stick. This is bound to be even more the case when no very precise circumstances are in view. When a nation prepares its military capabilities, on the contrary, it has a responsibility to be ready for almost anything. Even an apparently stable and friendly power may suffer, perhaps, a dramatic change of government and direction. What a nation is able to threaten justly as a deterrent, or be capable of threatening and carrying out, may therefore legitimately be out of proportion to any present cause or likely need.

All this means that we must be very careful to distinguish between a definitely, or actually, or categorically disproportionate act, and one which is merely apparent, contemplated or hypothetical. It is perhaps the major weakness of Ramsey's discussions that he does not make this distinction sufficiently clear. Unless this distinction is made, the Proposition that "a threat of something disproportionate is not necessarily a disproportionate threat" could never be acceptable. If something is definitely disproportionate, then it is immoral. To threaten an immoral act is always immoral, and it is beside the point to discuss whether such a threat is disproportionate or not. Of course, it still could be a "proportionate" threat, at least in the sense that an indiscriminate act could perhaps be proportionate.[20]

Once we have this point clearly established, we can consider another way in which the relation between threat and action may widen the scope of judgments of proportionality. Another of Ramsey's explanations of his Proposition leads us to offer interpretation (c):

(c) The threat of something disproportionate is not necessarily a disproportionate threat, because the gains and costs of the threat are not the same as those of the action itself.

This interpretation draws attention to the fact that a threat may well be made in quite different circumstances to the prospective act, and aimed at a different goal. The judgment of proportion or disproportion has therefore to be made in a different way. In particular, a deterrent threat is aimed at preserving world peace and security. The limits of what is threatened can therefore reasonably go quite high. Our second and third interpretations lead us to say:

When a disproportionate action is transposed *in mente* into a deterrent threat, we ought not thoughtlessly to continue to speak of the *threat* as disproportionate. This may or may not be the case. We need to remember the evil which the threat is ordered to prevent and with which it must be compared. A threat of something that would be disproportionate, and which would exceed any of the reasonable purposes of fighting if carried out, may be *proportionate* when weighed against the graver evil that is prevented by the threat. It can fall within the purposes to which deterrence should reasonably be ordered, namely, the prevention of the much graver evil of general war and the enforcing of limits upon disproportionate military actions by either side.

If we were to take (c) on its own, it would overlook the basic point that to threaten something definitely disproportionate is an immoral threat. It is beside the point that it may not be a disproportionate threat, but we do not need to dismiss what Ramsey has to say on this.

We may read point (c) in conjunction with point (b). Let us remind ourselves what ends deterrence has in view in the nuclear age. If we go back again to *The Limits of Nuclear War,* we remember that the problem Ramsey is tackling is the maintenance of limits on warfare, so that an enemy may be dissuaded from using his force unjustly, or from threatening to do so.[21] It is clear that in this context the aims of actually using nuclear weapons would be similar to the aims of threatening their use—namely, enforcing limits on warfare, and preserving or restoring peace. With this in mind, let us return to (c) to see if it should be reworded more accurately. Our first attempt read:

(c) The threat of something disproportionate is not necessarily a disproportionate threat, because the gains and costs of the threat are not the same as those of the action itself.

It is clear that we should rather put:

(c1) A threat of something apparently disproportionate (in terms of traditional military utility) is not necessarily a disproportionate threat, because the threat is not necessarily disproportionate when measured against the goal of world peace and security.

In this sense we can accept Ramsey's Proposition. When it is understood in this sense, we can also accept his point about the vagueness of intention that may lie behind such threatening. It may be a right political and military judgment to threaten excessive destruction which is neither indiscriminate nor yet definitely disproportionate (excessive, that is, in the likely circumstances of the threat being executed), while still believing that the threat need never be carried out. Whether the risks involved in such threats are politically appropriate or justifiable cannot be easily demonstrated, let alone in advance. Ramsey believed these risks to be an inherent aspect of deterrence, not only in the nuclear age. He also offered this explanation of disproportionate threats:

The issuance of threats of disproportionate destruction is ever the nature of deterrence under any conditions of warfare. One has to reject deterrence in general or in any war in order to reject this account of justifiable deterrence in a nuclear age. At the same time, it must be granted that herein lies the tragedy of war, namely, that threats of disproportionate damage, although proportionate to the end of deterrence, may be disproportionately actualized, and on both sides (as in the politically disproportionate countercombatant destruction in World War I). But this is a question of the immorality of warfare that has lost its objective or become disoriented from it. It is not a question of the morality of deterrence oriented upon *its* objective.

. . . of course, there is an obligation never to mean to do and accept damage disproportionate to political goals; but I suppose no military commander would actually calculate on doing any such thing.[22]

It is doubtful whether the World War I illustration helps Ramsey's point, for it is not clear that the destruction then was connected to any deterrent threats. One must also question whether a threat that is likely to be "disproportionately actualized" is one that is either necessary or helpful to genuine deterrence. Instead, we should remember Ramsey's own powerful critique of the uselessness of "unshootable" and irrational weapons (which is not withdrawn), and O'Brien's sober reminder about the realistic value of only making genuinely intended threats.[23]

Ramsey's statement that "A threat of something disproportionate is not necessarily a disproportionate threat" has unavoidably led us into a protracted discussion. We can now review the whole of his argument for a "graduated deterrent."

It is possible to mount a moral deterrent in the nuclear age, claims Ramsey, even against an opponent prepared to threaten indiscriminate, countercity use of his own weapons. A possible moral deterrent rests on two considerations. There is the deterrence gained from the prospect of the destruction inevitable in the counterforce (or countercombatant) use of nuclear weapons.[24] There is also deterrence inherent in the possession of such weapons, for no enemy can finally be sure that such weapons would never be used against cities (though that is never our intention, plan, or threat[25]).

A brief expansion of the meaning of these two ways of justly deterring an enemy will serve to summarize the main results of this chapter. There is justified deterrence arising from the threat of massive, apparently disproportionate, destruction of military targets, and the unavoidably associated collateral civilian destruction. In considering what is disproportionate here, we should bear in mind that (b) the threat of an apparently disproportionate act is not necessarily a disproportionate threat, until made in a specific well-defined situation, and specifically (c1) it may not be necessarily disproportionate when measured against the goal of world peace and security. Given that we legitimately possess these weapons, they themselves deter by their very existence. It is clear from Ramsey's analysis that this type of deterrence could only be moral if there were possible moral and rational uses for the weapons possessed. This argument cannot stand alone, but in Ramsey's analysis it does not need to.[26]

Is this moral method of nuclear deterrence sufficient to preserve world peace and security? Can the moralist be in a position to square the circle of this, the great political question of our age? We can now appreciate Ramsey's answer to this question.

Moral Theory and Political Reality

All this is a theoretical formulation, and it is necessary to ask what relation these moral limits have to political reality. This question is presented in two forms. What is the relation of all this to contemporary Western defense strategy? And how far does this moral limit allow the West to mount an effective deterrent that will preserve world peace and stability?

The first form of the question is whether this argument justifies contemporary U.S. policy, or whether it is intended to justify it. What relation does Ramsey think his argument bears to the criticism of actual political and strategic reality? To explore this question requires us to examine more closely his attitude to the actual military necessities confronting the United States. What is the moral duty of the United States in military terms? How does this moral duty meet the moral duty to limit the use of weapons, the threat of their use, and their possession for deterrence? Ramsey did not think it possible or desirable for the moralist to attempt to answer these questions directly. Ultimately, the morality of any action can only be fully decided by one with knowledge of all the relevant circumstances, and very often in political life, though of course not always, only the actor himself has that knowledge. The moralist's duty is to clarify as much as possible the terms of such decisions, or, in other words, to attend to questions of doctrine or thought (moral, political, etc.).

These questions thus lead us on to another of a more theoretical character. We recall, on one hand, Ramsey's views of the moralist's task. As moralists, our duty is to refrain from giving specific directives or pronouncements on actual or technical matters. We do not have the ability or the right to make definite applications, or diagnoses of technical matters or actual political decisions and actions. On the other hand, moral theory must be realistic, that is to say it must be conformed to the realities of the situation. Surely to make any moral pronouncement requires that we analyze "the facts" of the matter? Ramsey faces a real tension here, if not an actual contradiction.

Now it would be possible for Ramsey to satisfy this tension by keeping the discussion at a sufficiently theoretical level, using hypothetical arguments and so on. In theory, this is what Ramsey claims he is trying to do:

> The only way to tell whether a supposed factual situation is morally tolerable or intolerable is to be concerned primarily with the determination of what would be morally tolerable or intolerable in a specific area of action supposing certain conditions of fact.

In practice he does actually want to go further than that, and he admits that this has to be done. In discussing with Stein what would be a sufficiently effective deterrent, he admits:

> To raise this question is to come to a final assessment of where we are in connection with the respective judgments of fact to which neither of us is quite entitled but which nevertheless are unavoidably interwoven with our moral argument.[27]

The proponent of nuclear pacifism has also to make judgments of fact, Ramsey reminds us. Stein assumes that "a government resolve to treat non-combatant populations as inviolable" would mean "the dismantling . . . of the whole ultimate foundation of deterrence."[28] It is precisely this assumption that Ramsey challenges, and he believes that governments are moving in the direction he advocates:

> In fact, it can well be argued that the nuclear powers have already moved a long way toward placing the counter-city use of nuclear weapons in a class by itself, as a "war plan" (if such it can still be called) intended to be *not* used; . . .
> It ill behooves [*sic*] "moralists" to go about imbedding in the minds of people foolish and immoral notions of the necessary nature of deterrence or of modern war.[29]

Ramsey wants quite definitely to argue that it may be possible to find a nuclear deterrence policy that is both effective and moral. We can give another instance which indicates his belief that the United States was quite close to this sort of deterrence in the early 1960s:

> When at one of those famous Washington cocktail parties I was told by a man in the next to top echelons of the Pentagon, in the early days of the Kennedy administration and at the beginning of our policy of limited, flexible, graduated response, that the President had been briefed that *no*

matter what happened it didn't make sense to start striking cities, I was inclined to believe this; and to believe that our policy was the ambiguous no-cities one it should, at most, be.[30]

These statements are rather carefully phrased, and I think make clear that these are his own personal judgments of the particular situations. Ramsey's first purpose was always a theoretical one.

That it is a theoretical debate is a point that seems to have been overlooked by some of Ramsey's critics. Curran, for instance, simply avers that "there is too much deterrence" justified by these arguments. But this is not the point. The point must be not "how much" deterrence does Ramsey authorize. After all, deterrence is either effective and adequate, or inadequate and ineffective. Nor is the quantity of weapons held the first moral concern. It might be "too much" to give every soldier in the infantry two machine-guns for everyday maneuvers, but it would probably be quite reasonable to have as many weapons and more to hand in the armories for possible emergencies. It is not the stockpiles of weapons the moralist should first object to, so much as the policies for their use—the intentions and plans of generals, politicians and voters. The point rather is *what* deterrence does Ramsey think is morally justified.

Theoretician Ramsey may be, but there need be no mistaking that his theory has some very straightforward criticisms to make of existing policy and policy statements. For instance:

I have no cause to defend the tessellation of statements Stein cites from government officials. . . . We need to clean up our deterrence system, of course. . . . That commitments to genocide, built-in or intended-in, should be dismantled is also beyond question."[31]

All this follows from a simple agreement with Stein on a point from which Ramsey does not waver:

The question turns entirely upon what commitments are inherent in the Deterrence State. If this is now and must remain a *commitment* to execute city-hostages, as Stein supposes, then as long as we may allow any nuclear deterrence to stand we are all involved in and, in various degrees, responsible for constantly doing something that is most wicked.[32]

This quotation makes it even clearer that a moral analysis must make some assumptions about the facts if we are not all to be left in total moral suspense about our present situation. The claim that we can stand back as professional moralists from the specific judgments we each make does not really stand up: "Professionally, I should have no interest in proving a moral deterrent to be an effective one; and Stein should have no interest in proving the only effective deterrent to be necessarily immoral." It is clear that Ramsey is not prepared to leave it there. It is in any case not possible to remain in a purely hypothetical moral world. "But, of course, our ethical reflection begins with the facts we know or think we know, and it returns some judgment upon them."[33] The main fact to be debated is what actually constitutes a sufficient and effective deterrent. When we have examined this, we must ask if it falls within the outer limits of what may be a justifiable deterrent.

We saw earlier that Ramsey was concerned to press to the outer limits of a possibly moral deterrent.[34] Especially when he was advocating a policy of ambiguity or bluff, he was always somewhat reluctant, but there was a strong felt pressure to find a justifiable nuclear deterrent which would also be an effective one in the real world. This reluctance, and the pressure that overcame it, was evident in *The Limits of Nuclear War:*

> If the first two points above [deterrence from threat of collateral civilian damage, and from mere possession] do not seem to the military analyst sufficiently persuasive, or *able to be made so,* then an *apparent* resolution to wage war irrationally or at least an *ambiguity* about our intentions may have to be our expressed policy.

and

> Perhaps we should say that we ought to be conditionally willing to strive for this ingredient in deterrence, that is, *on the condition that it is necessary to deter and to save life.*[35]

We can see in these two quotes a serious concern with the political necessities. These necessities present their own moral requirements; morality is not only concerned with the limits on just war. Our moral duty includes "the responsibility to preserve, if and so long as we can, an ordered justice in the world by just and limited means," though these are still subject to particular moral limits:

> The precarious peace and security of the world depends on the effectiveness of a moral deterrent. . . . But since peace is not the only political

value, this should be no man's sole concern. Deterrence is not the sole or always an unqualified good in politics.[36]

At this point then we are presented by Ramsey with an argument identical in structure to that with which he opposed pacifism. The use of armed force is a moral requirement, not merely a moral permission, if and when it is permissible. In dealing with nuclear weapons we are immediately at the boundaries of what may be permitted by the test of discrimination—certainly by this test in particular, and also by any test of just means of war. These are the apparently divergent moral arguments that he seeks to reconcile, and that make the driving force of the debate. We have now moved from the question of the nature of the moralist's theoretical role, to seeing whether determining the possibility of a justified nuclear deterrent is a theoretical or a practical question. Ramsey believed that it was at least possible to press much further toward that possibility, in theoretical terms, that is usually attempted. He believed this because of the account he gave of the principle of proportion. The question of a justified nuclear deterrent, once indiscriminate intentions are disavowed, because a proper matter for political prudence. We might say that it becomes a political rather than a moral question. Let us now try to sum up Ramsey's resolution of the problem.

In the first place, we know that no policy that is avowedly indiscriminate can be moral, either in action or in deterrence. Ramsey did not believe that only such a policy can be an effective deterrent. In debate with Stein he admitted that this is his own "judgment of fact":

> Is he [Stein] committed factually and in principle to the proposition that *only* a plus-city-hostages deterrent deters and that this atrocity is what alone is at work in any of the seemingly effective lower levels of deterrence? Or will he look with me into the possibility that a minus-city-hostages deterrent would be quite enough shared danger to place adequate limits upon political and military decisions in this age? To raise this question is to come to a final assessment of where we are in connection with the respective judgments of fact to which neither of us is quite entitled but which nevertheless are unavoidably interwoven with our moral argument.[37]

If there is a moral dilemma, then, it is clear that Ramsey would definitely not abandon the principle of discrimination, but is it possible to reconcile this dilemma? This is perhaps *the* moral question of our day. It is clear that Ramsey wants to answer it positively—is it possible for him to show that he can?

Ramsey's answer relies on the observation that, long before nuclear warfare is indiscriminate, it is likely to be disproportionate. The test of proportion is what in practice must place the upper limit on nuclear weapons and nuclear deterrence. This test, though, is the test of political wisdom and reason. On the other wing of the dilemma there is also a political judgment to be made, namely, what is a sufficient deterrent to keep the peace. It is from this that Ramsey deduces that the moral requirements can be reconciled, or meshed together:

> I simply note that modern war, including nuclear war, would cause *disproportionate* civil damage long before it would be indiscriminate (*and that therefore effective deterrence need stem from nothing inherently immoral*).[38]

and

> Deterrence from disproportionate combatant and collateral civilian damage and from the other ingredients of deterrence that may morally be in prospect provides a way of meshing together the moral requirements and the force requirements.[39]

Therefore, provided that a counterforce policy, with city-avoidance, is a sufficient deterrent, there is no insuperable moral dilemma to be faced. Ramsey has argued that it is sufficient because of the deterrence to be gained from threats of (apparently) disproportionate action. To say that it is sufficient is not to say that it is guaranteed. There can be no such guarantees in politics, and there may or may not finally be any answer to the problem of deterring an irrational and immoral opponent by moral and rational means. But we may go to the outer limits of what is morally legitimate in order to deter such an opponent.

It is not, in the final analysis, a moral dilemma we are confronted with, but a political one—a great one, probably the greatest political dilemma, but no different in principle from the other tragic dilemmas always encountered in politics. What level of military threat, and inevitable risk, can be accepted for the sake of world stability and peace? To this the moralist has no easy answers, nor is giving answers to such questions his business. All he can do is to help the political actor to think through the right basis on which such questions can be put, and decisions made.

Conclusion

This book set out with the claim that Ramsey has offered us a coherent and theological account of Christian political ethics. This may not seem the most likely claim to make, but if it can be vindicated, it will also demonstrate Ramsey's power to penetrate dark moral crevices and enlighten them with the truths of Christian faith. Ramsey's work reached from the basis for moral thought in Christian teachings through to detailed engagement with moral questions of great difficulty and even greater concern. If it can be shown to be coherent, as well as theological, across this range, then it is indeed a large claim that is established. There are, as Ramsey admitted, senses in which his work was not complete.[1] But in terms of the range of his thought, that is hardly to be held against him.

Let us try to set out in brief the structure we have uncovered. Ramsey started with fundamental convictions about the love of God as providing the pattern and the warrant for Christian love to determine the shape of Christian morality. Christian love is covenant love, which both underlies the work of God in creation and is expressed in the realities of the created order. In both love and creation, we learn continuities, persisting patterns, and regularities that enable us to formulate principles and rules of morality. However, human nature in a fallen world is not wholly to be governed by rules; there are, as well as things never to be done, occasions where choices to be made are morally indeterminate. Not only are there hard choices which are obscure, but human action and intentionality also has its obscurities. One of Ramsey's strengths was the way in which he continued recognition of the obscurities of human action and human choices with clarity and firm objectivity about morally prohibited types of action.

We moved from an analysis of Ramsey's ethical theory to his

political thought, and his conviction that force may and should be used in politics for good ends. The use of force, even in warfare, is an institution of God (even if an "alien" one). Whether and when to resort to force may be an indeterminate decision, for who can say how much justice is worth so many human lives? Nevertheless, there are times, tragically, when the use of force is warranted in the cause of justice. The manner of the use of force is subject to moral conditions; these flow from the nature of the warrants for its use. Force that sets out to protect the innocent and to fight for justice cannot then directly work injustice and oppress innocent lives.

Ramsey's just war theory was presented with nuclear deterrence especially in mind. This aim was to reason from the basic purposes of politics, and the limits which flowed from those purposes. He sought to apply the just war theory of the discriminate and proportionate use of force to nuclear deterrence. This, as we traced his argument, set out a possibility for justified nuclear deterrence at its outer limits, which rested on a justification for the possible use of nuclear weapons in some circumstances (if deterrence were to fail).

I have tried to test the links in Ramsey's chain of argument. Apart from occasional obscurities in presentation, it is hard to find weak spots. The structure is solid and in place. The strength and coherence of his thought is surely a product of his way of criticizing other thinkers. In a letter to D. H. Smith, who was editing *Love and Society,* Ramsey wrote this:

> I hope . . . that people . . . [writing for *Love and Society*] . . . will be stimulated to emulate my way of dealing with the thought of another person, in *Nine Modern Moralists:* i.e. close order work, adopting the author's point of view so far and as sympathetically as possible in order to exhibit what goes on in it, until a criticism emerges: internal criticism, I call it.[2]

The method he employed to find cracks in others' thought, he himself applied to his own work. (He would return to correct and revise, elaborate or reword, positions and formulations already set out.)

Ramsey was determined that his task was *Christian* ethics. His interest in natural law, and his use of the work of philosophers, or his detailed wrestlings in politics or medical ethics with leading experts— all these mislead us if we think that they find Ramsey away from his Protestant theological foundations. Rather, at all points, the leading edge is the determination to find what love requires—any tool that is of service in this enterprise may be used.

The connecting element in all these assistants is surely the power of rigorous human reason. Reason is at the heart of natural law, it is a central philosophical concern, and it is essential to any "expert" knowledge. Rigor is indispensable to clear thought. Ramsey's purpose was not first to spur people on to better moral behavior, or even to shore up the crumbling walls of a once Christian civilization. His purpose was to find out what was entailed by Christian truth. The truth of the Christian faith is not to be made menial to other causes.

How does reason work? To this there can be no simple answer. There is not a set of rules of logic, or of grammar, which can specify in advance how to think. What we can say, however, is that there is no substitute for the careful and accurate use of language. Ramsey deplored the efforts of those who would change the usage of words like "violence."[3] This was not because he disagreed with their objectives, but because such redefinitions could only make the work of careful moral analysis harder or even impossible. On the contrary, the chief work of the Christian moralist, and the Christian church in its public speech, is to reshape and clarify the prevailing ethos, to enlighten and transform it.

Ramsey's concern for language was by no means a conservative one, as a casual acquaintance might suggest. Rather he attempted to transform the usage of key words such as "discrimination" in just war, or "care" in medical ethics. Such usage, while largely underwriting a conservative use, set out to do two things. First, to relate key categories to a theology of Christian love; second, to deepen and refine the categories to make them useful tools in detailed moral analysis. The importance of the careful use of language for Ramsey can scarcely be overestimated. See, for instance, our analysis of the vital significance of the accurate description of human action.

Ramsey's vigorous thought combined together in a remarkable way not only to cover a range of theological and moral issues, but also drew upon a wide range of Christian tradition. Here again we mistake his aim if we see his work as essentially conservative. Conservative his conclusions may appear, but his use of tradition is eclectic and radical, reaching to the roots of Christian theology in a fresh and powerful way.

To read and reread Ramsey's writings is continually to be impressed with the strength of his insight and with the power of detailed application that he brings to bear. It is also to reveal a coherence of thought, an integrity and deep consistency of structure which runs from one end of his work to the other. This essay has sought to vindicate that along one cross-section.

Ramsey's example, and his moral method, inspires his reader to want to press past him in discernment of the urgent moral questions of our age. Clearly these questions are among the major tasks facing Christian theologians, but going beyond Ramsey is not so easy as it might appear. Oliver O'Donovan shrewdly observes of Ramsey's careful readers that they "will find Ramsey a companion *sans pareil,* who, on a second or third reading, will turn out to have anticipated all the moves by which they had thought they were advancing beyond his tuition."[4]

Christian ethics faces its twofold task: to be both determinedly theological and rigorously rational. The world is not served by Christian ethics which are less than theologically honest and uncompromising or which are not sufficiently fresh and rigorous to bring Christian thought to bear accurately on the heart of the issues that are raised. If this is difficult, it needs to be remembered that the common generalities and pious exhortations so often on offer do little honor to those most closely facing the issues, and very little honor to the Christian faith. To honor them properly in the face of genuinely perplexing and new moral questions, Christian ethics will need all the help afforded by Ramsey's demanding tuition.

Notes

Books and articles are referred to by author and title in the notes; publication details are in the bibliography. Paul Ramsey's books and articles are referred to by title, and articles also with bibliographical reference (e.g., 1935a).

Abbreviations

AJD	*Again, The Justice of Deterrence*
BCE	*Basic Christian Ethics*
CESI	*Christian Ethics and the Sit-In*
DEAG	*Doing Evil to Achieve Good*
D&R	*Deeds and Rules in Christian Ethics*
JW	*The Just War*
LNW	*The Limits of Nuclear War*
L&S	*Love and Society*, J. T. Johnson and D. H. Smith (eds.)
MUA	"More Unsolicited Advice to Vatican II"
NMM	*Nine Modern Moralists*
PCB	*Peace, the Churches and the Bomb*, J. Finn (ed.)
SU	*Speak Up for Just War or Pacifism*
WCC	*War and the Christian Conscience*

Introduction

1. Apart from Ramsey's editing of two volumes of Edwards's works (*Freedom of the Will* and *Ethical Writings*), he made few references to Edwards in his own work (for these see the end of Chapter One below), but this should not obscure his admiration for Edwards, "America's greatest theologian."

2. Ramsey published no articles on Karl Barth, but he referred to him fairly frequently. These references are more a mark of respect than agreement, for Ramsey took issue with Barth's approach to ethics and to politics. Ramsey's understanding of the nature of man and woman is, however, very

close to Barth. Ramsey referred warmly to Barth in "The Marriage of Adam and Eve," 1960e.

3. *NMM*, 235 and fn.

4. These themes are most prominent in Ramsey's work on marriage and on medical ethics. One of their fuller, most rhetorical statements may be found in "The Biblical Norm of Righteousness," 1970b. Cf. also *CESI*, 33–36, where Ramsey says "Man has rights because fellow humanity is precarious in him."

5. There is a fine expression of this theme in "Marriage Law and Biblical Covenant," 1964d, 69–72, and another in "A Christian Approach to the Question of Sexual Relations Outside of Marriage," 1965a, 113–17 (*One Flesh*, 1975, 19–22). Ramsey's writings on sexuality and marriage are rather scattered. He wrote a good deal in this area in the 1950s when he projected a book on the topic. Much of this was subsequently published separately. Still unpublished is "Sex and the Order of Reason in Thomas Aquinas." (Both are in the Paul Ramsey papers in Perkins.) Published papers, which had been written as chapters for the book, are "The Marriage of Adam and Eve," 1960e, "Human Sexuality in the History of Redemption," 1988a, and "Jean-Paul Sartre: Sex in Being," *NMM*, ch. 4. In addition, on marriage, there is "Community of Two," 1962b, "Marriage Law and Biblical Covenant," 1964d, "A Christian Approach to the Question of Sexual Relations Outside Marriage," 1965a, the discussions in *D&R*, and more briefly in *CESI*. On parenthood, there is "Sex and People: A Critical Review," 1960d, and the discussion in *Fabricated Man*. In addition to these, there is also a series of adult Sunday School lessons, containing many of these themes, "God and the Family," 1955a, and the articles "A Proposal to the New Moralists," 1968, and "Do You Know Where Your Children Are?" 1979b.

6. Cf. especially *The Patient as Person*, xii–xv.

7. See, e.g., *JW*, 143–46, 150–53.

8. "Love and Law," 1956b. This article is reprinted as ch. 5 of *NMM*, "Reinhold Niebuhr: Christian Love and Natural Law."

9. This claim is the burden of "The Case of the Curious Exception," 1968a. Ramsey's ethical theory only came to full expression in this article.

10. See, for instance, "War and the New Morality," 1968o, or "Justice In War" (1964c, *JW*, ch. 6).

11. See especially "The Uses of Power" (1964j, *JW*, ch. 1).

12. The tension between order and justice is a leitmotif of Ramsey's political writings. For two examples, see "Election Issues 1968," 1968e, 27, and "The Uses of Power" (1964j, *JW*, 10–13).

13. Consider two recent books: Finnis et al., *Nuclear Deterrence, Morality and Realism*, and Kenny, *The Logic of Deterrence*. Finnis is very close to the position of Stein, who was Ramsey's chief "nuclear pacifist" antagonist. Kenny's argument, on the other hand, is very close in structure to that of Ramsey. For all the differences of detail, illustration, style, etc., the moral arguments of these two major books are almost identical with their predecessors.

14. Ramsey's shifts are helpful to the student, who is alerted to the moves made in argument, and the paramount need for verbal care and accuracy. Ramsey draws attention to explicit shifts and changes in his book (e.g., viii–ix, 78n, and 252n). The shift on the "bluff" argument, which *can* be found in the volume, is not explicitly noted in the same way. See the discussion below, ch. 14.

15. For some of the complaints, see Curran, *Politics, Medicine and Christian Ethics*, 8–9; O'Connor, "War in a Moral Perspective," v–vi; and Fry, *The Immobilized Christian*, 149. Fry himself is a defender of Ramsey's style. He defends Ramsey's convoluted sentences and style by pointing to his concern for rigor and exactness, and his concern to correct sloppy and inexact thinking and writing.

16. "The Case of the Curious Exception" and "Incommensurability and Indeterminacy in Moral Choice" (1968a and 1978d) are two such essays. In the Preface to *Ethics at the Edges of Life* Ramsey argues that perfection of style is not an overriding concern: "clarity of statement [might have been] improved if there had been time." But this could have been a year, and Ramsey claims "I regard publication as only another form of communication. One reaches a larger audience, but the printed word is only a little less perishable than good conversation. I do not write for ages to come" (xvi). With this excuse one can only sympathize (as a fellow-writer) and disagree (as a student).

17. These debates are surveyed below in chs. 7–8 and 14–15.

18. "Some Rejoinders," 1976g, 191.

19. Many examples of this could be adduced. Here are three. In the Introduction to *D&R* Ramsey referred to a place where he was "mistaken" (7). In "Some Rejoinders," 1976g, he called his work "unfinished in several meanings of that word" (186). He referred to *Doing Evil to Achieve Good*, which he co-edited and contributed to, as a "failed book" ("A Letter to James Gustafson," 1985a, 77).

20. To give a full analysis of Ramsey's various characteristic tactics and styles in criticizing, analyzing, and reviewing others would easily become complex and tedious, but a good example of the way he endeavored to make the most of his opponents' work can be found in his critique of Robinson in *D&R*, 21–42. See especially the argument at 41, leading to the conclusion "Robinson has drawn a correct boundary."

21. *The London Times*, Monday, March 7, 1988.

22. Cf., e.g., Fry, *The Immobilized Christian*, 151–52, 156–57, or O'Brien, in *L&S*, 180. Gustafson, however, called Ramsey a "rigorist," which is perhaps more an accusation than a compliment. Ramsey contested the implication that his inquiry into questions of ethics is prejudiced by an assumed rigorist starting point. He claimed, rather, that "covenant love drives on to some rigorist deontic principles." (See Gustafson, *Ethics and Theology*, 84–85, and "A Letter to James Gustafson," 1985a, 83.)

Chapter 1. 1913–1951

1. "Non Solum in Memoriam Sed in Intentionem: A Tribute to the Late John W. Ramsey," 1949b, 9.
2. See *JW*, Preface, viii–ix.
3. "Christianity and War," 1935a, 203.
4. He actually remained a pacifist well into World War II. His change of mind is probably to be traced to his time teaching at Garrett Biblical Institute, from 1942 to 1944, where he reacted against the prevailing "liberal-pacifist" ethos. In a letter to Sidney Macaulay (March 20, 1976), Ramsey wrote about his theological development: "Two things were at work, I suppose, or happened to me. One was my gradual growth out of Millsaps liberalism into a more orthodox theological outlook at Yale, where the influence of the Niebuhrs had its steady effect long before any change of position on my part. The second was the 'culture shock' of going to teach for two years at Garrett where I found myself in the midst of a hotbed of that same Methodist liberal-pacifist background of mine. That accomplished the overturning of my position, more than when I was defending it at Yale." (See Macaulay's M.Th. dissertation on "The Use of Scripture.")
5. Although Ramsey often refers to pacifist views, he has few extended discussions of them. *JW* contains "Can a Pacifist Tell a Just War?" (ch. 12), a critique of James Douglass. Here are a few pages (261–65) of general discussion of pacifism. The nub of Ramsey's argument is that "A genuinely sectarian Christian who is a universal pacifist prescinds from the history of nations in prescinding from the history of warfare" (263). However, the only really full discussion is to be found in the discussion of Yoder in *SU*.
6. Ramsey believed a consistent pacifism to be a defensible Christian way. Christ's example in enduring suffering "may have been the better path to take in His discipleship away back yonder when Christian non-political pacifism and Christian political responsibilism came to this enduring fork in the road" ("Can a Pacifist Tell a Just War?" *JW*, 278). Ramsey did not attempt to prove the way of just war to be the right interpretation of Christian discipleship. Nevertheless he believed that it is, and that the pacifist way is not.
7. For instance the discussions of human rights, and of sovereignty and social contract theories, in *BCE* chs. IX and X (351–66 and 367–88). Ramsey maintained that he stood by the book as a whole in a letter to O'Connor, November 5, 1970 (O'Connor, "War in a Moral Perspective, 7n.").
8. I use the words "*agape*" and "Christian love" interchangeably. On occasion I also put "love," with the same meaning, where that is clear in the context.
9. *BCE*, 2, 21.
10. The importance of "faithfulness" is clear in the published versions of the Clarence D. Ashley Lectures on Law and Theology, which Ramsey gave in 1958. Revised versions of the first two lectures form chs. 8 and 9 of *NMM*.

The third lecture was published in 1964 as "Marriage Law and Biblical Covenant," 1964d.

11. *BCE*, 209–13.

12. See especially "Love and Law," the essay on Reinhold Niebuhr, 1956b, ch. 5 of *NMM*.

13. *BCE*, 99–102, 157–66.

14. Cf., e.g., *BCE*, 189.

15. Tillich is quoted from *The Protestant Era*, 154–55, at *BCE*, 90–91; Ramsey himself from *BCE*, 184.

16. Especially, of course, ch. II, "Christian Liberty: An Ethic Without Rules."

17. Gustafson, "How Does Love Reign?" 655, repeated in *Ethics and Theology*, 88–89.

18. "A Letter to James Gustafson," 1985a, 75, referring to *NMM*, 149–50.

19. See *D&R*, 112–13, 117–19.

20. *BCE*, 160.

21. *BCE*, 181–84. Ramsey had a very "tough-minded" approach to bloody dilemmas. Cf. his discussions of the possible destruction of life on earth (*WCC*, ch. 9); possible deaths in nuclear war (*LNW*, *JW*, ch. 11, 213); the bombing of concentration camps in World War II (*AJD*, *JW*, ch. 15, 351–52); the discussion "Incapacitating Gases," (*JW*, ch. 19, 465–78); and the dilemmas of "Shelter Morality" (1961h). In the latter article, Ramsey argued that it would be right for a householder in possession of a shelter in times of civil breakdown following a nuclear attack to be armed and to repel would-be intruders by force for the sake of his family.

22. On Ramsey's early pacifism, see ch. 1; for a fuller consideration see ch. 10.

23. Ramsey himself makes this claim at *BCE*, xi.

24. "The Biblical Norm of Righteousness," 420, 421, 422, 426.

25. Cf., e.g., the section "The Righteousness of God," 2–24, or ch. VII, "The Work of Christian Love," 234–48.

26. Gustafson, *Ethics and Theology*, 91.

27. Ramsey's most common Bible references are allusive rather than directly expository. Numerous examples might be given. See, e.g., "Counting the Costs," 1967a, *JW*, ch. 24, or "Force and Political Responsibility," 1972c. Ramsey's objective quality will become clear as we proceed. Meanwhile, the contrast between Gustafson and Ramsey on abortion, or more clearly between Fletcher and Ramsey on euthanasia, would indicate what I have in mind here. McCormick is, of course, rather trickier to epitomize in such a fashion!

28. Augustine, Aquinas, and Luther (among others) are treated in *BCE*; the twentieth-century thinkers in this list in *NMM*.

29. In "A Letter to James Gustafson," 1985a, 74, Ramsey compliments Gustafson on his accounts of theologians, saying: "Your discussion in these chapters is better than most secondary accounts—*none* of which should ever

be relied on without acknowledging that God has not ordered our finitude and the time-limits that press down upon us so as to make adequate understanding of one another possible."

30. For instance, on Augustine, see R. S. Hartigan, "Non-combatant Immunity: Reflection on its Origins and Present Status." It should be noted that Ramsey's use of other writers in his own exposition is based on a capacity and a care for detailed interpretation and exegesis. For an example of his work on Augustine, see the posthumously published essay on sex in Augustine, 1988a.

31. See *WCC*, ch. 3, and *BCE*, ch. VI, especially 203–13.

32. *Freedom of the Will* (1957) is vol. 1 of the Yale edition of Edwards's *Works; Ethical Writings* is vol. 8.

33. "A Letter to James Gustafson," 1985a, 97–100.

34. Edwards, *Ethical Writings*, 572.

Chapter 2. 1951–1961

1. *NMM*, 7.

2. Though it should be noted that *Nine Modern Moralists* was mostly written in the 1950s and published in articles dated between 1951 and 1959.

3. See note (5) to the Introduction.

4. *NMM*, 4, 194–95.

5. *NMM*, 244.

6. E.g., *NMM*, 213.

7. *NMM*, 5. For Ramsey's review of his use of the phrase "Christ transforming natural justice," see "Some Rejoinders," 1976g, 189–91.

8. "A Letter to James Gustafson," 1985a, 74.

9. *CESI*, 22 n. "The development of a philosophy of law and an analysis of 'natural' justice on the basis of covenant-creation is imperative even for a Barthian theological ethics."

10. *CESI*, 25–26.

11. *CESI*, 125, 127, 125.

12. Brief references occur only a handful of times after 1961, perhaps most significantly in the preface to *The Patient as Person*, xii.

13. "The Case of the Curious Exception," 1968a, 119. The sentence is quoted and affirmed in "A Letter to James Gustafson," 1985a, 74.

14. 1960a.

15. *CESI*, 26.

16. See especially *Ethics at the Edges of Life*.

17. Ramsey's ability to work in this way in the public arena without overt theological reference often misled his readers, who sometimes thought he had moved away from a Christian covenant love basis for moral reasoning.

18. *NMM*, 235, and 235n, from the chapters which are a revised version of lectures given in 1958.

19. See especially *The Patient as Person*, xii–xiii, and *Ethics at the Edges of Life*, xiii.

20. The fullest exposition of "non-combatant immunity" is to be found in "The Case for Making 'Just War' Possible" (1962a, *JW*, ch. 7). See especially 150–51. See also ch. 11.

21. This is most fully explored in "The Case of the Curious Exception," Section IV, "Canons of Loyalty," 120–35.

22. Cf. Ramsey's gibe that Fletcher is "the last Puritan," in *D&R*, 176–92. Ramsey argued that Fletcher's consequentialism is always concerned with doing good, i.e., bringing about good. Against this Ramsey argued that acts can be good in themselves. See especially *D&R*, 185–87.

23. Especially in "The Uses of Power" (1964j, *JW*, ch. 1) 16–18.

24. *BCE*, 182. "A selfish act is the most unlovely thing."

25. See, e.g., *WCC*, ch. 9, "The politics of fear, or, the end is not yet," especially 192–95, and *SU*, 20–31. Cf. also the discussion of the "end of the world" in *Fabricated Man*, 22–32.

26. Cf. *JW*, 461, 15, and also *CESI*, generally, e.g., 48–51, 67–68.

27. Cf. *Fabricated Man*, for instance in its conclusion, 159–60.

28. "A Christian Approach to the Question of Sexual Relations Outside of Marriage," 1965a, 113–17. See also *CESI*, 48–51, where Ramsey uses the phrase "garments of skin" as a metaphor for social institutions and their protective function. The same phrase is applied to marriage.

29. Ramsey's concern "to save politics (and war) for purposefulness" is given as one of three main purposes of *JW*, in the Introduction, x. The mistake of trying to abolish war is certainly a common theme of the volume. See, e.g., 50–54, 148–67, etc. At the same time (the early 1960s) he was still advocating world government, but he had decisively changed his mind on this by the early 1970s. See further in ch. 4.

Chapter 3. Developing a Protestant Casuistry

1. See "The Case of the Curious Exception," 1968a, 74–93, especially 91.

2. Fletcher, *Situation Ethics*, and "What's in a Rule?: A Situationist's View."

3. E.g., by Gustafson (*Ethics and Theology*, 85, 90–93). Apart from the sentence cited by Gustafson in *BCE*, "Certainly Christian ethics is a deontological ethic, not an ethic of 'the good' " (116), Ramsey never used the word without careful qualification, or at least hesitation. See, e.g., *D&R*, 108, *DEAG*, 141 n. 32, and "A Letter to James Gustafson," 1985a, 76–78.

4. See, for example, "Faith Effective Through In-Principled Love," 1960a, "Protestant Casuistry Today," 1963f, "On Taking Sexual Responsibility Seriously Enough," 1964f.

5. From this point I will generally use the word "situationism" to include

a variety of related approaches to ethics. They have in common an opposition to rules, to casuistry, etc., as determinative or authoritative in Christian ethics.

6. 1956b, in Kegley and Bretall, (eds.), *Reinhold Niebuhr: His Religious, Social and Political Thought*. Ramsey's chapter is reprinted in *NMM* as ch. 5: "Reinhold Niebuhr: Christian Love and Natural Law."

7. Reprinted as ch. 11 of *The Essential Reinhold Niebuhr*, 142–59, edited by R. McA. Brown.

8. *NMM*, 150.

9. *NMM*, 121.

10. *The Essential Reinhold Niebuhr*, 147, quoted in *NMM*, 119.

11. Miller, "Unprincipled Living: The Ethics of Obligation," 28, 30, and 31. Is it possible that the title of this article provoked the title and wording of Ramsey's critique: "Faith Effective Through In-Principled Love," 1960a?

12. "Faith Effective Through In-Principled Love," 1960a, 77.

13. Heron (ed.), *Towards a Quaker View of Sex*, and Robinson, *Honest to God* and *Christian Morals Today*.

14. *Towards a Quaker View of Sex*, 45, *D&R*, 12, 15.

15. *D&R*, 41.

16. It is common to find Ramsey's opponents attacking a position he does not hold, but which he has rethought and revised. This, perhaps, is sometimes to be attributed to the difficulty of his presentation, but more, I think, to the combination of depth, subtlety, and rigor in his writing.

17. See, e.g., "Protestant Casuistry Today," 1963f, and the unpublished "Apologia Pro Vita Sua—One Decade, That Is," 40–41 (1972): "Now it is a fact worthy of contemplation—if only with frustration and outrage—that in the present age academic and church liberals who have the podia and the power have become ever more unsure of the meaning of doing the ethical thing in personal morality, in sex and marital ethics, in filial piety, in piety toward the unborn, in respect for the sources of life which forbid technological alienation, while waxing ever more sure they know the exact meaning of just solutions in the complexities of international affairs and conflict of a technological age."

18. "Protestant Casuistry Today," 1963f, 24. Cf. *D&R*, 94, commenting on Paul Lehmann.

19. We have already seen this with respect to marriage. For the same point with respect to truth-telling, see *D&R*, 77–80, and "The Case of the Curious Exception," 1968a, 89.

20. Frankena, "Love and Principle in Christian Ethics," 210–14. Frankena's introduction of the ugly word "agapism" into the discussion enabled him to employ the distinctions between different types of utilitarianism and apply them to an analysis of theories of Christian ethics.

21. "Love and Principle in Christian Ethics," 212, quoted in *D&R*, 110.

22. See *D&R*, ch. VII.

23. He also tried to use the language of John Rawls of "rules of practice," but this did not help. Rawls's rules of practice were designed to provide a utilitarian justification of, for instance, punishment. Though this has many

points in common with Ramsey's critique of situationism, it does not help to answer the question now in front of us. Ramsey admits in a footnote that he is "probably too dependent on Rawls's article" ("Two Concepts of General Rules in Christian Ethics," 1966h, *D&R*, ch. VI. Cf. 123n3).

24. Ramsey's defense of some exceptionless moral rules is carefully qualified. It is more accurate to say that he defends the existence of some *virtually* exceptionless moral rules.

Chapter 4. Political Ethics and the Just War Theory

1. For instance, *CESI*, 49, "quite properly the Christian should aim *ahead* of the flying bird of justice in order actually just to strike it," and *JW*, 12, "*Justitia* refers to the regulative ideal of all political action summed up, I suppose, in the word 'humanitarianism.' "

2. In addition to their own writings, I have found R. H. Stone's *Reinhold Niebuhr: Prophet to Politicians* helpful on Niebuhr, and the account of Courtney Murray in G. Weigel's *Tranquillitas Ordinis* also most helpful.

3. See *Speak Up for Just War or Pacifism*, 72.

4. This is so widespread that it barely needs noting. In 1944 Ford was already aware that the principle of discrimination needed a full defense and clarification. At the same time he was able to write that "even in the circumstances of a modern war every Catholic theologian would condemn as intrinsically immoral the direct killing of innocent non-combatants" (273). For a more recent view see O'Brien in *L&S*, and his critique, 173–80. Cf. also his comment, "In the world of moralists and experts concerned with war, Ramsey is virtually alone in this understanding of and emphasis on the principle of discrimination" (167).

5. "The Case for Making 'Just War' Possible," 1962a, *JW*, 151.

6. See especially *JW*, 153–65.

7. *We Hold These Truths*, 265.

8. *We Hold These Truths*, 271, 272.

9. *We Hold These Truths*, 265.

10. *Nuclear Policy for War and Peace*, 41–42.

11. *WCC*, ch. 12, 273–304.

12. *Nuclear Policy for War and Peace*, 223–24, 42, 40. We return to Ramsey's discussion of Thomas Murray in ch. 14.

13. For the charting of Niebuhr's phases of thought, his changes and continuity, see Stone, *passim,* but briefly summarized at 131.

14. "Reinhold Niebuhr: Leader in Social, Political and Religious Thought," 1960c.

15. Stone, *Reinhold Niebuhr: Prophet to Politicians,* 166, summarizing the essay on realism and idealism in *Man's Nature and His Communities*, 1965.

16. See Ramsey's tribute, 1960c.

17. *JW*, 260.
18. On pure and summary rules, see ch. 6.
19. *JW*, 429.
20. Ramsey complained in 1966 about a comment made by Niebuhr: "What warrant in either theology or politics has Niebuhr ever given us for accepting such a simplicist [*sic*] analysis?" ("Farewell to Christian Realism," 1966a, *JW*, 487.)
21. Ramsey admitted that Karl Barth and Reinhold Niebuhr were exceptions to his general contention, *JW*, 484.
22. Cf. O'Brien's comment, n. 4 above.
23. 1956b, *NMM*, ch. 5.
24. E.g., *An Interpretation of Christian Ethics*, 100–104; *The Nature and Destiny of Man*, II, 247–56. For Ramsey's summary, see *NMM*, 123.
25. *An Interpretation of Christian Ethics*, 136, cited in *NMM*, 126. NB: I am referring to an edition of this book with a different pagination from that used by Ramsey.
26. *NMM*, 135–36; cf. *BCE*, 163–66.
27. *NMM*, 128. Cf. also *CESI*, 25–30, or the critique of Brunner's "dualistic" account of the relationship between love and justice, *NMM*, 196–208, or Ramsey's cutting answer to Brunner's view "that there is room for love . . . not in the actual activity of the institution itself, but 'between the lines' " (*Justice and the Social Order*, 117). Ramsey replies: "What man nurtured in the Bible can be content with love effective only through the interstitial spaces?" (*BCE*, 3).
28. See especially *Moral Man and Immoral Society, passim*, e.g., "The moral obtuseness of human collectives makes a morality of pure disinterestedness impossible. There is not enough imagination in any social group to render it amenable to the influence of pure love" (272). Cf. also Niebuhr's congratulation of the wisdom of the children of darkness, *The Children of Light and the Children of Darkness*, 10–13.
29. *NMM*, 139, 138.
30. It is not only pacifists who call politics immoral, and say that politics necessarily involves undertaking immoral acts. In "Farewell to Christian Realism," 1966a, *JW*, 479, Ramsey protested against John Bennett's use of such language.
31. For this awkward expression, see, "The Uses of Power," 1964j, *JW*, 4.
32. *JW*, 4–5.
33. See "The Ethics of Intervention," 1965c, *JW*, ch. 2, especially 22–23, where Ramsey insists that failure to use force to fulfill political responsibilities may be just as blameworthy as misusing force. Ramsey's remarks on conservative and liberal perspectives are to be found in *JW*, 3–4.
34. "Does the Church Have Any Political Wisdom for the 70's?" 1972b, 30.
35. Ramsey discusses the question of the use of economic sanctions in *CESI*, ch. 3, 99–123.

36. See "A Letter to James Gustafson," 1985a, 89.

37. See especially "How Shall Counter-Insurgency Warfare Be Conducted Justly?" *JW*, 455–58, and *Who Speaks for the Church?*

38. See especially *SU*, 52–55 and 81–92. Ramsey takes issue in these pages with those who put a presumption against violence, or against war, at the head of just war theory. Just war theory begins instead with a presumption against injustice, following this with the concern to act prudently (raising questions of proportion, last resort, and so on). It is the tension between these, exacerbated by the nature of modern warfare, which leads to the moral anguish of facing choices between the cause of justice and the cause of peace. (See also ibid. 72–73.)

39. 1964j, *JW*, ch. 1, 3–18.

40. *JW*, 7–8.

41. *JW*, 10.

42. *SU*, 83.

43. *JW*, 11. It is necessary to note that Ramsey uses the words "just" and "justice" in two different senses. In the phrase "the just conduct of war," for instance, the word is used to refer to a quality of action, and is a synonym for "right" or "justified." When contrasted with order, or peace, justice refers to a state of affairs and to the need to remedy injustices done or established.

44. Cf., for instance, some remarks of Reinhold Niebuhr about the world community in ch. 5 of *The Children of Light and the Children of Darkness*, 168: "The international community . . . must find its first unity through coercive force to a larger degree than is compatible with the necessities of justice. Order will have to be purchased at the price of justice; though it is quite obvious that if too much justice is sacrificed to the necessities of order, the order will prove too vexatious to last."

45. *JW*, 11.

46. Cf., e.g., *JW*, 15, or "Turn Toward Just War," 1962g, e.g., *JW*, 179, 187. See also Ramsey's complaint about inaccurate moral objections to the Vietnam war in "Over the Slope to Total War?" 1967g, *JW*, 534–36, and *CESI*, especially the discussion of "The Law and Civil Disobedience," 75–98.

47. Especially "The Ethics of Intervention," 1965c. Of course, Ramsey did not think that intervention per se was always right. Cf. his discussion of the alternatives facing the United States in Vietnam in 1965, in "How Shall Counter-Insurgency War be Conducted Justly?" *JW*, 440–52.

48. Especially "What Americans Ordinarily Think about Justice in War," 1961e, *JW*, ch. 2, e.g., 51–53.

49. See *CESI*, 37–38, 47–51; quotations are from 38 and 50.

50. Cf. *CESI*, 40–45, 83–87.

51. "Election Issues 1968," 1968e, 27.

52. Although we will consider Ramsey's views on Vietnam a little more fully later, we should indicate here that his view, in hindsight, was that Vietnam was a disproportionate war, and therefore unjustified. He also condemned particular U.S. actions during the war.

53. Particularly, of course, over Vietnam. See "Farewell to Christian Realism," 1966a, and "Vietnam: Dissent from Dissent," 1966j, *JW,* 479–88 and 489–96. He writes here: "Perhaps it is understandable that a consensus of vocal liberal religious opinion finds itself unable to look an arbitrament of arms squarely in the face" (493).

54. *Who Speaks for the Church?,* 29–45.

55. *Who Speaks for the Church?,* 58–118, on the Geneva Conference. Ramsey had a particular concern not to unchurch those serving in the armed forces (131–35).

56. *Who Speaks for the Church?,* 45–46.

57. *WCC,* 12, 310–11.

58. Ramsey claims this in "Some Rejoinders," 1976g, 209–10. While this is a defensible claim for *WCC,* it should be noted that he uses the same expression, with respect to complicity in S. African apartheid, in *CESI,* 116.

59. Finnis et al. also advance somewhat similar considerations in relation to the same issue. See *Nuclear Deterrence, Morality and Realism,* e.g., 345–46 (though they do not use Ramsey's expression or refer to him).

60. This reluctance is exemplified in Ramsey's handling of the cases proposed by situationists, and of cases in medical ethics, as well as in politics, where nuclear deterrence and counterinsurgency are the topics often labeled "dilemmas."

61. On doing evil that good may come, see, e.g., *JW* 147. Ramsey returns several times to Kahn's advocacy of "rationality of irrationality" policies. See *WCC,* 265–72, "The Hatfields and the McCoys," 1962a revised, *JW,* 174–77, and *The Limits of Nuclear War,* 1963, *JW,* 216–25.

62. *WCC,* 125–27.

63. "Selective Conscientious Objection," 1968n revised, *JW,* ch. 5. One of the hidden ironies of this discussion is that although Ramsey wished to argue for selective conscientious objection, he did so for very different reasons from many others who also pleaded for it. Cf. *JW,* 94.

64. In the decision given in the case *United States v. Seeger,* which allowed that a general humanitarianism could count as religious grounds for conscientious objection.

65. For an account of the debate in the 1960s, and an assessment of Ramsey's contribution to it, see John Rohr, *Prophets Without Honor.*

66. "*Pacem in Terris,*" 1963e, *JW,* ch. 4, especially 83–90; "When 'Just' War Is Not Justified," *JW,* ch. 10, especially 199–200.

67. Quoted by Ramsey, *JW,* 78–79, 191–92.

68. *JW,* 86.

69. Other references to a world public authority in *JW* include 15, 25, 36, 135–37, 181, 187, 381–83, 390. I do not think that it can be shown that Ramsey argues decisively in *JW* for or against a world public authority. He argues elsewhere in both directions, as we will see directly.

70. "The Just War Theory on Trial," 1963b, 484. Cf. also "Morgenthau on Nuclear War," 1963c.

71. "A Political Ethics Context for Strategic Thinking," 1973j, 105.
72. *Theological Ethics,* Vol. II, *Politics,* 435, 440–41.
73. "Does the Church Have Any Political Wisdom for the 70's?" 1972b, 30.

Chapter 5. Political Ethics in Debate: Nuclear Deterrence

1. *WCC,* 270–72, 301–4.
2. The work of Kahn, Schelling, and others can be seen as attempts to provide a reasoned account of nuclear deterrence, and to render it credible in spite of appearances. See H. Kahn, *On Thermonuclear War* and *On Escalation;* T. Schelling, *Arms and Influence;* see also Freedman, *The Evolution of Nuclear Strategy.* Cf. his remark: "This represented the central problem in all deterrence theory. How credible was a threat of punishment that would literally, as the schoolmaster says as he prepares to spank a naughty schoolboy, 'hurt me as much as it hurts you?' " (80).
3. The difficulty is stated in another way by Kenny in *The Logic of Deterrence,* 37–38. The one who is to be deterred must believe the deterring power to be either mad or lying—so how is this deterrent effective?
4. *WCC,* 234.
5. *On Thermonuclear War,* 184, cited in *WCC,* 263–64.
6. *WCC,* 263–72.
7. "The Hatfields and the McCoys," 1962a revised, *JW,* 171–72. Ramsey's bizarre analogy to deterrence is cited by Maguire, *The Moral Choice,* 156–57.
8. *WCC,* 291–92.
9. *WCC,* 303.
10. Analysis of the main lines of Ramsey's proposal will form the subject of Part Four.
11. Both were published in 1965.
12. Cf. Lawler's two essays in *Peace, The Churches and the Bomb,* quotations from 33 and 93.
13. Ramsey's withdrawal of the "bluff" argument for nuclear deterrence is covered in ch. 14.
14. "Others" include most prominently Finnis, Boyle, and Grisez, *Nuclear Deterrence, Morality and Realism.*
15. Ramsey several times described the principle of discrimination as "the natural law of warfare." See, e.g., *WCC,* 304 and *JW,* 60, 164.
16. How much the city-avoidance policy was really fulfilling the principle of discrimination may be doubted, of course. McNamara gave as the reason to avoid striking cities the thought of keeping them as useful hostages for bargaining purposes. See Freedman, *The Evolution of Nuclear Strategy,* 235. As Schelling put it: "The reason for not destroying the cities is to keep them at our mercy," *Arms and Influence,* 193.
17. In "The MAD Nuclear Policy," 1972f; *Speak Up for Just War or Pacifism,* 55–56.

18. E.g., "A Political Ethics Context for Strategic Thinking," 1973j, 142.

19. But Ramsey wrote significant articles on political ethics after 1968.

20. See *The Patient as Person*, preface, xviii–xxii.

21. In addition to Ramsey's four books of medical ethics, his articles on abortion and on in-vitro fertilization should be noticed. See, e.g., *Three on Abortion*, 1978, and "Shall We 'Reproduce'?" 1972h and 1972i.

22. *SU*, 20–28.

23. *Ethics at the Edges of Life*, 139–42, 222–23 n. 50.

24. A label Ramsey might have used here. Cf. *Ethics at the Edges of Life*, 140–42.

25. See especially *Fabricated Man, passim*, e.g., 36–39, 87–93, 130–38.

26. See "What Americans Ordinarily Think about Justice in War," 1961e, *JW*, 48–50.

27. "A Letter to James Gustafson," 1985a, 74. See ch. 2.

28. "Some Rejoinders," 1976g, 190–91.

Chapter 6. Love and Rules

1. See "The Case of the Curious Exception," 1968a, 88–90.

2. "A Letter to James Gustafson," 1985a, 74.

3. Joseph Fletcher, "What's in a Rule?: A Situationist's View," 328, 325.

4. *BCE*, 54.

5. *BCE*, 65.

6. *BCE*, 89.

7. *BCE*, 142.

8. *BCE*, 84.

9. *BCE*, 88.

10. *BCE*, 78.

11. *BCE*, 79.

12. *BCE*, 344.

13. *BCE*, 344.

14. *BCE*, 9.

15. *BCE*, 345.

16. As Ramsey wrote in a letter to O'Connor, see O'Connor, 7n: Ramsey "indicated that his thought had changed very little since he wrote *Basic Christian Ethics*."

17. Curran, *Politics, Medicine and Christian Ethics*, 83; Gustafson, *Ethics and Theology*, 90.

18. Curran, *Politics, Medicine and Christian Ethics*, 85.

19. E.g., "Notice here the lack of any transforming aspect of charity or love on the political situation" (*Politics, Medicine and Christian Ethics*, 22, and repeated in *L&S*, 55). Curran has also noticed that there are questions surrounding the use of the "love transforming justice" motif, thinking that

transformation is not a theme very evident in Ramsey's political thought (*Politics, Medicine and Christian Ethics*, 5, 39, etc.).

20. "Some Rejoinders," 1976g, 191.

21. "A Letter to James Gustafson," 1985a, 83.

22. Hoitenga, "Development of Paul Ramsey's Ethics," 282 (quoting *BCE*, 77–78).

23. Ibid., 283.

24. Ibid., 287.

25. *D&R*, 120.

26. Hoitenga, "Development of Paul Ramsey's Ethics," 285.

27. "On Taking Sexual Responsibility Seriously Enough," 1964f, *D&R*, ch. II, 12.

28. Ramsey uses Frankena's typology, from "Love and Principle in Christian Ethics," 211–13, adding the fourth type to Frankena's three (*D&R*, 106–7).

29. *D&R*, 107.

30. *D&R*, 112.

31. *D&R*, 112–13.

32. Hoitenga is, however, clearly mistaken when he misquotes *D&R* to allege that Ramsey makes a clear distinction between private morality and social ethics, the former governed by love alone, the latter mainly by rules. See Hoitenga, "Development of Paul Ramsey's Ethics," 286, referring to *D&R*, 107. Hoitenga says that this is Ramsey's "general suggestion." But Ramsey is careful to write: "Someone *might* say, for example, that act agapism . . . governs private morality," etc. (italics in original).

33. This claim, with an admission of ambiguity or weakness in *BCE*, is made in *D&R*, 122, n. 41.

Chapter 7. The Rule of Double Effect

1. Although Ramsey often refers to the rule of double effect (cf., e.g., the index to *JW* under "double effect"), he has in fact comparatively few full discussions of it. It must be admitted that some of these are rather involved. They are: *WCC*, chs. 3, 4, and 8; "The Morality of Abortion," 1968g, 80–86, and "Incapacitating Gases," *JW*, ch. 19, 470–72, both originally presented as papers in 1966; "Abortion: A Review Article," 1973a; "Some Rejoinders," 1976g, 191–204; and "Incommensurability and Indeterminacy in Moral Choice," 1978d.

2. Mangan, "An Historical Analysis of the Principle of Double Effect," 43. This is the standard work referred to by both Ramsey and McCormick (*WCC*, 46; and *DEAG*, 50n1). McCormick slightly amplifies Mangan's terse wording: "There are conflict situations where an evil can be avoided or a more or less necessary good achieved only when another evil is reluctantly caused.

In such situations the evil caused as one goes about doing good has been viewed as justified or tolerable under a fourfold condition. (1) The action is good or indifferent in itself; it is not morally evil. (2) The intention of the agent is upright, that is, the evil effect is sincerely not intended. (3) The evil effect must be equally immediate causally with the good effect, for otherwise it would be a means to the good effect and would be intended. (4) There must be a proportionately grave reason for allowing the evil to occur" (*DEAG*, 7).

3. At least since the treatment of Bouscaren, *The Ethics of Ectopic Operations*. See *WCC*, ch. 8, especially 172–76.

4. McCormick reviews this revision in "Ambiguity in Moral Choice," reprinted as ch. 1 of *DEAG*.

5. *AJD, JW*, 315, 316.

6. O'Donovan notes that the principle of double effect is most applicable and helpful in the area of the taking of human life. Cf. *Resurrection and Moral Order*, 193.

7. Ch. 8 of *WCC*, and "The Morality of Abortion," 1968g. (The latter was presented at a symposium on "The Sanctity of Life," March 11–12, 1966 at Reed College, Portland, Oreg.)

8. *JW*, ch. 19; see 465n.

9. "Some Rejoinders," 1976g, 194.

10. *Summa Theologiae*, II, ii, Q.64, art. 7.

11. In ch. 3 of *WCC*, 43–44.

12. *L&S*, 63.

13. *Summa Theologiae*, II, ii, Q.64, art. 7., Reply to first Objection.

14. *Summa Theologiae*, II, ii, Q.43, art. 3.

15. See, e.g., *Summa Theologiae*, II, ii, Q.64, art. 2; Augustine, *Earlier Writings, "On Free Will,"* 117.

16. *WCC*, 57. Cf. also 46–47, where Ramsey follows Mangan, 42, 54.

17. Ramsey continued to defend this in "Some Rejoinders," 1976g, 194–95, but cf. also the comment made in response to Yoder in *SU*, 102.

18. Ramsey used T. L. Bouscaren's *Ethics of Ectopic Operations*, the standard text.

19. *WCC*, 176.

20. *WCC*, 179.

21. *WCC*, 178.

22. *WCC*, 188–89.

23. *WCC*, 190.

24. "The Morality of Abortion," 1968g, 81.

25. "The Morality of Abortion," 1968g, 84, 85.

26. *SU*, 102.

27. In 1973 he included a critique of Grisez in "Abortion: A Review Article," which somewhat refined the language he had used in 1968, but maintained the same stance. In "Some Rejoinders" (1976g) he responded to Curran's and Smith's essays (David H. Smith, "Paul Ramsey, Love and

Killing''; Charles Curran, "Paul Ramsey and Traditional Roman Catholic Natural Law Theory''; chs. 1 and 3 respectively of *L&S*). Curran accused Ramsey of departing from traditional doctrine (a move Curran would also make, though in a different way). Smith's main charge concerned some unclarity or ambiguity in Ramsey's use of the word "direct." Again, although Ramsey amplified and clarified his views a little, I think his response did not add anything of substance.

Although I will continue to use the terms "double effect," and "the rule of double effect," the recent debates have made it clear that it should be known as the rule of "double intent," or of "direct and indirect voluntariety," etc. The point is that the rule covers not only cases where there are two (or more) separate effects (such as the bombing of a military target which also kills civilians foreseeably, but "unintentionally" or "unwillingly"). It also covers cases where there is only one "effect" (such as abortion to save the mother's life). Here, however, there are two legitimate descriptions of the action, "saving a life" and "aborting a fetus," of which one is "willed" and "intended," and one is not.

28. "A Letter to James Gustafson," 1985a, 77. Ramsey's comment should not lead us to overlook the book, which is fairly widely cited on its subject. There are three helpful, if short, commentaries in Joseph Allen, "Paul Ramsey and His Respondents since *The Patient as Person*''; L. S. Cahill, "Within Shouting Distance: Paul Ramsey and Richard McCormick on Method''; and John Langan, "Direct and Indirect—Some Recent Exchanges Between Paul Ramsey and Richard McCormick."

29. For instance, in a most revealing passage, McCormick accused Schüller of offering a possible justification for the bombing of Hiroshima (*DEAG*, 260).

30. See McCormick's account of Schüller, *DEAG*, 29–33. See also Schüller's essay in that book, 165–92.

31. The varying terminology used by those who wish to avoid deontological accounts of ethics needs to be carefully noted. Both Schüller and McCormick avoid the word consequentialism on the whole, Schüller preferring the word teleological, and McCormick proportionate reason. Schüller's consequentialism is not at issue, though the question is more complicated with McCormick. That they are "subtle" forms of consequentialism goes without saying.

32. *DEAG*, 42–45.

33. *DEAG*, 166.

34. *DEAG*, 44; cf. 42–45, 259–61.

35. The three arguments are to be found on 75–83, 83–92, and 92–95 of *DEAG* respectively.

36. *DEAG*, 136.

37. For instance, McCormick, *DEAG*, 207, draws attention to Ramsey's statements at *DEAG*, 71, 73–74, and 93. There is a mistake, or at least a serious omission, in Ramsey's presentation here. On 71, he calls lives commensurate with each other, which he expressly denies at 93. It is the first

statement he should have revised in some way. This inconsistency is noted by Levy, "Paul Ramsey and the Rule of Double Effect," 70 n. 4. Levy's careful article concentrates too narrowly on the issue of incommensurability. This is understandable, but in consequence he fails to grasp Ramsey's aim accurately.

38. *DEAG,* 93.

39. *DEAG,* 69.

40. Ramsey questions value-language rather mildly (*DEAG,* 92). For a passage showing what can be proved using the language of values, cf. a passage from R. W. Tucker, in *Force, Order and Justice,* 234: "If it is held that . . . certain acts of war may never be justified—. . .—the meaning of this argument is that the evil such acts entail by their very commission must prove disproportionate to whatever good they are intended to serve and might in fact serve. To declare that certain acts are absolutely forbidden is to insist that the value sacrificed in committing such acts is equally absolute and, by definition, disproportionate to any value their commission may conserve or promote."

41. *DEAG,* 261.

42. *DEAG,* 104.

43. *DEAG,* 260.

44. *DEAG,* 260.

45. Talk of "undermining values" surely originated in debates over contraception, where it is perfectly clear and proper. See, for instance, Ramsey's remarks at the end of his essay, where he agrees that the use of proportionate reason is applicable to this question (and not the rule of double effect). The question to be asked about contraception is: "Will not the manner of protecting the good (procreation) undermine it in the long run by serious injury to an associated good (the communicative good)?" (*DEAG,* 136). It is, I think, instructive to compare this sentence with the argument of McCormick about the principle of discrimination just quoted in the text above. Finnis, *Fundamentals of Ethics,* draws attention to this talk of "undermining values" in his elegant and devastating critique of proportionalism (see 100–104).

46. Perhaps the sharpest critic is Finnis, in *Fundamentals of Ethics.*

Chapter 8. The Analysis of Action

1. *JW,* 453.

2. *JW,* 453.

3. This is a key point at issue in discussions with Tucker, or with Smith on the rule of double effect—which are important in the analysis of nuclear deterrence.

4. "Robert W. Tucker's *Bellum Contra Bellum Justum,*" 1966g, *JW,* 400, 402. Ramsey's clarification of the distinction between motive and intention in this article is particularly important for my analysis here and in what follows.

5. *Summa Theologiae* II, i, Q.1, art. 3.

6. This illustration of motive, aim, and final goal is my own.

7. This sequence is a simplified version of a similar sequence given by Ramsey to analyze a case of judicial murder in *D&R*, 196.

8. *L&S*, 10–14.

9. "Abortion: A Review Article," 1973a, 220–21, in "Three on Abortion," 54.

10. "Some Rejoinders," 1976g, 200.

11. *L&S*, 15.

12. "Some Rejoinders," 1976g, 203. Cf. also the claim made by Ramsey (*DEAG*, 69, quoted in ch. 7) that his understanding of the rule of double effect does not aspire to eliminate ambiguity, but rather locate it correctly and reduce it.

13. *D&R*, 37; cf. "The Case of the Curious Exception," 1968a, 87–89. Ramsey's claim that this has been the method of Christian casuistry probably cannot be sustained. This, rather, is his own constructive suggestion.

14. 1968a. This powerful essay has received two important critiques by D. Evans and O. M. T. O'Donovan. See Evans, "Paul Ramsey on Exceptionless Moral Rules," *L&S*, ch. II; O'Donovan, *Resurrection and Moral Order*, 196–97. Evans gives a working summary of the argument for exceptionless moral rules, and professes himself convinced by Ramsey's main contention. (There is a misunderstanding of the view of marriage held by Ramsey, who corrects this in "Some Rejoinders.") In the course of the argument Ramsey gives a fairly full account of the work of casuistry in clarifying and refining principles and rules, and in the work of application or subsumption. It is this that O'Donovan summarizes incisively in *Resurrection and Moral Order*, 196–97, drawing attention to what he perceives as a "lacuna" in Ramsey's article, namely, the lack of a fully articulate doctrine of creation.

15. "The Case of the Curious Exception," 1968a, 67–93.

16. "The Case of the Curious Exception," 85.

17. "The Case of the Curious Exception," 71.

18. See "The Case of the Curious Exception," 88. For this much discussed case, see Ramsey's outline on 83.

19. "The Case of the Curious Exception," 88.

20. *L&S*, 30, quoting from "The Case of the Curious Exception," 91–92.

21. *L&S*, 30.

22. *L&S*, 32.

23. *AJD, JW*, 326–27.

Chapter 9. The Unity of Christian Ethics

1. "The Structure of Justification in the Political Ethics of Paul Ramsey," *L&S*, ch. VII, 146.

2. *L&S*, 148.

3. Cf. *D&R*, 159–65.
4. *L&S*, 149, 150.
5. Gustafson, *Ethics and Theology*, 90.
6. Others include, for example, D. H. Smith and Paul Camenisch.
7. *DEAG*, 107 n.
8. Gustafson, *Ethics and Theology*, 92, 93.
9. "Paul Ramsey's Task: Some Methodological Clarifications and Questions," *L&S*, ch. IV. See especially 80–85.
10. *D&R*, 44, 112.
11. *L&S*, 81–82, 84.
12. Ramsey himself accepts Camenisch's summary in "Some Rejoinders," 1976g, 186.
13. "The Case of the Curious Exception," 1968a, 124.
14. *D&R*, 112, 164, Cf. also the full argument of *D&R*, 162–65 about "summary rules"; and the references to Brunner, Bonhoeffer et al., ibid., 118–20, 154–55.
15. "The Case of the Curious Exception," 1968a, 125.

Chapter 10. A Christian Ethic of Resistance

1. See *WCC*, xv–xvii, and Bainton, *Christian Attitudes Toward War and Peace*, ch. 5, 66–84. But Ramsey makes no acknowledgment of Bainton, whom he must have known and whose book he surely uses.
2. *WCC*, 67–68.
3. *WCC*, xvi. See Bainton, *Christian Attitudes*, 77–84, where he makes the same argument: "The primary ground of their aversion was the conviction of its incompatibility with love. The quality of love set forth by Jesus and by Paul had not been lost in the early church" (77). "All varieties of early Christian pacifism had in common an emphasis on love and an aversion to killing" (81).
4. The phrase "wrestle with pacifism" is adapted from a letter from Ramsey to Oliver O'Donovan (December 8, 1980).
5. See at the beginning of ch. 2.
6. *WCC*, xvii.
7. See "Reinhold Niebuhr: Christian Love and Natural Law," 1956b, *NMM*, ch. 5.
8. See ch. 8.
9. Cf. especially Ramsey's quotation of Augustine in *BCE*, 157–58. Noting the italics Ramsey adds, and his comment: "The permanent relationships he has established with other persons within the limits of his particular calling have also to be taken into account." The idea of covenants of life with life is to be found in the medical writings in particular.
10. *L&S*, 71.
11. *BCE*, 165.

12. We have already seen that it may be justified to "incapacitate" an unconscious aggressor, as the unborn child may sometimes be.

13. *WCC*, xviii.

14. It is also worth noting that there was much less scholarly literature available to Ramsey than there is now in this area.

15. On intervention see "The Ethics of Intervention," 1965c, *JW*, ch. 2; on defense see "What Americans Ordinarily Think about Justice in War," 1961e, *JW*, ch. 3. Note also the repeated concern of *SU* that the just war theory has a presumption against injustice at its root.

16. See the discussion in *SU*, 83–94, of Potter and Childress, and Ramsey's comments on their influence on Hehir and through him on the U.S. Catholic Bishops' Pastoral Letter.

17. *SU*, 109–10.

18. *SU*, 83.

19. See, for instance, "How Shall Counter-Insurgency War Be Conducted Justly?" *JW*, 452–54.

20. *BCE*, 188.

21. This is a common theme, especially in Ramsey's writings on Vietnam. See, e.g., "Counting the Costs," 1967a, *JW*, 525–29.

22. *BCE*, ch. I, section III: "In What Way, Then, Are the Teachings of Jesus Valid?"

23. This account of what Ramsey claims perhaps telescopes his train of thought too abruptly. For Ramsey's view of the unjustified optimism held in common between pacifists and deterrentists, see *JW*, e.g., xi, 53–54, 271–72.

24. D. T. O'Connor, "War in a Moral Perspective," 15. The quotation is from *BCE*, 38.

25. Cf. *BCE*, 166–69.

26. Sanders, *Jesus and Judaism*, 75.

27. *BCE*, 168.

28. *BCE*, 171.

29. Ambrose, *Duties of the Clergy*, ch. iv, 27. Quoted *BCE*, 173, Ramsey's italics.

30. Augustine, *Letters* Vol. I, 181.

31. I do not try to avoid conflating the thoughts expressed in *WCC* with my exposition here. The reader should perhaps be warned that this exposition does read *BCE* with the benefit of hindsight.

32. *BCE*, 173.

33. *BCE*, 172.

34. "War and the New Morality," 1968o. In this piece Ramsey is one of a number of respondents to an article by Dewey Hoitenga. Hoitenga advocates a somewhat legalistic sounding pacifism; and claims to find common ground between just war theory and situation ethics, both of which he opposes.

35. *BCE*, 182.

36. Douglass, *The Non-Violent Cross*, 160–61, cited in *JW*, 266, 273.

37. *SU,* 96–111.

38. The U.S. Catholic Bishops' Pastoral Letter. *SU* has extensive comments on the Pastoral Letter (37, 41–49, 62–63, 72, 81–96, 109–10, 120, 132–34, 136, 138–39).

39. It is characteristic of Ramsey's comments on authoritative church documents, especially Roman Catholic ones, that he puts the best construction on them, from his point of view. In commenting on paragraphs 93 and 120, in particular, he appears not to read them in their plain sense. Instead he calls them "misleading"! (*SU,* 90, 91).

40. *The Challenge of Peace,* paragraphs 81, 120. See *SU,* 81–83.

41. That is, under the test of proportion, which comes after the test of discrimination in Ramsey's lexical ordering of just war criteria. See ch. 11.

42. The chain of references here is *City of God,* IV, 15, *The Challenge of Peace,* paragraph 82 and note, *SU,* 83.

43. Niebuhr, "Why the Christian Church Is Not Pacifist" in Brown (ed.), *The Essential Reinhold Niebuhr,* especially 106–11. See *BCE,* 67–70. It is not clear that "non-resistance" is precisely the right word for the quality Ramsey has in mind. It does not consist well with the argument of *BCE* that Jesus resisted the religious leaders. Hauerwas queries the use of the word for the characterization of Jesus' life (*SU,* 177–78), and continues to insist on the use of "nonviolence." But we should not locate the source of their disagreement in this verbal argument.

44. See especially *SU,* 74–75.

45. *SU,* 118 (in the middle of a discussion of this point, 115–20). On 120 Ramsey attributes this equivocation to Yoder and the Methodist and Catholic bishops. A clear example of the confusion can be found in *The Challenge of Peace,* paragraph 120. For Hauerwas's response to Ramsey on this, see *SU,* 177–78.

46. *SU,* 37 commenting on United Methodist Bishops, *In Defense of Creation,* and *The Challenge of Peace.* The Methodist Bishops provided the occasion for *SU.* Ramsey demolished both the theological and moral arguments of his bishops in his book, in which the more valuable debating partners for Ramsey were the U.S. Catholic Bishops, and J. H. Yoder.

47. *SU,* 111–15.

48. *SU,* 112.

49. *SU,* 115. Hauerwas agrees with Ramsey that the issue is Christological and eschatological (e.g., *SU,* 162, 178). Hauerwas's substantive response to Ramsey raises too many issues to be satisfactorily dealt with here.

50. *SU,* 122–23.

51. "Christian pacifism is not a doctrine *addressed* to states. It is, is it not, a doctrine addressed *to the church*" (*SU,* 120).

Chapter 11. The Twin Principles of Just War

1. J. T. Johnson, *Ideology, Reason, and the Limitation of War,* and "Morality and Force in Statecraft: Paul Ramsey and the Just War Tradition,"

L&S, ch. V. Johnson's claim (e.g., *L&S,* 98–99) that the development of *jus in bello* owes more to secular than to church sources seems to me a little misleading. It overlooks, surely, the inextricable connection between both the chivalric code and *jus gentium,* on the one hand, and the Christian (and churchly) beliefs and energies, on the other, which underlay them in the period he discusses.

2. *JW,* 1962a, ch. 7.

3. "Incapacitating Gases," *JW,* ch. 19. The key paragraphs are at *JW,* 471–72. Cf. also ch. 7.

4. *JW,* ch. 7.

5. *JW,* 150.

6. *JW,* 151.

7. *JW,* 151.

8. For an example of this common theme, see "Is Vietnam a Just War?" 1967e, *JW,* 508–9 and note.

9. "A Political Ethics Context for Strategic Thinking," 1973j. The same points were expressed not quite so concisely in 1960, *JW,* 156.

10. "Over the Slope to Total War?" reprinted as part of *JW,* ch. 24. The quotation is from 533.

11. *JW,* 534.

12. *JW,* 154.

13. *JW,* 154.

14. *JW,* 155, 156. In the second of these two quotations the grammar seems to give way in the heat of Ramsey's emotion, but the sense of the emotion is clear enough.

15. *JW,* 154–55.

16. "Over the Slope to Total War?" 1967g, *JW,* 535.

17. "Robert W. Tucker's *Bellum Contra Bellum Justum,*" 1966g, *JW,* 404.

18. "Counting the Costs," 1967a, *JW,* 525.

19. *JW,* 527.

20. *AJD, JW,* 349–50.

Chapter 12. Just War in Debate

1. Unpublished, 1972, 34. The "Apologia" was originally part of the paper published as "Does the Church Have Any Political Wisdom for the 70's?" 1972b.

2. The paper presented in January 1966 was published as chs. 18 and 19 of *JW:* "How Shall Counter-Insurgency Warfare Be Conducted Justly?" and "Incapacitating Gases." I shall refer to them as chapters in *JW.* The published articles were "Farewell to Christian Realism," 1966a, April 1966; "Vietnam: Dissent from Dissent," 1966j, July 1966; "Counting the Costs," 1967a, April 1967; "Over the Slope to Total War?", 1967g, June 1967; and "Is Vietnam a

Just War?'', 1967e, Winter 1967. *JW*, chs. 20–22, 24. See also *Who Speaks for the Church?*

3. Maclear, *Vietnam: The Ten Thousand Day War*, 178–79.

4. The relevant paragraphs are quoted in full in *Who Speaks for the Church?* 83–84.

5. Weigel, *Tranquillitas Ordinis*, 217–19, 233.

6. See Maclear, *Vietnam*, ch. 14, especially 313–24. For instance, he quotes Rusk's estimate that the swing of U.S. opinion against the war took place in the first half of 1968, 322.

7. *JW*, ch. 18.

8. *JW*, 435.

9. Ramsey occasionally objected to the word absolute in this connection, pointing out that God alone is truly described by this word. Nevertheless, Ramsey himself did also use it, in *SU*. When Finnis et al. use the word, they gloss it, in effect, as exceptionless. They define absolutes as "norms which exclude as immoral certain kinds of acts regardless of the circumstances in which and ulterior purposes for which they are chosen" (*Nuclear Deterrence, Morality and Realism*, 275).

10. *JW*, ch. 18, 455.

11. *JW*, 441.

12. He mentions Thailand, among a variety of other places in S.E. Asia, in at least four articles (*JW*, 448, 485, 491, 532).

13. *JW*, 449.

14. Especially "Vietnam: Dissent from Dissent," 1966j, *JW*, ch. 21.

15. Sincerely mistaken policies can, of course, be immoral in different ways.

16. *JW*, 441.

17. *JW*, 455.

18. "Farewell to Christian Realism," *JW*, 482.

19. *JW*, ch. 18, 446.

20. 1967g, *JW*, 533–36.

21. *JW*, 535.

22. Ramsey's chief opponent was John Bennett, but he took on what he called the "liberal consensus" of the Protestant churches.

23. On the question of title changes, see Curran, *Politics, Medicine and Christian Ethics*, 71, and Ramsey's unpublished "Apologia" (1972).

24. *JW*, ch. 19.

25. *JW*, 476.

26. *JW*, 478.

27. "Abortion: A Review Article," 1973a, in *Three on Abortion*, 59.

28. E. J. Laarman, *Nuclear Pacifism*, 166, 167–68, 173–74, 183.

29. I mean here only to repeat Ramsey's point that moral issues are not settled by quantities of horror. Surely this is even more true when horrible threats are intended to avoid the horrors themselves. All this is not to enter the substantial moral argument (e.g., as debated by Stein and Ramsey).

30. W. V. O'Brien, "Morality and War: The Contribution of Paul Ramsey," *L&S*, ch. VIII, 174. O'Brien's works include *Nuclear War, Deterrence and Morality; War and/or Survival; The Conduct of Just and Limited War.*

31. *L&S*, 165, 174.

32. It is not clear, however, that O'Connor correctly understands Ramsey's use of the phrase "Love transforming natural justice" for he writes that it is very close to a Niebuhrian understanding of love and justice ("War in a Moral Perspective," 66). At times he is an opportunist critic, taking either side of a question in order to score points. In doing so he not infrequently misunderstands or distorts Ramsey's position.

33. O'Connor, "War in a Moral Perspective," 79–80. Cf. also 82–86.

34. "Love and Law," 1956b, *NMM*, 118.

35. O'Connor, "War in a Moral Perspective," 204–5.

36. O'Connor, "War in a Moral Perspective," 235.

37. Cf. e.g., *JW*, 432–33, 480–81.

38. O'Connor, "War in a Moral Perspective," 242.

39. O'Connor, "War in a Moral Perspective," 245.

40. Cf. especially *JW*, ch. 18, sec. III, 432–40.

41. O'Connor, "War in a Moral Perspective," 240.

42. Ch. 9 above.

43. "*Bellum Justum* and the Second Vatican Council: A Critique." It is surprising that O'Connor makes no reference to this essay, or, I think, to Ramsey's reply to it (1966g, *JW*, ch. 17).

44. Tucker, "*Bellum Justum*," 39.

45. Tucker, "*Bellum Justum*," 27.

46. Cf. note 9 to this chapter.

47. "Tucker's *Bellum Contra Bellum Justum*," 1966g, *JW*, ch. 17.

48. Tucker, "*Bellum Justum*," 35, 39.

49. *JW*, 391. Ramsey also quoted this passage twice in the Vietnam essays (*JW*, 482, 510).

50. Langendörfer, "Abschreckung und Sittlichkeit" ("Deterrence and Morality"); Walzer, *Just and Unjust Wars* will also be considered in Part Four.

51. Langendörfer, op. cit. 183.

52. E.g., "absolutes Gebot" ("an absolute command"), 164.

53. Langendörfer, "Abschreckung und Sittlichkeit," 175.

Chapter 13. Rational Nuclear Armament?

1. *The Limits of Nuclear War* and *Again, the Justice of Deterrence* were separately published by the CRIA as Occasional Papers in 1963 and 1965. "More Unsolicited Advice to Vatican Council II," 1965f, is contained in *Peace, The Churches and the Bomb*. They are chs. 11, 15, and 14 of *JW*, respectively.

2. *JW*, 306.

3. *JW,* viii–ix.

4. *WCC,* 277.

5. Quoted by Ramsey, *WCC,* 277 from Murray, *Nuclear Policy,* 223, 224.

6. Ramsey here builds on his argument in the same direction in the previous chapter of *WCC.*

7. Although this is now twenty-five years ago, the basic principles and possibilities of nuclear weaponry may not have changed very greatly, if we also include the projected and imagined advances covered here. That is to say, e.g., that SDI and the neutron bomb are foreshadowed in *WCC* (221 and 288 respectively), as well as "the dream of a nuclear bullet that can be fired with extreme accuracy at a target" (292).

8. *WCC,* 275.

9. *WCC,* 283–97.

10. *WCC,* 283.

11. *WCC,* 286.

12. *WCC,* 288ff.

13. *WCC,* 291, 292.

14. *WCC,* 293, 294.

15. *WCC,* 295.

16. *WCC,* 296.

17. *WCC,* ch. 11, "Two Deep Truths about Modern Warfare."

18. *WCC,* 260.

19. *WCC,* 269.

20. Both quotations are from *WCC,* 303.

21. The footnote on 211 of *JW* giving the date as 1965 is an error.

22. *JW,* 223.

23. *JW,* 235.

24. References for the first five steps are *LNW, JW:* 1. 235–36; 2. 236–41; 3. 241–42; 4. 242–43; 5. 243–44. The two final sections are on 245–48 and 248–58 respectively.

25. *JW,* 248.

26. *JW,* ix.

Chapter 14. The Justice of Deterrence

1. *JW,* 252–53.

2. *JW,* 253, 254.

3. See note 1 to ch. 13 above.

4. Walzer, *Just and Unjust Wars,* 279.

5. "A Political Ethics Context for Strategic Thinking," 1973j, 142.

6. As we have seen, in *LNW* Ramsey analyzes our points (2), (3), and (4) as 1, 2, and 3 (*JW,* 252–58). Stein sets out Ramsey's proposals as (A), (B), (C), and (D)—four points in the same order as our (1)–(4)—in "The Limits of

Nuclear War: Is a Just Deterrence Strategy Possible?'' in *PCB*, 73–84. Stein's criticism on *LNW* is at 78–84.

7. The link between threat and intention is discussed below, 229–32. See, e.g., Stein's implicit concession of this in "Would You Press the Button?" *PCB*, 24.

8. *PCB*, 24.

9. E.g., *JW*, 321.

10. *AJD, JW*, 314.

11. "A Political Ethics Context for Strategic Thinking," 1973j, 142. This article is substantially reprinted in *SU*, 183–212. References here are to the original publication.

12. Cf. *WCC*, ch. 11, especially 236–47, and see also the discussion above.

13. *LNW, JW* 252 and note, and *AJD, JW*, 317. Ramsey's first use of the word "effect" (the *deterrent effect*) is misleading since it *may* confuse us to think *this* effect (deterrence) is to be considered among the consequences to be weighed in planning a morally targeted weapons policy. See further below, and note 21 to this chapter.

14. "War and Murder," in *Nuclear Weapons and Christian Conscience*, 57.

15. "War and Murder," 58. Cf. Stein in *PCB*, 80–81.

16. *AJD, JW*, 322–28.

17. McCormick, *Notes on Moral Theology 1965–1980*, 106.

18. McCormick, *Notes on Moral Theology 1965–1980*, 106.

19. *AJD, JW*, 318.

20. *Just and Unjust Wars*, 280.

21. We should perhaps say that Ramsey could be *misread* to this effect, if that were not begging the question. This misreading may perhaps be partly excused because Ramsey did not sufficiently clearly underline the point that the deterrence flows from the *prospect* of unwanted consequences, not from the consequences themselves. Unfortunately Ramsey called the "prospect" of war an "effect" of military planning and policy, which is confusing.

22. "A Political Ethics Context for Strategic Thinking," 1973j, 141–42.

23. "How Shall Counter-Insurgency War Be Conducted Justly?" *JW*, 437–38.

24. For intricate argument, see for example *JW*, 317–28. Clearly, not all commentators have found it clear and accurate. Laarman, *Nuclear Pacifism*, 85–86, appears to accept Ramsey's defense, although he is otherwise a staunch opponent of Ramsey's views. Finnis et al., *Nuclear Deterrence*, 161–63, on the other hand, claim both Laarman and Stein as fellow critics of Ramsey. In rejecting Ramsey on collateral civilian damage, they merely assert that deterrence in war will force military commanders to want to threaten cities—a reply that misses altogether Ramsey's point about the *prospect* of such damage. O'Connor, "War in a Moral Perspective," 222–23, reads McCormick's carefully worded caution (which we noted above) as spelling defeat for Ramsey's proposal. This is a pity, for McCormick's objection (if such it is) is easily

answered, and O'Connor is otherwise happy with Ramsey's answer to Stein on this point (i.e., collateral civilian damage). Curran follows O'Connor in seeing this point of McCormick as identifying a fallacy in Ramsey's argument. (It is not clear to me whether Curran also thinks Stein was right in identifying "the decisive flaw" in Ramsey's argument. See Curran, *Politics, Medicine and Christian Ethics*, 95–97.)

25. It is not just the fear of retaliation which has deterred nations from using nuclear weapons. In the early 1950s, when the Soviet Union had only just begun to acquire nuclear weapons, there was some consideration by the United States of their use in Korea. This brought a quick reaction from America's allies, especially British Prime Minister Attlee. Freedman comments: "The experience suggested that when it came to the crunch, atomic weapons were not perceived as ordinary weapons but as something special to be handled with care, almost as if a taboo prevented their use" (*The Evolution of Nuclear Strategy*, 72).

26. Finnis et al. (*Nuclear Deterrence*, 105–10, 162) confuse this distinction. At 162 they lump deterrence of mere possession together with deterrence of bluff in order to refute Ramsey. In the earlier argument (V. 2, to which they refer), they had carefully distinguished these, although claiming that all variants of bluff were all either impractical or immoral.

27. "A Political Ethics Context for Strategic Thinking," 1973j, 146. Ramsey's reference to Kahn is a covert reference to a statement made by Kahn in *On Escalation*. Kahn admitted there that "the deterrence of a rational enemy [is] almost a simple philosophic consequence of the existence of thermonuclear bombs." (See "Can a Pacifist Tell a Just War?" *JW*, 269 and note.)

28. Kenny's proposal there differs importantly from the kind of proposal Ramsey made or would have made. See note 26 to ch. 15 below.

29. *LNW, JW*, 254.

30. *AJD, JW*, 333–36.

31. *AJD, JW*, 358–59, quoting *PCB*, 80.

32. *JW*, 361–62.

33. *JW*, 362.

34. *JW*, 364.

35. "A Political Ethics Context for Strategic Thinking," 1973j, 142; the first half of the quotation first appeared in "The MAD Nuclear Policy," 1972f, 18.

36. *Newsweek*, June 14, 1982, 84.

37. From Ramsey's letter to *Newsweek*, which was published in an edited form on July 5, 1982; reprinted in *SU*, 206–9.

Chapter 15. Deterrence, Threats, and Disproportion

1. *PCB*, 30.

2. *MUA, JW*, 303.

3. Laarman (*Nuclear Pacifism*, 91) also offers a gloss to the Proposition. He suggests: "A threat of something disproportionate [in the military realm] is not necessarily a disproportionate threat [in the political realm]." This is close to the gloss (c1) that I shall offer below; there is a measure of truth in it, although, and as I shall argue, it is not quite defensible on its own.

4. MUA, *JW*, 304–5; "The MAD Nuclear Policy," 1972f, 19.

5. See ch. 14.

6. For instance, he did so in the typescript of his letter to *Newsweek*, which was published in an edited form on July 5, 1982.

7. MUA, *JW*, 306–7.

8. *PCB*, 99. Ramsey cites this in part as a footnote in *AJD*, *JW*, 335 n.

9. *JW*, 252.

10. *JW*, 328.

11. *JW*, ch. 12.

12. *JW*, 268.

13. "The Limits of Nuclear War: Is a Just Deterrence Strategy Possible?" *PCB*, 79. Stein takes the wording of both points A) and B) from MUA, *JW*, 294. He adds points C) and D), which are not our concern at this moment.

14. MUA, *JW*, 303. Ramsey's first, fullest, discussion and defense of the Proposition is at 302–7.

15. *AJD*, *JW*, 361; my italics.

16. Chs. 4 and 11.

17. Cf. *DEAG*, 72–73.

18. My example.

19. E.g., *JW*, 404, 454, 526.

20. This, of course, is to continue to assume that proportionality is not the single ultimate judge of the morality of anything, which some consequentialists propose. Nothing could be further from Ramsey's mind than this!

21. See *JW*, 245, 248–50, and our discussion above.

22. "The MAD Nuclear Policy," 1972f, 19.

23. Earlier in this chapter, above.

24. Types (1) and (2) in our summary, ch. 14.

25. Type (3).

26. Here is the major difference between Ramsey and Kenny (*The Logic of Deterrence*). Ramsey would never have made such specific proposals as Kenny, and he would have demurred from some of Kenny's ideas. Kenny's proposal is that the "existential deterrent" be kept as a transitional arrangement pending disarmament, and it seems also to be too closely connected to weapons designed chiefly for countercity use to be easily justified as a possibly discriminately aimed system (an essential feature of Ramsey's proposal).

27. *AJD*, *JW*, 336.

28. *PCB*, 22; quoted by Ramsey, MUA, *JW*, 295.

29. MUA, *JW*, 295–96.

30. *AJD*, *JW*, 342. Ramsey's optimism in the 1960s was shortlived. See, for instance, his condemnation of MIRV-ed nuclear missiles (*SU*, 55–56).

31. These sentences are taken from a section of MUA, *JW,* 291, 293, 295.
32. MUA, *JW,* 291.
33. *AJD, JW,* 336.
34. Ch. 14 above.
35. *LNW, JW,* 254, 257; my italics. The italicized condition is of course foundational for any just war or preparation for war or deterrence, according to Ramsey. It is significant that it is spelled out here.
36. *AJD, JW,* 357, 356.
37. *AJD, JW,* 342.
38. "Can a Pacifist Tell a Just War?" *JW,* 267; my italics for the concluding clause.
39. *AJD, JW,* 355.

Conclusion

1. "Some Rejoinders," 1976g, 186.
2. Letter to David H. Smith, June 18, 1973 (in the Paul Ramsey papers at Duke University, Durham, N.C.).
3. See, for instance, "The Betrayal of Language," 1971a.
4. "Obituary," 87.

Bibliography

Allen, Joseph L. "The Discriminating Realism of Paul Ramsey." *Worldview* 12/12 (December 1969): 13–17.

———. "Some Introductory Remarks about Paul Ramsey's Ethics." *Perkins Journal* (Fall 1972): 25–28.

———. "Paul Ramsey and his Respondents Since *The Patient as Person.*" *Religious Studies Review* 5/2 (April 1979): 89–95.

Ambrose, *On the Duties of the Clergy,* Nicene and Post-Nicene Fathers, 2d Series, Vol. X. Grand Rapids, Mich.: Eerdmans, 1955.

Anscombe, G. E. M. "War and Murder." In Stein (ed.) *Nuclear Weapons and Christian Conscience,* edited by Walter Stein, 45–62. London: The Merlin Press, 1961, 1965.

Aquinas. *Summa Theologiae.* Edited by T. Gilby. London: Eyre and Spottiswoode, 1963–.

Augustine. *The City of God.* Works, Vols. I & II, Edited by Marcus Dods. Edinburgh: T&T Clark, 1871–.

———. *Letters,* Vol. I. *Works,* Vol. VI. Edited by Marcus Dods. Edinburgh: T&T Clark, 1871– .

———. *On Free Will (De libero Arbitrio).* Library of Christian Classics, Vol. VI, *Augustine: Earlier Writings.* London: SCM, 1953.

Bainton, Roland H. *Christian Attitudes Toward War and Peace.* London: Hodder & Stoughton, 1961.

Bennett, John C. (ed.) *Nuclear Weapons and the Conflict of Conscience.* London: Lutterworth Press, 1962.

———. "Christian Realism in Vietnam." *America* (April 30, 1966): 616–17.

———. [Editorials on Vietnam], *Christianity and Crisis* (February 21, 1966, 13–14; March 7, 1966, 33–34; March 6, 1967, 32–33; August 7, 1967, 182–184).

------. "A Critique of Paul Ramsey." *Christianity and Crisis* 27/18 (October 30, 1967): 247–50.

Bouscaren, T. Lincoln. *The Ethics of Ectopic Operations*. Milwaukee, Wis.: Bruce Publishing Co., 1943.

Brown, Richard McAfee (ed.). *The Essential Reinhold Niebuhr: Selected Essays and Addresses*. New Haven and London: Yale University Press, 1986.

Brunner, Emil. *Justice and the Social Order*. London: Lutterworth, 1945.

Cahill, Lisa Sowle. "Within Shouting Distance: Paul Ramsey and Richard McCormick on Method." *The Journal of Medicine and Philosophy* 4/4 (1979): 398–417.

Cahn, Edmond. *The Moral Decision: Right and Wrong in the Light of American Law*. Bloomington, Ind.: Indiana University Press, 1955.

------. *The Sense of Injustice*. New York: New York University Press, 1949.

Camenisch, Paul F. "Paul Ramsey's Task: Some Methodological Clarifications and Questions." In *Love and Society: Essays in the Ethics of Paul Ramsey*, edited by James T. Johnson and David H. Smith, 67–89. Missoula, Mont.: Scholars Press, 1974.

Childress, James F. "Just-War Criteria." In *War or Peace? The Search for New Answers*, edited by Thomas A. Shannon, 40–58. New York: Orbes, 1980.

Curran, Charles E. *Politics, Medicine and Christian Ethics*. Philadelphia: Fortress Press, 1973.

------. "Paul Ramsey and Traditional Roman Catholic Natural Law Theory." In *Love and Society: Essays in the Ethics of Paul Ramsey*, edited by James T. Johnson and David H. Smith, 47–65. Missoula, Mont.: Scholars Press, 1974.

Douglass, James. *The Non-Violent Cross*. New York: Macmillan, 1968.

Edwards, Jonathan. *Freedom of the Will*. Edited by P. Ramsey. New Haven: Yale University Press, 1957.

------. *Ethical Writings*. Edited by P. Ramsey. New Haven: Yale University Press, 1989.

Evans, Donald. "Paul Ramsey on Exceptionless Moral Rules." In *Love and Society: Essays in the Ethics of Paul Ramsey*, edited by James T. Johnson and David H. Smith, 19–46. Missoula, Mont.: Scholars Press, 1974. First published in *The American Journal of Jurisprudence* 16 (1971): 184–214.

Finn, James (ed.). *A Conflict of Loyalties: The Case for Selective Conscientious Objection*. New York: Pegasus, 1968.

------. (ed.). *Peace, the Churches and the Bomb*. New York: The Council on Religion and International Affairs, 1965.

Finnis, John. *Fundamentals of Ethics*. Oxford: Clarendon Press, 1983.

Finnis, John, Joseph Boyle, and Germain Grisez. *Nuclear Deterrence, Morality and Realism*. Oxford: Clarendon Press, 1987.

Fletcher, Joseph. *Situation Ethics*. London: SCM, 1966.

———. "What's in a Rule?: A Situationist's View." In *Norm and Context in Christian Ethics*, edited by Gene H. Outka and Paul Ramsey, 325–49. New York: Charles Scribner's Sons, 1968.

Ford, John C. "The Morality of Obliteration Bombing." *Theological Studies* 5/3 (September 1944), 261–309.

Frankena, William K. "Love and Principle in Christian Ethics." In *Faith and Philosophy*, edited by Alvin Plantinga, 203–225. Grand Rapids: Eerdmans, 1964.

Freedman, Lawrence. *The Evolution of Nuclear Strategy*. London: Macmillan, 1981.

Fry, John R. *The Immobilized Christian: A Study of his Pre-Ethical Situation*. Philadelphia: Westminster Press, 1963.

Gessert, Robert A., and J. Bryan Hehir. *The New Nuclear Debate*. New York: CRIA, 1976.

Green, Philip. *Deadly Logic*. Columbus, Ohio: Ohio State University Press, 1966.

Gustafson, James M. *Ethics from a Theocentric Perspective*. Vol. Two, *Ethics and Theology*. Chicago and London: University of Chicago Press, 1984.

———. "Context Versus Principle: A Misplaced Debate in Christian Ethics." *Harvard Theological Review* 58 (1965): 171–202.

———. "How does Love Reign?" *The Christian Century* 83/20 (May 18, 1966): 654–55.

Hartigan, Richard S. "Noncombatant Immunity: Reflection on its Origins and Present Status." *Review of Politics* 29 (1967): 204–20.

Hauerwas, Stanley. *Against the Nations*. Minneapolis: Winston Press (Seabury), 1985.

———. "Can Ethics Be Theological?" *Hastings Center Report* 8/5 (October 1978): 47–49.

Hehir, J. Bryan. "The Just-War Ethic and Catholic Theology." In *War or Peace? The Search for New Answers*, edited by Thomas A. Shannon, 15–39. New York: Ordiss, 1980.

Hehir, J. Bryan, and Robert A. Gessert. *The New Nuclear Debate*. New York: CRIA, 1976.

Heron, Alistair (ed.). *Towards a Quaker View of Sex*. London: Friends Home Service Committee, 1963.

Hoitenga, Dewey J., Jr. "Development of Paul Ramsey's Ethics." *Gordon Review* 11 (1970): 282–90.

———. "War and the New Morality." *Reformed Journal* 18/2 (February 1968): 10–15. [The subsequent discussion includes Ramsey, 1968o.]

Hollenbach, David S.J. *Nuclear Ethics: A Christian Moral Argument.* New York/Ramsey: Paulist Press, 1983.

John XXIII. *Pacem in Terris,* Encyclical Letter of 11 April 1963. Trans. by H. E. Winstone. *Acta Apostolicae Sedis* 55 (1963): 257–304; London: Catholic Truth Society, 1965.

Johnson, James Turner. *Ideology, Reason, and the Limitation of War.* Princeton, N.J.: Princeton University Press, 1975.

———. "Morality and Force in Statecraft: Paul Ramsey and the Just War Tradition." In *Love and Society: Essays in the Ethics of Paul Ramsey,* edited by James T. Johnson and David H. Smith, 93–114. Missoula, Mont.: Scholars Press, 1974.

———. "The Cruise Missile and the Neutron Bomb: Some Moral Reflections." *Worldview* 20/12 (December 1977): 20–26; "James T. Johnson Responds" [to "Reader's Response"—(Paul Ramsey)], *Worldview* 21/4 (April 1978): 57–58.

Johnson, James T., and David H. Smith (eds.). *Love and Society: Essays in the Ethics of Paul Ramsey.* Missoula, Mont.: Scholars Press, 1974.

Kahn, Herman. *On Thermonuclear War.* Princeton, N.J.: Princeton University Press, 1960.

———. *On Escalation.* London: Pall Mall Press, 1965.

Kegley, Charles W., and Robert W. Bretall (eds.). *Reinhold Niebuhr: His Religious, Social and Political Thought.* New York: Macmillan, 1956.

Kenny, Anthony. *The Logic of Deterrence.* London: Firethorn Press, 1985.

Knauer, Peter. "The Hermeneutic Function of the Principle of Double Effect." *Natural Law Forum* 12 (1967): 132–62.

Laarman, Edward J. *Nuclear Pacifism: Just War Thinking Today.* New York and Berne: Peter Lang, 1984.

Langan, John. "Direct and Indirect—Some Recent Exchanges Between Paul Ramsey and Richard McCormick." *Religious Studies Review* 5 (1979): 95–101.

Langendörfer, Hans. "Abschreckung und Sittlichkeit." In *Politik und Ethik der Abschreckung,* edited by Franz Böckle and Gert Krell, 163–185. Mainz: Grünewald; München: Kaiser, 1984.

Lawler, Justus George. "The Council Must Speak," and "Moral Issues and Nuclear Pacifism." In *Peace, the Churches and the Bomb,* edited by James Finn, 32–36, 85–94. New York: CRIA, 1965.

————. "Review of Ramsey's *The Limits of Nuclear War.*" *Continuum* 1/2 (Summer 1963): 198–210.

Lehmann, Paul. *Ethics in a Christian Context.* London: SCM, 1963.

Levy, Sanford S. "Paul Ramsey and the Rule of Double Effect." *Journal of Religious Ethics* 15 (Spring 1987): 59–71.

Little, David. "The Structure of Justification in the Political Ethics of Paul Ramsey." In *Love and Society: Essays in the Ethics of Paul Ramsey,* edited by James T. Johnson and David H. Smith, 139–62. Missoula, Mont.: Scholars Press, 1974.

McCormick, Richard A., S.J. *Notes on Moral Theology 1965–1980.* Lanham and London: University Press of America, 1981.

————. "Proxy Consent in the Experimentation Situation." In *Love and Society: Essays in the Ethics of Paul Ramsey,* edited by James T. Johnson and David H. Smith, 209–27. Missoula, Mont.: Scholars Press, 1974.

————. "Experimentation in Children: Sharing in Sociality." *Hastings Center Report* 6/6 (December 1976): 41–46.

————. "Ambiguity in Moral Choice" and "A Commentary on the Commentaries." In *Doing Evil to Achieve Good: Moral Choice in Conflict Situations,* edited by Richard A. McCormick, S.J., and Paul Ramsey, 7–53, 193–267. Lanham, New York and London: University Press of America, 1985.

Macaulay, Sidney S. "The Use of Scripture in the Ethics of Paul Ramsey." Unpublished M.Th. dissertation, Columbia Theological Seminary, 1976.

Maclear, Michael. *Vietnam: The Ten Thousand Day War.* London: Thames/ Methuen, 1981.

Maguire, Daniel. *The Moral Choice.* Minneapolis: Winston Press, 1979.

Mangan, Joseph T., S.J. "An Historical Analysis of the Principle of Double Effect." *Theological Studies* 10/1 (March 1949): 41–61.

Maritain, Jacques. *Man and the State.* Chicago: University of Chicago Press, 1981.

Miller, Alexander. "Unprincipled Living: The Ethics of Obligation." *Christianity and Crisis* 20/5 (March 21, 1960): 28–31.

Murray, John Courtney, S.J. *We Hold These Truths.* New York: Sheed and Ward, 1960.

————. "War and Conscience." In *A Conflict of Loyalties: The Case for Selective Conscientious Objection,* edited by James Finn, 19–30. New York: Pegasus, 1968.

Murray, Thomas E. *Nuclear Policy for War and Peace.* Cleveland and New York: The World Publishing Co., 1960.

Niebuhr, Reinhold. *The Children of Light and the Children of Darkness.* New York: Charles Scribner's Sons, 1944 and 1960.

————. *An Interpretation of Christian Ethics*. (Living Age edition.) New York: Meridian Books, 1956; first published by Harper & Brothers, 1935.

————. *Moral Man and Immoral Society*. London: SCM, 1963; first published by Charles Scribner's Sons, 1932.

————. *The Nature and Destiny of Man*. 2 Vols. New York: Charles Scribner's Sons, 1943 and 1964.

————. [see also Brown, R. McA., (ed.), *The Essential Reinhold Niebuhr*].

O'Brien, William V. *Nuclear War, Deterrence and Morality*. New York: Newman, 1967.

————. *War and/or Survival*. New York: Doubleday, 1969.

————. *The Conduct of Just and Limited War*. New York: Praeger, 1981.

————. "Morality and War: The Contribution of Paul Ramsey." In *Love and Society: Essays in the Ethics of Paul Ramsey,* edited by James T. Johnson and David H. Smith, 163–84. Missoula, Mont.: Scholars Press, 1974.

O'Connor, D. Thomas. "War in a Moral Perspective: A Critical Appraisal of the Views of Paul Ramsey." Unpublished Ph.D. dissertation. Claremont (Calif.) Graduate School, 1972.

O'Donovan, Oliver. *Resurrection and Moral Order*. Leicester: IVP, 1986.

————. "Obituary: Paul Ramsey (1913–1988)." *Studies in Christian Ethics* 1/ 1 (1988): 82–90.

Osgood, Robert E., and Robert W. Tucker. *Force, Order and Justice*. Baltimore, Md.: Johns Hopkins Press, 1967.

Outka, Gene. *Agape: An Ethical Analysis*. New Haven and London: Yale University Press, 1972.

Potter, Ralph. *War and Moral Discourse*. Richmond, Va.: John Knox Press, 1969.

Quade, Quentin L. "Selective Conscientious Objection and Political Obligation." In *A Conflict of Loyalties: The Case for Selective Conscientious Objection,* edited by James Finn, 195–218. New York: Pegasus, 1968.

Rawls, John. "Two Concepts of Rules." *Philosophical Review* 64/1 (January 1955): 3–32.

Robinson, John A. T. *Honest to God*. London: SCM, 1963.

————. *Christian Morals Today*. London: SCM, 1964.

Rohr, John A. *Prophets Without Honor: Public Policy and the Selective Conscientious Objector*. New York: Abingdon Press, 1971.

Sanders, E. P. *Jesus and Judaism*. London: SCM, 1985.

Schelling, Thomas C. *Arms and Influence*. New Haven and London: Yale University Press, 1966.

Schüller, Bruno, S.J. "The Double Effect in Catholic Thought: A Reevaluation." In *Doing Evil to Achieve Good: Moral Choice in Conflict Situations,* edited by Richard A. McCormick, S.J., and Paul Ramsey, 165–192. Lanham, New York and London: University Press of America, 1985.

Sellers, James. "Mr. Ramsey and the New Morality." *Religion in Life* 37 (1968), 282–91.

Shannon, Thomas A. (ed.). *War or Peace? The Search for New Answers*. New York: Orbis, 1980.

Shinn, Roger L. "Paul Ramsey's Challenge to Ecumenical Ethics." *Christianity and Crisis* 27/18 (October 30, 1967): 243–47.

Smith, David H. "Paul Ramsey, Love and Killing." In *Love and Society: Essays in the Ethics of Paul Ramsey,* edited by James T. Johnson and David H. Smith, 3–17. Missoula, Mont.: Scholars Press, 1974.

Stein, Walter. "Would You Press the Button?" and "The Limits of Nuclear War: Is a Just Deterrence Strategy Possible?" In *Peace, the Churches and the Bomb,* edited by James Finn, 20–25, 73–84. New York: CRIA, 1968.

———. (ed.). *Nuclear Weapons and Christian Conscience*. London: Merlin Press, 1961, 1965.

Stone, Ronald H. *Reinhold Niebuhr: Prophet to Politicians*. Washington, D.C.: University Press of America, 1981.

Thielicke, Helmut. *Theological Ethics*. Vol. 2 *Politics*. Ed. and trans. by William H. Lazareth. Grand Rapids, Mich.: Eerdmans, 1979.

Tucker, Robert W. *The Just War: A Study in Contemporary American Doctrine*. Baltimore, Md.: Johns Hopkins Press, 1960.

———. *Just War and Vatican Council II: A Critique*. New York: Council on Religion and International Affairs, 1966. [This piece is also titled "*Bellum Justum* and the Second Vatican Council: A Critique." Substantial parts of it are also used in Osgood and Tucker, *Force, Order and Justice.*]

The United Methodist Council of Bishops. *In Defense of Creation: The Nuclear Crisis and a Just Peace*. Nashville, Tenn.: Graded Press, 1986.

United States National Conference [Catholic Bishops]. *The Challenge of Peace: God's Promise and Our Response*. London: Catholic Truth Society, 1983. Reprinted in Murnion (ed.), *Catholics and Nuclear War*.

Walzer, Michael. *Just and Unjust Wars*. Harmondsworth: Penguin Books, 1980.

Weigel, George. *Tranquillitas Ordinis: The Present Failure and Future Promise of American Catholic Thought on War and Peace*. Oxford and New York: Oxford University Press, 1987.

Wogaman, Philip. "The Vietnam War and Paul Ramsey's Conscience." *Dialog* 6 (Autumn 1967): 292–98.

Yoder, John H. *The Politics of Jesus*. Grand Rapids, Mich.: Eerdmans, 1972.

———. *The Original Revolution*. Scottdale, Pa.: Herald Press, 1971.

Bibliography: Paul Ramsey

Books and Occasional Papers

1950   *Basic Christian Ethics*. New York: Charles Scribner's Sons.

1961   *Christian Ethics and the Sit-In*. New York: Association Press.

1961   *War and the Christian Conscience: How Shall Modern War Be Conducted Justly?* Durham, N.C.: Duke University Press.

1962   *Nine Modern Moralists*. Englewood Cliffs, N.J.: Prentice-Hall.

1963   *The Limits of Nuclear War: Thinking about the Do-able and the Un-Do-Able*. New York: Council on Religion and International Affairs.

1965   *Again, the Justice of Deterrence*. New York: Council on Religion and International Affairs.

1965,   *Deeds and Rules in Christian Ethics*. Edinburgh and London: Oliver
1967   and Boyd, 1965 (*Scottish Journal of Theology* Occasional Papers, No. 11); New York: Charles Scribner's Sons, 1967. [Note: The 1967 edition is substantially enlarged from the 1965 edition.]

1967   *Who Speaks for the Church? A critique of the 1966 Geneva Conference on Church and Society*. Nashville and New York: Abingdon Press.

1968   *The Just War: Force and Political Responsibility*. New York: Charles Scribner's Sons.

1970   *Fabricated Man: The Ethics of Genetic Control*. New Haven: Yale University Press.

1970   *The Patient as Person: Explorations in Medical Ethics*. New Haven: Yale University Press.

1975   *The Ethics of Fetal Research*. New Haven: Yale University Press.

1975   *One Flesh: A Christian View of Sex Within, Outside and Before Marriage*. Bramcote, Nottingham: Grove Books.

1978   *Ethics at the Edges of Life: Medical and Legal Intersections*. New Haven: Yale University Press.

1978   *On In Vitro Fertilization*. Studies in Law and Medicine, No. 3. Chicago: Americans United for Life, Inc.

1978   *Three on Abortion*. (Child and Family Reprint Booklet Series.) Oak Park, Ill.: Child and Family.

1988   *Speak Up for Just War or Pacifism. A Critique of the United Methodist Bishop's Pastoral Letter "In Defense of Creation."* (With an Epilogue by Stanley Hauerwas.) University Park and London: Pennsylvania State University Press.

Edited by Paul Ramsey

1957   *Freedom of the Will* (ed., with critical introduction), *Works of Jonathan Edwards* Vol. 1. New Haven: Yale University Press.

1957   *Faith and Ethics: The Theology of H. Richard Niebuhr.* New York: Harper and Brothers.

1965   *Religion* (ed.) *The Princeton Studies: Humanistic Scholarship in America.* Englewood Cliffs, N.J.: Prentice-Hall.

1968   *Norm and Context in Christian Ethics* (ed. with Gene H. Outka). New York: Charles Scribner's Sons.

1970   *The Study of Religion in Colleges and Universities* (ed. with John F. Wilson). Princeton, N.J.: Princeton University Press.

1978   *Doing Evil to Achieve Good: Moral Choice in Conflict Situations* (ed. with Richard McCormick). Chicago: Loyola University Press.

1989   *Ethical Writings* (ed., with critical introduction). *Works of Jonathan Edwards* Vol. 8. New Haven: Yale University Press.

Articles, Chapters, etc.

This listing follows the bibliography prepared by James T. Johnson and included in *Love and Society.* I am deeply in debt to Professor Johnson for the help his meticulously careful work has been to me in researching Ramsey's work. Johnson's bibliography extended to 1974 (up to and including 1974b); the remaining entries are my own. His 1960e is a reference to a 1961 article which I have renumbered 1961i. The new entries for 1960e and 1960f were not included by Johnson; I have also added three references to published letters: 1966k, 1967k, and 1967l.

1935a   "Christianity and War." *Christian Advocate* 110/4 (February 15): 202–3.

1943a   "The Great Commandment." *Christianity and Society* 8/4 (Fall).

1943b   "The Manger, the Cross, and the Resurrection." *Christianity and Crisis* 3/6 (April 16): 2–5.

1944a   "Natural Law and the Nature of Man." *Christendom* 9/3 (Summer): 369–81.

1944b   "A Social Policy for Liberal Religion." *Religion in Life* 13/4 (Autumn): 495–507.

1946a   "The Idealistic View of Moral Evil: Josiah Royce and Bernard Bosanquet." *Philosophy and Phenomenological Research* 6/4 (June): 554–89.

1946b   "Religious Instruction Problematically Christian." *Journal of Religion* 26/4 (October): 243–62.

1946c   "A Theology of Social Action." *Social Action* 23/2 (October 15): 4–34.

1946d   "The Theory of Democracy: Idealistic or Christian?" *Ethics* 56/4
         (July): 251–66.

1947a   "Beyond the Confusion of Tongues." *Theology Today* 3/4 (January):
         446–58.

1947b   "Religion at Princeton." *Religious Education* 42/2 (March–April):
         65–69.

1947c   "A Theory of Virtue According to the Principles of the Reformation."
         Journal of Religion 27/3 (July): 178–96.

1948a   *"Existenz* and the Existence of God: A Study of Kierkegaard and
         Hegel." *Journal of Religion* 28/3 (July): 157–76.

1949a   "Elements of a Biblical Political Theory." *Journal of Religion* 29/4
         (October): 258–83.

1949b   "Non Solum in Memoriam Sed in Intentionem: A Tribute to the Late
         Rev. John W. Ramsey." *The Mississippi Methodist Advocate* (March
         23): 8, 9, 12.

1950a   "In This is Love. . . ." *Motive* 11/1 (October): 21–23.

1951a   "God's Grace and Man's Guilt." *Journal of Religion* 31/1 (January):
         21–37.

1951b   "The Revealer of Many Hearts." *Adult Teacher* (General Board of
         Education of the Methodist Church) 4/6 (June): 7–9.

1952a   "God and the Family." Sunday School Lesson for May 18. *Cross-
         roads* (Board of Christian Education of the Presbyterian Church in
         the U.S.), April–June: 59–61.

1952b   "God's Estimate of Human Life." Sunday School Lesson for May
         25. *Crossroads* (Board of Christian Education of the Presbyterian
         Church in the U.S.), April–June: 62–64.

1953a   "Paul and Some of His Letters." A series of seven Sunday School
         lessons for adult classes, May 17–June 28. *Crossroads* (Board of
         Christian Education of the Presbyterian Church in the U.S.), April–
         June: 77–79; together with the exegesis of scripture and instruction
         for teachers. *Westminster Teacher,* April–June.

1955a   "God and the Family." A series of five adult lessons. *Crossroads*
         (Presbyterian Board of Publications), July: 13–30; together with in-
         structions to teachers. *Westminster Teacher,* July–September: 5–14.

1956a   "Freedom and Responsibility in Medical and Sex Ethics: A Protestant
         View." *New York University Law Review* 31/7 (November): 1189–
         204.

1956b   "Love and Law." In *Reinhold Niebuhr: His Religious, Social and
         Political Thought,* edited by Charles W. Kegley and Robert W. Bretall,
         80–123. New York: Macmillan.

1956c   "Marriage and the Kingdom of God." *Crossroads* (Presbyterian Board of Publications), January: 13–16, 19.

1956d   "No Morality Without Immortality: Dostoevsky and the Meaning of Atheism." *Journal of Religion* 36/2 (April): 90–108.

1957a   "Christian Ethics." In *Collier's Encyclopedia,* Vol. 5. New York: P. F. Collier and Son Corporation, 227.

1957b   "The Church Is You." *Growing* (Presbyterian Board of Education), October–December: 14–16; also in *Victory* (Presbyterian Church of Canada), October–December: 4–6.

1957c   "Mysticism." In *Collier's Encyclopedia,* Vol. 14. New York: P. F. Collier and Son Corporation, 343.

1958a   "A Fable." *The Chaplain* 15/5 (October): 27–28; reprinted in *Motive* 18/7 (April, 1959): cover, and *The Christian Advocate* 136/1 (January 5, 1961): 11.

1959a   "Freedom and Responsibility in Medical and Sex Ethics: A Protestant View." In *Readings in Legal Methods,* edited by Burke Shartel and B. J. George, Jr., 284–99. Ann Arbor, Mich.: Overbeck.

1959b   "The Legal Imputation of Religion to an Infant in Adoption Proceedings." *New York University Law Review* 34/4 (April): 649–90.

1959c   "Religious Aspects of Marxism." *Canadian Journal of Theology* 5/3 (July): 143–55.

1959d   "Right and Wrong Calculation." *Worldview* 2/12 (December): 6–9.

1960a   "Faith Effective Through In-Principled Love." *Christianity and Crisis* 20/9 (May 30): 76–78.

1960b   "Male and Female He Created Them." *Victory* (Presbyterian Church of Canada), January–March: 1–4.

1960c   "Reinhold Niebuhr: Leader in Social, Political and Religious Thought." *New York Herald Tribune Book Review,* June 19:4.

1960d   "Sex and People: A Critical Review." *Religion in Life* 30/1 (Winter): 53–70.

1960e   "The Marriage of Adam and Eve." *Moravian Theological Seminary Bulletin,* 1960: 35–56.

1960f   "Religious Aspects of Marxism." *Moravian Theological Seminary Bulletin,* 1960: 57–75.

1961a   "The Case for Just or Counterforces Warfare." *Pittsburgh [Theological Seminary] Perspective* 2/3 (September): 7–20.

1961b   "Dream and Reality in Deterrence and Defense." *Christianity and Crisis* 21/22 (December): 228–32.

1961c   "The New Papal Encyclical—I." *The Christian Century* 78/36 (September 6): 1047–50.

1961d   "The New Papal Encyclical—II." *The Christian Century* 78/37 (September 13): 1077–79.

1961e   "The Nuclear Dilemma." In *Christian Ethics and Nuclear Warfare*, edited by U. S. Allers and W. V. O'Brien, 108–34. Washington, D.C.: Georgetown University Institute of World Polity.

1961f   "Preface." In *The Death of God: The Culture of Our Post-Christian Era*, Gabriel Vahanian, xiii–xxix. New York: George Braziller.

1961g   "Right and Wrong Calculation." In *The Moral Dilemma of Nuclear Weapons*, edited by William Clancy, 47–54. New York: The Church Peace Union.

1961h   "Shelter Morality." *Presbyterian Life*, November 15: 7–8, 41–42; discussion, January 1, 1962: 4–5, 42.

1961i   "Theological Studies in College and Seminary." *Theology Today* 17/4 (January): 466–84.

1962a   "The Case for Making 'Just War' Possible." In *Nuclear Weapons and the Conflict of Conscience*, edited by John C. Bennett, 143–70. New York: Charles Scribner's Sons.

1962b   "Community of Two." *Crossroads* (Presbyterian Board of Education) 12/3 (April–June): 92–94.

1962c   "Death's Duel." *Motive* 22/7 (April): 2–5; also available from the Office of the University Chaplain, Pennsylvania State University, University Park, Pennsylvania.

1962d   "Life, Death and the Law." *Journal of Public Law* 11 (1962): 377–93.

1962e   "Porcupines in Winter." *Motive* 22/8 (May): 6–11.

1962f   "Princeton University's Graduate Program in Religion." *Journal of Bible and Religion* 30/4 (October): 291–98.

1962g   "Turn Toward Just War." *Worldview* 5/7–8 (July–August): 8–13.

1962h   "U.S. Military Policy and 'Shelter Morality.' " *Worldview* 5/1 (January): 6–9; discussion 5/3 (March): 6–9.

1963a   "Church and Academy: A Tension in Theological Education." *The Garrett Tower* 39/1 (December): 8–15.

1963b   "The Just War Theory on Trial." *Cross Currents* 13/4 (Fall): 477–90.

1963c   "Morgenthau on Nuclear War." *Commonweal* 78/21 (September 20): 554–57.

1963d   "On Taking Sex Seriously Enough." *Christianity and Crisis* 23/19 (November 11): 204–6.

1963e   "*Pacem in Terris.*" *Religion in Life* 33/1 (Winter): 116–35.

1963f   "Protestant Casuistry Today." *Christianity and Crisis* 23/5 (March 4): 24–28.

1963g "Toward a Test-Ban Treaty: Is Nothing Better than On-Site Inspection?" *Worldview* 6/7–8 (July–August): 4–10.

1964a "How Shall We Sing the Lord's Song in a Pluralistic Land? The Prayer Decisions." *Journal of Public Law* 13/2 (1964): 353–400.

1964b "Is God Mute in the Goldwater Candidacy?" *Christianity and Crisis* 24/15 (September 21): 175–78.

1964c "Justice in War." *New Wine, A Christian Journal of Opinion* 2 (Spring): 21–25.

1964d "Marriage Law and Biblical Covenant." In *Religion and the Public Order*, edited by D. A. Giannella, 41–77. Chicago: University of Chicago Press.

1964e "Morals and Nuclear Weapons." In *A Study of Morals and the Nuclear Program*, 23–41. Albuquerque, N.M.: Headquarters Field Command, Defense Atomic Support Agency, Sandria Base.

1964f "On Taking Sexual Responsibility Seriously Enough." *Christianity and Crisis* 23/23 (January 6): 247–51.

1964g "The Status and Advancement of Theological Scholarship in America." *The Christian Scholar* 47 (Spring): 7–23.

1964h "Teaching 'Virtue' in the Public Schools." In *Religion and the Public Order*, edited by D. A. Giannella, 336–39. Chicago: University of Chicago Press.

1964i "Theological Studies in College and Seminary." In *The Making of Ministers*, edited by K. R. Bridgston and D. W. Culver, 21–114. Minneapolis: Augsburg Press.

1964j "The Uses of Power." *Perkins [School of Theology] Journal* 18/1 (Fall): 13–24.

1965a "A Christian Approach to the Question of Sexual Relations Outside Marriage." *Journal of Religion* 45/2 (April): 100–18.

1965b "The Church and the Magistrate." *Christianity and Crisis* 25/11 (June 28): 136–40.

1965c "The Ethics of Intervention." *Review of Politics* 27/3 (July): 287–310.

1965d "Lehmann's Contextual Ethics and the Problem of Truth-Telling." *Theology Today* 21/4 (January): 466–75.

1965e "Modern Papal Social Teachings." In *The Heritage of Christian Thought* (*Festschrift* for R. L. Calhoun), edited by Robert E. Cushman and Egil Grislis, 202–38. New York: Harper and Brothers.

1965f "More Unsolicited Advice to Vatican Council II." In *Peace, the Churches and the Bomb*, edited by James Finn, 37–66. New York: Council on Religion and International Affairs.

1965g "The Uses of Power." *Catholic Mind* 63/1196 (October): 11–23.

1966a   "Farewell to Christian Realism." *America* 114/18 (April 30): 618–22.

1966b   "A Letter from Canon Rhymes to John of Patmos." *Religion in Life* 35/2 (Spring): 218–29.

1966c   "Living with Yourself." *The Pulpit* 37/7 (July–August): 4–8.

1966d   "Moral and Religious Implications of Genetic Control." In *Genetics and the Future of Man,* edited by John D. Roslansky, 107–69. Amsterdam: North-Holland Publishing Co. (distributed in U.S. by Appleton-Century-Crofts).

1966e   "Nuclear War and Vatican Council II." *Theology Today* 23/2 (July): 244–63.

1966f   "Responsible Parenthood: A Response to Fr. Bernard Haering." In *The Vatican Council and the World of Today.* Providence, R.I.: Office of the Secretary, Brown University.

1966g   "Tucker's *Bellum Contra Bellum Justum.*" In *Just War and Vatican Council II: A Critique,* edited by Robert W. Tucker, 67–101. New York: Council on Religion and International Affairs.

1966h   "Two Concepts of General Rules in Christian Ethics." *Ethics* 76/3 (April): 192–207.

1966i   "The Vatican Council on Modern War." *Theological Studies* 27/2 (June): 179–203; *Theology Today* 23/2 (July): 244–63.

1966j   "Vietnam: Dissent from Dissent." *The Christian Century* 33/29 (July 20): 909–13.

1966k   "To Speak the Whole Political Truth." *Christianity and Crisis* 26 (June 13, 1966): 134–35.

1967a   "Counting the Costs." In *The Vietnam War: Christian Perspectives,* edited by Michael B. Hamilton, 24–44. Grand Rapids, Mich.: William B. Eerdmans Publishing Co.

1967b   "Death's Duel." *The Pulpit* 38/3 (March): 16–19.

1967c   "Discretionary Armed Service." *Worldview* 10/2 (February): 8–11.

1967d   "From Princeton, with Love." *Reflection* (Yale Divinity School) 64/1 (January): 5–6.

1967e   "Is Vietnam a Just War?" *Dialog* 6/1 (Winter): 19–29.

1967f   "On Sexual Responsibility." *The Catholic World* 205/1228 (July): 210–16.

1967g   "Over the Slope to Total War?" *The Catholic World* 205/1225 (June): 166–68.

1967h   "Responsible Parenthood: An Essay in Ecumenical Ethics." *Religion in Life* 26/3 (Autumn): 343–54.

1967i   "The Sanctity of Life—In the First of It." *The Dublin Review* 511 (Spring): 1–21.

1967j   "Two Extremes." *Dialog* 6/3 (Summer): 218–19.

1967k   "Abortion and the Law." *Christianity and Crisis* 27 (August 7, 1967): 195–96.

1967l   "Paul Ramsey Replies" [to Shinn and Bennett]. *Christianity and Crisis* 27 (November 27, 1967): 280–82.

1968a   "The Case of the Curious Exception." In *Norm and Context in Christian Ethics*, edited by Gene H. Outka and Paul Ramsey, 67–135. New York: Charles Scribner's Sons.

1968b   "Christian Ethics Today." *Rockford College Alumni Magazine*, Spring: 3–6, 23.

1968c   "Christianity and Modern War." *Theology Digest* 16/1 (Spring): 47–53.

1968d   "Dissent, Democracy and Foreign Policy: A Symposium." *Headline Series* 190 (August): 40–44. New York: Foreign Policy Association.

1968e   "Election Issues 1968." *Social Action/Social Progress* 35/2//59/1 (September–October): 18–28.

1968f   "Election 1968, and Beyond." *Worldview* 11/12 (December): 16–19.

1968g   "The Morality of Abortion." In *Life or Death: Ethics and Options*, edited by Daniel Labby, 60–93. Seattle: University of Washington Press.

1968h   "Naturrecht und Christliche Ethik bei N.H. Søe." *Zeitschrift für Evangelische Ethik* 12/2 (March): 80–98.

1968i   "On Taking Sexual Responsibility Seriously Enough." In *Social Ethics*, edited by Gibson Winter, 44–45. New York: Harper and Row; London: S.C.M. Press.

1968j   "Political Repentance Now." *Christianity and Crisis* 28/18 (October 28): 247–52.

1968k   "Politics as Science, Not Prophecy." *Worldview* 11/1 (January): 18–21.

1968l   "A Proposal to the New Moralists." *Motive* 28/7 (April): 38–44.

1968m   "A Reaction to 'Black Power and the Shock of Recognition' by James Luther Adams." *Action/Reaction* (San Francisco Theological Seminary), Summer: 5–6.

1968n   "Selective Conscientious Objection: Warrants and Reservations in the Just War Doctrine." In *Conflict of Loyalties: Selective Conscientious Objection*, edited by James Finn, 31–77. New York: Pegasus, Western Publishing Co.

1968o   "War and the New Morality." *Reformed Journal* 18/2 (February): 25–28, with subsequent discussion.

1969a   "Introduction." In *War and/or Survival*, edited by William V. O'Brien, xi–xvii. Garden City, N.Y.: Doubleday.

1969b   "Medical Ethics: A Joint Venture." *Reflection* (Yale Divinity School) 66/3 (March): 4–5.

1969c   "On Up-Dating Death." In *The Religious Situation*, edited by Donald R. Cutler, 253–75. Boston: Beacon Press. Also (as "On Updating Death") in *Up-dating Life and Death: Essays in Ethics and Medicine*, edited by Donald R. Cutler, 31–54. Boston: Beacon Press.

1970a   "Abortion: A Theologian's View." *AORN* (Journal of the Association of Operating Room Nurses), November: 55–62. Also in *In Defense of Life*, edited by Valerie Vance Dillon. Trenton, N.J.: New Jersey Right to Life Committee.

1970b   "The Biblical Norm of Righteousness." *Interpretation* 24/4 (October): 419–29.

1970c   "Christian Love in Search of a Social Policy." In *The Christian and His Decisions*, edited by Harmon L. Smith and Louis W. Hodges, 184–196. Nashville and New York: Abingdon Press.

1970d   "Christianity and Modern War." In *Christian Witness in the Secular City*, edited by Everett J. Morgan, S.J., 275–85. Chicago: Loyola University Press.

1970e   "Feticide/Infanticide Upon Request." *Child and Family* 9/3 (Fall): 257–72; *Religion in Life* 39/2 (Summer): 170–86.

1970f   "Panel Discussion." *Annals of the New York Academy of Sciences* 169/2 (January 21): 576–83.

1970g   "Reference Points in Deciding about Abortion." In *The Morality of Abortion: Legal and Historical Perspectives*, edited by John T. Noonan, Jr., 60–100. Cambridge, Mass.: Harvard University Press.

1970h   "Shall We Clone a Man?" In *Who Shall Live? Medicine, Technology, Ethics*, edited by Kenneth Vaux, 79–113. Philadelphia: Fortress Press.

1971a   "The Betrayal of Language." *Worldview* 14/2 (February): 7–10.

1971b   "Christian Ethics and the Future of Humanism." In *God, Man and Philosophy*, edited by Carl W. Grindell, 83–91. New York: St. John's University Press.

1971c   "Church Stand Should Be Withdrawn." *The Christian Advocate*, 15/21 (November 11): 11–12.

1971d   "The Ethics of a Cottage Industry in an Age of Community and Research Medicine." *New England Journal of Medicine* 284/13 (April 1): 700–6.

1971e   "The Morality of Abortion," In *Moral Problems: A Collection of Philosophical Essays*, edited by James Rachels, 1–27. New York: Harper and Row.

1971f   "A Proposal to the New Moralists." In *Moral Issues and Christian Responses,* edited by Paul T. Jersild and Dale A. Johnson, 47–54. New York: Holt, Rinehart and Winston.

1971g   "Some Moral Problems Arising in Genetic Medicine," *Linacre Quarterly* 38/1 (February): 15–20.

1971h   "The Wedge: Not So Simple." *The Hastings Center Report,* No. 3 (December): 11–12.

1971i   "Who Speaks for the Church?" In *Moral Issues and Christian Responses,* edited by Paul T. Jersild and Dale A. Johnson, 117–25. New York: Holt, Rinehart and Winston.

1972a   "Author-Reviewer Symposia." *Philosophy Forum* 12: 149–64.

1972b   "Does the Church Have Any Political Wisdom for the 70's?" *Perkins* [School of Theology] *Journal* 26/1 (Fall): 29–40.

1972c   "Force and Political Responsibility." In *Ethics and World Politics,* edited by Ernest W. Lefever, 43–73. Baltimore: Johns Hopkins Press.

1972d   "Genetic Engineering." *Bulletin of the Atomic Scientists* 28/10 (December): 14–17.

1972e   "Genetic Therapy: A Theologian's Response." In *The New Genetics and the Future of Man,* edited by Michael Hamilton, 157–75. Grand Rapids, Mich.: William B. Eerdmans Publishing Co.

1972f   "The MAD Nuclear Policy." *Worldview* 15/11 (November): 16–20.

1972g   "The Morality of Manipulation." *Worcester Polytechnic Institute Journal* 76/1 (August): 11–13.

1972h   "Shall We 'Reproduce'? I. The Medical Ethics of *In Vitro Fertilisation.*" *Journal of the American Medical Association* 220/10 (June 5): 1346–50.

1972i   "Shall We 'Reproduce'? II. Rejoinders and Future Forecast." *Journal of the American Medical Association* 220/11 (June 12): 1480–85.

1973a   "Abortion: A Review Article." *The Thomist* 37/1 (January): 174–226.

1973b   "The Abstractness of Concrete Advice." In *Contemporary Religion and Social Responsibility,* edited by Norbert Brockman and Nicholas Piediscalzi, 335–45. New York: Alba House.

1973c   "The Just Revolution." *Worldview* 16/10 (October): 37–40.

1973d   "Medical Progress and Canons of Loyalty to Experimental Subjects." *Proceedings* (Institute for Theological Encounter with Science and Technology), 51–77.

1973e   "Military Service as a Moral System." *Military Chaplains' Review* 2/1 (January): 8–21.

1973f   "The Moral and Religious Implications of Genetic Control." In *Heredity and Society: Readings in Social Genetics,* edited by Adela S. Baer, 364–82. New York: Macmillan.

1973g "Morals and the Practice of Genetic Medicine." In *The Pilgrim People: A Vision with Hope,* edited by Joseph Papin, 71–84. Villanova, Pa.: Villanova University Press.

1973h "The Nature of Medical Ethics." In *The Teaching of Medical Ethics,* edited by Robert M. Veatch, Willard Gaylin and Councilman Morgan, 14–27. Hastings-on-Hudson, N.Y.: The Hastings Centre, Institute of Society, Ethics and the Life Sciences.

1973i "Should Medicine Today Be Taught Without Medical Ethics?" *Connecticut Medicine* 37/8 (August): 420–21.

1973j "A Political Ethics Context for Strategic Thinking." In *Strategic Thinking and Its Moral Implications,* edited by Morton A. Kaplan, 101–47. Chicago: University of Chicago Center for Policy Study.

1973k "Screening: An Ethicist's View." In *Ethical Issues in Human Genetics: Genetic Counselling and the Use of Genetic Knowledge,* edited by Bruce Hiltonn, Daniel Callahan, Maureen Harris, Peter Condliff and Burton Berkley, 147–67. New York: Plenum Publishing Corporation.

1973l "Shall We 'Reproduce'?" In *New Theology No 10,* edited by Martin E. Marty and Dean G. Peerman, 87–120. New York: Macmillan.

1974a "Conceptual Foundations for an Ethics of Medical Care: A Response." In *Ethics and Health Care: Proceedings of the Conference of Health Care and Changing Values.* Washington, D.C.: National Academy of Sciences.

1974b "The Indignity of 'Death with Dignity.' " With Response by Leon R. Kass and Robert Morison. *Hastings Centre Studies* 2/2 (May): 47–62.

1974c "Beyond Relief and Liberation" *Worldview* 17/12 (December): 12–13.

1974d "Death's Pedagogy" *Commonweal* 100 (September): 497–502.

1974e "Protecting the Unborn: Testimony Before the Subcommittee of the Senate Judiciary Committee, 8th March 1974." *Commonweal* 100/13 (May 31): 308–14.

1975a "The Indignity of Death with Dignity" In *Death Inside Out,* edited by Peter Steinfels and Robert M. Veatch, 81–96. New York: Harper & Row.

1975b "Moral Issues in Fetal Research: Statement submitted to the National Commission for the Protection of Human Subjects in Biomedical and Behavioral Research." In *Transcript of the Meeting Proceedings, March 14, 1975,* 1–21. Springfield, Va.: National Technical Information Service.

1975c "Some Ethical Reflections on Prospective Studies of Families at High Risk of Schizophrenia." In *Proceedings of Conference, World Health Organization.* Copenhagen, Denmark, May 28, 1975.

1975d "Theological Table-Talk: The Bicentennial Began Last August; The Church's Role to Celebrate; 'Unfound' Theologians." *Theology Today* 31 (January): 331–38.

1976a "Abortion After The Law." *Journal of the Christian Medical Society* 7/3 (Summer): 150–52.

1976b "Conceptual Foundations for an Ethics of Medical Care: A Response." In *Ethics and Health Policy,* edited by R. M. Veatch and R. Branson, 35–55. Cambridge, Mass.: Ballinger Publishing Co.

1976c "Death as an Ethical Issue for the Professions." (Columbia University Seminar Reports, 3/8, General Education Seminar). New York: Columbia University (1975/76): 150–52.

1976d "The Enforcement of Morals: Non Therapeutic Research on Children." *Hastings Center Report* 6/4 (August): 21–30.

1976e "Prolonged Dying: Not Medically Indicated." *Hastings Center Report* 6/1 (February): 14–17.

1976f "The Right Care of Karen Quinlan." *Crucible* (April–June): 66–71.

1976g "Some Rejoinders." *Journal of Religious Ethics* 4/2 (Fall 1976): 185–237.

1977a "Abortion: Last Resort." In *Ethics for Modern Life,* edited by R. Abelson and M. Frequegnon, 61–75. New York: St. Martin's Press.

1977b "Children as Research Subjects: A Reply." *Hastings Center Report,* 7/4 (April): 40–41.

1977c "Death's Pedagogy." In *Death, Dying and Euthanasia,* edited by D. J. Horan and D. Hall, 331–43. Washington, D.C.: University Publications of America.

1977d " 'Euthanasia' and Dying Well Enough." *Linacre Quarterly* 44/1 (February): 37–46.

1977e "Excursus: Korean Creeds and the Rejection of Old Heresies." *Worldview* 20/11 (November): 27–28.

1977f "A Human Lottery?" In *Ethical Issues in Modern Medicine,* edited by R. Hunt and J. Arras, 444–51. Palo Alto, Calif.: Mayfield Publishing.

1977g "The Indignity of Death with Dignity." In *Death, Dying and Euthanasia,* edited by D. J. Horan and D. Hall, 305–30. Washington, D.C.: University Publications of America.

1977h "Kant's Moral Theology or a Religious Ethics? Response to Alasdair MacIntyre." In *Knowledge, Value and Belief,* edited by H. T. Engelhardt, Jr., and D. Callahan, 44–74. Hastings-on-Hudson, N.Y.: Hastings Center.

1977i   "Observation: Consider the Morning Glory." *Worldview* 20/12 (December): 41–44.

1977j   "Observation: The Dade County Vote and Our Crisis of Community." *Worldview* 20/10 (October): 32–34.

1977k   "Protecting the Unborn." In *Liberty: Selected Readings*, edited by J. Feinberg and H. Gross, 143–50. Belmont, Calif.: Dickenson Publishing.

1977l   "Research Involving Children or Incompetents." In *Ethical Issues in Modern Medicine*, edited by R. Hunt and J. Arras, 297–304. Palo Alto, Calif.: Mayfield Publishing.

1977m   "The Same Old Illusions." *Worldview* 20/9 (September): 42–43.

1977n   "Screening: An Ethicist's View." In *Ethical Issues in Modern Medicine*, edited by R. Hunt and J. Arras, 110–17. Palo Alto, Calif.: Mayfield Publishing

1978a   "Can the 1973 Abortion Decisions Be Justly Hedged?" *Human Life Review* 4/3 (Summer): 77–110.

1978b   " 'The Cruise Missile and the Neutron Bomb': Some Critical Reflections." *Worldview* 21/4 (April): 2, 56–57.

1978c   "Ethical Dimensions of Experimental Research on Children." In *Research on Children: Medical Imperatives, Ethical Quandaries, and Legal Constraints*, edited by Jan van Eys, 57–68. Baltimore, Md.: University Park Press.

1978d   "Incommensurability and Indeterminacy in Moral Choice." In *Doing Evil to Achieve Good*, edited by Richard McCormick and Paul Ramsey, 69–114. Chicago: Loyola University Press.

1978e   "Manufacturing Our Offspring: Weighing the Risks." *Hastings Center Report* 8/5 (October): 7–9.

1978f   *On In Vitro Fertilisation.* Studies in Law and Medicine no. 3. Chicago, Ill.: Americans United for Life, Inc.

1978g   "The Saikewicz Precedent: What's Good for an Incompetent Patient?" *Hastings Center Report* 8/6 (December): 36–42.

1978h   "Self-Conflict in Ethical Decisions: Response to Eric Cassell." In *Morals, Science and Sociality*, edited by H. T. Engelhardt, Jr., and D. Callahan, 234–46. Hastings-on-Hudson, N.Y.: Hastings Center.

1979a   "The Background Music: Symposium on Civil Defense." *Worldview* 22/1–2 (January–February): 46–48.

1979b   "Do You Know Where Your Children Are?" *Theology Today* 36/1 (April): 10–21.

1979c   "Liturgy and Ethics." *Journal of Religious Ethics* 7/2 (Fall): 139–71.

1979d   "On In Vitro Fertilisation." *Human Life Review* 5 (Winter): 17–30.

1979e   "Washington Knows . . . ?" *Theology Today* 35/4 (January): 428–37.

1981a   "Kant's Moral Theology or a Religious Ethics." In *The Roots of Ethics,* edited by Daniel Callahan and H. Tristram Engelhardt, 139–69. New York: Plenum Press.

1981b   "On *In Vitro* Fertilisation." *Crucible* (October–December): 175–84.

1981c   "Two-Step Fantastic: The Continuing Case of Brother Fox." *Theological Studies* 42 (March): 122–34.

1982a   "Adolescent Morality: A Theologian's Viewpoint." *Post-Graduate Medicine* 72/1 (July): 233–36.

1982b   "Do You Know Where Your Children Are." *Journal of Psychology and Christianity* 1/4 (Winter): 7–16.

1982c   Foreword, to Arthur C. McGill, *Suffering: A Test of Theological Method.* Philadelphia: The Westminster Press. Pp. 7–15.

1982d   Introduction, to *Infanticide and the Handicapped Newborn,* Dennis J. Horan and Melinda Delahoyde (eds). Provo, Utah: Brigham University Press. Pp. vii–xvi.

1982e   "Tradition and Reflection in Christian Life." *Perkins* [School of Theology] *Journal* 35 (Winter–Spring): 46–56.

1983a   Response, to Richard John Neuhaus, *Speaking to the World; Four Protestant Perspectives.* Washington, D.C.: Ethics and Public Policy Centre. Pp. 17–24.

1984a   "The Issues Facing Mankind." In *The Question of In Vitro Fertilisation,* Studies in Medicine, Law and Ethics. SPVC Education Trust, 7 Tufton Street, Westminster, London.

1985a   "A Letter to James Gustafson." *Journal of Religious Ethics* 13 (Spring): 71–100.

1988a   "Human Sexuality in the History of Redemption." *Journal of Religious Ethics* 16 (Spring): 56–86.

Unpublished writings

A few important articles and papers remain unpublished. The three most significant of these are:

- Chapter Three: "Sex and the Order of Reason in Thomas Aquinas."

- "War and Peace as a Religious Issue: On Extricating the Church from Liberal Disillusionment." This dates from c.1968.

- "Apologia Pro Vita Sua—One Decade, That Is," (1972).

Paul Ramsey's papers are held by the Manuscript Department, William R. Perkins Library, Duke University, Durham, N.C. There are brief notes on the papers in the unpublished Ph.D. thesis of which this thesis is a revision. The thesis ("The Theological Basis for Political Ethics in the Thought of Paul Ramsey" CNAA, Trinity College, Bristol, England) also contains a fuller bibliography of book reviews and articles responding to Ramsey's work.

Index

About the Author

David Attwood teaches Christian Ethics at Trinity College, Bristol, England. Previously he worked in parish ministry for eight years. He was awarded his doctorate for his thesis on Paul Ramsey, for which he studied under Professor Oliver O'Donovan at Oxford. This is his first book; previous writings include the Grove booklet *The Spade and the Thistle*, on the ethics of work.

Acknowledgments

Grateful acknowledgment is hereby made to the following for permission to reprint quotations from books by Paul Ramsey:

Basic Christian Ethics. Copyright 1980 by University of Chicago Press. Reprinted with the permission of the publisher.

Nine Modern Moralists. Copyright 1983 by Paul Ramsey. Reprinted with the permission of University Press of America, Inc.

Speak Up for Just War or Pacifism, pp. 37, 83, 115, 122–23. Copyright 1988 by The Pennsylvania State University (University Park and London: Pennsylvania State University Press, 1988). Reproduced by permission of the publisher.

The Just War. Copyright 1983, 1968 by Paul Ramsey. Reprinted with the permission of University Press of America, Inc.

War and the Christian Conscience. Copyright 1961 by Duke University Press. Reprinted by permission of the publisher.